the redbird sings the song of hope:
and other stories of love through loss

KANDY NOLES STEVENS

WESTBOW
PRESS®
A DIVISION OF THOMAS NELSON
& ZONDERVAN

WestBow Press books may be ordered through booksellers or by contacting:

WestBow Press
A Division of Thomas Nelson & Zondervan
1663 Liberty Drive
Bloomington, IN 47403
www.westbowpress.com
1 (866) 928-1240

Scripture taken from the NEW AMERICAN STANDARD BIBLE®, Copyright © 1960, 1962, 1963, 1968, 1971, 1972, 1973, 1975, 1977, 1995 by The Lockman Foundation. Used by permission.

ISBN: 978-1-5127-5282-3 (sc)
ISBN: 978-1-5127-5283-0 (hc)
ISBN: 978-1-5127-5281-6 (e)

Library of Congress Control Number: 2016912924

Print information available on the last page.

WestBow Press rev. date: 9/28/2016

For Emilee, Hunter, Jesse, and especially Reed,
and for all the hearts that love them.

Contents

Part One
What Are You, a Bunch of Idiots?
In Nicer Terms: Things That Are Not Really Helpful

PART TWO
ONE SIZE FITS MOST–THINGS THAT MIGHT BE HELPFUL

PART THREE
BLOW YOUR SOCKS OFF–
THINGS THAT ARE MOST DEFINITELY HELPFUL

Foreword: And I Didn't Even Pledge …

WHEN I WAS IN COLLEGE, THE SMALL TOWN WHERE WE LIVED was preparing to celebrate the upcoming centennial. By that time in my life, my family had relocated for a second time from our roots in the Deep South to the amber prairies of North Dakota. I had grown to love these Scandinavians and Germans, who came to call me one of their own. One of the town matriarchs penned a beautiful play about the settling of our community one hundred years earlier. I had once dated the playwright's nephew, and I really wanted to be in the production. My brother and I went to the audition, reading for several different parts. Eventually, I landed the role of the lead female character, personifying those beautiful and challenging pioneer days. The opening of the play involved a soliloquy in which I was required to agonize over how I loved the land and how I had lost so much in our journey to homestead. My character's angst had less to do with the backbreaking work (she expected that) and much more to do with the heart-wrenching loss of her children. I went to two practices and realized I simply could not play the part. No matter how hard I tried to pull from a wellspring of emotion, at that point in my life, I had the world in the palm of my hands. I had only lost two elderly family members and one classmate, and other than the sadness stemming from moving all over the country, I didn't really know loss. The playwright, who also happened to be the director, wanted a depth and range of emotion that I simply could not produce. The whole town was counting on this play to be a success, and I knew I had no choice but to step down from the role. My performance would not have been authentic. The director assumed the role, and she gave a stunning opening performance, including genuine tears over her

1

scripted loss. She understood the pain of the prairie mother who had lost her children because she had walked in those shoes. Watching her pain exposed for all to see, I knew I had made the right choice.

During those same years, I joined a sorority. During pledge week, there were many fun activities, including teas and socials, and then there was the candlelit "Welcome to the club" installation ceremony. As you journey through this book, you will learn that through our loss, I learned to care less about dividing people into groups of *us* and *them*. After all, we are all part of God's family—each and every one of us. There should never be *we vs. they* mentalities. I wish I had realized that during my sorority days. I can only attribute my participation in that type of thinking to believing that God was still molding me. Thankfully, that is still true today. Even though there are bumps in the road—lots of bumps, bruises, and deep valleys—I am so thankful that God has used each broken moment to help mold me into the girl he wants me to be. Every time I fail, God's mercy has been extended as the lifeline to help me move forward.

About a decade ago, I had the opportunity to chaperone a group of students on a field trip to the Minneapolis Institute of Arts. While there, several students overheard that I was going to pay extra money to see the exhibit on the St. John's Bible. I was surprised when these students decided they wanted to join me. We were able to pick and choose some of our itinerary, and they too wanted to see the work that had gone into this handwritten and hand-illuminated version of the Bible. Before we had the opportunity to see the exhibit, there was a brief video of the work that had been done thus far on the project, which was slated to take years to complete. One of the things that captivated my heart was the process the artist and monks went through to prepare their hearts for handling a task of such significance. I had heard about this process in the work of Bible translation, but somehow seeing it played out at the institute that day was captivating.

Even though there was never another part for me in the centennial pageant, my opportunity to act came full circle years later. In an effort to make the Good Friday service more personal to the congregants, our pastors decided to have members portray first-person accounts of those who would have been present at the cross all those years ago—those who had denied him, betrayed him, sentenced him, befriended and followed him, and finally, the one who bore him and had to say good-bye that very day. I was to be Mary. Although I readily accepted the role, I still had reservations. The role of Mary felt so important, so precious, I was unsure whether I was the right girl for the job. But once I accepted the task, I dove into it with the same reverence as those who had illuminated the Bible my students and I had enjoyed years earlier. My research into the role—let's call it "character development"—uncovered that I was most likely the exact age Mary was at the time of Jesus's death. Well, that was one thing going for me. We were also both moms, and I like to believe that she was a brunette just like me. The big difference was that my son was not called to be the Savior of the world.

Somewhere in preparation for the evening, I began to realize that while I admired Mary for her bravery and strength, over the years, I had glossed over the fact that she was a grieving mom, which was something I could definitely wrap my head and heart around at that point in my life.

The night of the service, I poured my heart out in front of a church family who had walked through the shadow of the valley of death with us. There were very few dry eyes as anguished words poured deep from my soul, as I can only imagine poured from Mary while watching her son die.

My membership in a different kind of club—the one I never wanted to pledge in the first place—provided the character development I used that night. My membership in this club is for a lifetime with no chance for revocation. There is no place to cancel my subscription. Here is one place where I hope that *we vs. they* mentality does continue to exist. My deepest wish is to have no more pledge nights for new members in the club of grieving parents.

A Message From Kandy

WHENEVER I TRAVEL FOR SPEAKING ENGAGEMENTS, I TYPICALLY open by sharing the two dreams I had as a little girl. Compared to many of my friends who had huge lists of all they wanted out of life, my dreams of becoming a teacher and a momma seemed pretty small in comparison. Truly, though, they were all I wanted out of life. When my husband, Daniel, travels with me for these engagements, he usually cringes at this explanation, because I never mention that I wanted to be a wife. Don't get me wrong! I wanted to be married too, but my *big* aspirations were to have children and to teach other people's children.

Most of my childhood was idyllic. I loved my family and I adored school. I wore the cover right off my favorite childhood storybook, *Little Mommy*, from The Little Golden Book line. Playing school and house, the book fit perfectly with my future plans. Having parents who valued education gave me an incredible head start on learning, which carried me to great heights all through my schooling—including paving the road to becoming a teacher. I was, am, and perhaps always will be what some describe as a "high achiever." If I set my mind to it, it was attainable, and my life appeared to be one success after another.

After meeting and marrying the boy of the dreams I didn't know I had, we hoped to start a family right away. Two pink lines and my dreams, now *our* dreams, were well on their way. All was right with the world, until the day we were crib shopping. A pain like I had never experienced ripped through my abdomen. After waiting a week for the mobile ultrasound unit to come to the hospital in our rural community, we learned the worst outcome: a miscarriage. For the first time in my

5

life, I felt like a failure, believing I was to blame for this sadness. I wasn't equipped with how to handle something that didn't fit into my projected path to the future. Even more devastating, this grief caused me, for the first time, to doubt God's love. *How could a God who said he loved me allow a tiny baby, my baby, not to live?* Devastation, reality, and recognition led to the realization that my plans do not always match God's.

After what seemed like forever to me, we learned we were pregnant again, but after our first loss, I contained my joy until the first ultrasound, which showed a very healthy and thriving baby. Nine and a half months later, we brought home the tiniest baby boy, who was actually too small for the first car seat we had purchased for him. We loved this little ginger wonder we named Reed (which ironically means "red-haired"), and he was truly the sunshine of our world. Although all seemed right in the world again, the earlier loss of a baby we named Noah never went away.

Twenty months later, we brought home another absolutely delightful little boy, who became his big brother's best friend. Almost a full three pounds larger than Reed, Sawyer always seemed like a giant of a boy. Another two years passed, and we were ready to bring home another little one. Hearts were all a pitter-patter when, the day after Reed's fourth birthday, it was time to go back to the hospital for Stevens baby number 3. The anticipation of the moment was overshadowed by the rockiest delivery of all of our children. Erin Elisabeth arrived breach, purple, unresponsive, and in peril. After quite some time, the doctors and nurses were able to revive her, and she was whisked away to respiratory intensive care for four days.

Remember the part about God's plans not being my plans? The scare of almost losing another child led us to the conclusion that we didn't want to bear that type of heartache again. We had three beautiful children, and we were happy with our family.

Four years later, I was not feeling well, and we discovered we were unexpectedly expecting. My dreams were multiplying. (I forgot to mention I am a science and math teacher, so nerdy puns are one of my specialties.) On a family outing over a school break, the same experience from nine years earlier happened again. Overcome with intense abdominal cramping, I began praying what my heart knew to be true was wrong. But it wasn't. We learned a few days later that we were losing another sweet baby, whom we named Timothy.

Our plans for no more babies were further solidified. But God's plans were not as solid in our minds. Several months down the road, I wasn't feeling well at school. I went to the doctor, having left school earlier because I felt like I was going to pass out, a sensation I had never experienced. The doctor's diagnosis was not what we were expecting *at all*. We learned we were pregnant and miscarrying in the same day. This was a pain almost too deep to fathom. No time to celebrate. No time to anticipate. No time to dream.

For days we went through the motions, bereft of happiness. My mind could not fathom how my dreams could be so shattered. How could I have three children in my home and three children waiting in heaven? This couldn't have possibly been what God had in mind when he said he had plans for us to prosper. With splintered dreams and broken hearts we pressed on, not really sure how to take the next steps.

A month later, I was once again feeling horrible at school. It was during a teacher workshop day, and this time I did pass out. Thankfully, no students had to witness their teacher in such a predicament. I had an uneasy feeling and was able to call out to another teacher before collapsing. The principal called my husband, who came to school to get me, and back to the hospital we went. If the news just a few weeks before had been shocking, what came next seemed like it was made for a television special. After running some blood work, the medical staff asked us over and over if we could be pregnant. In pure distaste and genuine distress, I spewed out, "Look at my medical charts closer. Only a month ago we lost a baby. No! We are *not* pregnant." My heart ached more at the ridiculous question causing me to revisit the barely scabbed-over wound.

When all the tests came back, the doctor invited us to sit down for the explanations. I had prepared my heart for more calamitous news because it just seemed fitting. To be perfectly honest, I wasn't ready for more bad news, so I let my mind wander to another place, only hearing phrases like "blood work," "blah, blah, blah," "don't always catch," and "twins." My mind jolted back to reality on that final word. No, this can't be happening. Not another baby. Not another loss. Only, it wasn't a loss. It was a perfectly healthy little baby fighting to live.

During a prayer service with our pastor a month earlier, we had been too overcome with grief to name our third miscarried baby. But after an ultrasound confirming the doctor's diagnosis, we learned we were expecting a little girl. Baby number 7 was the twin we would hold, while baby number 6 went straight to Jesus's arms. We decided to name the girls after my grandmothers: Savannah *Kate* (number 6) and *Cloie* Ruth (number 7).

Although I don't think any of us breathed peacefully until the day she was delivered, Cloie's arrival was one of the most beautiful days of my life. From that moment forward, I began to see how God was using the story of our pain to minister to other moms who experienced pregnancy losses. Here and there, God would place in my path women who needed an understanding ear. Although I didn't blame God, I had come to a place of understanding. He had a plan, and even though I didn't like the pain we experienced, he was slowly turning my mourning into a mission.

For three years, our life was filled with the busyness of a family with four children and a bunch of pets. One Christmas, I shared in our annual card about my childhood dreams and how blessed we were because all we ever wanted out of life sat right in front of us at the dinner table. "Blessed" was a word that easily slipped off our tongues.

Our bigger kids were growing older, and we were beginning to see the dreams of their futures take hold. One day, Reed announced on a trip back from visiting family in North Dakota that he wanted to attend Yale University. I didn't even realize he knew the Ivy League school existed, let alone had plans to attend for postsecondary studies. Dreams—they are contagious. Sawyer, who has always been a big movie fan, chimed in with his intention to attend Marshall University, which wasn't surprising since we had watched *We Are Marshall* a week previous. Sister, who loves all things Irish, spoke up that she wanted to attend the University of Notre Dame. As a teacher, I could hardly contain my excitement to watch my children dream up amazing plans for learning. Our lives were busy but simple—typically focused on spending time together and serving others every chance we got.

Our life was about as idyllic as a postcard. Sure, we had some minor blips here and there, but just like my childhood, everything was what we had envisioned our lives to be when we were young and newly married.

But postcard images fade, which we learned in the most horrific of ways.

Everything I knew and believed to be good and right with the world changed on February 19, 2008. After a brief relocation for my husband's work the year prior, I decided to leave my career as an educator to be a stay-at-home mom. So after driving the big kids to school that frigid morning, Cloie and I settled in for a day of making homemade bread, reading stories, and dreading going back out in the cold to pick up the kids at the bus stop. We live in a town seventeen miles away from our children's school, and because of the agreement between the two school superintendents, our children could only ride the bus to the district line, not all the way to our neighborhood. At the normal time, we bundled up and headed to wait in the parking lot of the Catholic church in the tiny town in between home and school.

The bus had always been punctual. When no telltale yellow blur appeared in my rearview mirror at the usual time, I should have known something was amiss. *I didn't.* The other two moms waiting didn't seem too concerned either. Soon we began to notice a flurry of emergency vehicles, sirens blaring, and lights flashing, speeding toward the direction of the school. We continued to wait and wait and wait, but the bus never came. One mom, who was related to someone in local law enforcement, contacted her family member and learned a school bus had been involved in an accident. The thought that this could be our children's school bus never crossed my mind. Believing they were just held up by a traffic jam, we decided to journey toward the school to pick up our kids, leaving two vehicles to wait for the kids if we missed them.

Those unattended vehicles remained empty.

We learned before we were halfway to the school that the bus involved was not just some random school bus but the very one transporting our children. What we didn't know was how that one moment would change our lives forever.

I woke up that morning after spending a long President's Day weekend with my children, dreading sending them back to school. I loved every moment I was able to have my kiddos to myself. By late afternoon, I was jolted into a nightmare that has left scars so deep only God knows they exist.

When I finally attempted to rest at three in the morning, I was sitting in a rocking chair in the pediatric intensive care unit next to the bed, cradling our son Sawyer, who had undergone emergency surgery to repair his broken and dislocated right hip and broken left femur. While Daniel was sleeping on the chair that folded out into a bed, our Boy Wonder, was fighting to live, hooked to up to all kinds of machines. Three floors below us, Reed, the sunshine of our world, was waiting to be transported to another hospital because I had made a promise to him three years earlier. The vow was that we would honor his wishes to be an organ donor. Reed, along with three other beautiful children— classmate Jesse Javens, his younger brother, Hunter, and Emilee Olson, a 4-H friend and classmate of Erin, died that day. Erin, traumatized by what she had witnessed and by watching our sadness in the aftermath, kept her injuries quiet that night, only to be discovered six weeks later. But on that night, both of our girls were safely ensconced in a hotel room across the street with amazing friends who journeyed with us to the hospital ninety miles from home.

The scales then tipped in heaven's favor. Four of my children resided there, and three were on earth with us. It felt as if the earth had opened a deep black hole and grief sucked us right to the bottom.

Despite other children being hospitalized besides Sawyer, several days passed before we learned some of the details of the accident. None of what we discovered would alter or lessen the pain we (or any of the other families) were experiencing then or for years to come. I couldn't sleep or eat, but the desire to be my children's momma was strong. I knew they needed me, and that knowledge is what kept me going. Knowing I needed God more now than I had ever acknowledged before was a life-altering experience. The verses of my childhood became lifelines allowing us to cling to the faith we held dear.

Over the last eight years, I have had plenty of experience in what is and isn't helpful in this grieving journey that I will be on for the rest of my life. We have spent a lot of time since that fateful day working through our children's physical injuries and their emotional needs as well. We were left grieving one son (and three friends) and faced with the daunting task of not only raising three children, but also three grieving children.

Much to our surprise, not only did we have broken hearts to mend but we also had to develop thicker skin. Well-intentioned actions and well-meaning words sometimes cut us to the core. We also learned we were made of us some pretty tough stuff. I never imagined that anyone could survive what we have been and still are going through. To date, Sawyer has had over twenty surgeries/procedures, and Erin has had six. Because of our injured children's needs, at times we felt we weren't given the luxury of grieving. But our faith in God and the extraordinary kindness of people buoyed us. Even in the darkest moments, we could sense people praying and cheering for us. To each person who did, you have no idea how much the words from your mouths to God's ears helped us hang on and gave us the freedom to let go of tendencies that God never meant for us to have in the first place.

This book was written to provide hope and practical ideas for anyone who wishes to support someone on a grief journey.

Grief is messy, and recovering from grief is even messier. Many have asked what they can do to help. Others have been afraid to even talk to us, wanting to help but not knowing how to start the conversation.

A kind word, a prayer, or a hug goes a really long way, even farther some days than grandiose gestures. *I have decided that small acts of love are really revolutionary acts.* It takes courage to love someone when you don't know what to say. It takes guts to reach out to a complete stranger and say, "I have walked in your shoes. I can see in your eyes that you will survive this pain."

This book is also written for me. There is no manual on how to grieve, and people create their own formula for dealing with it. There is no magical formula, no set number of days after which the pain will go away, and no one way to work through it. What works for one person's healing may never work for another.

Grief is a horrible friend—the kind that makes you wear the hideous dress as a bridesmaid only to make herself look better. She tells you lies that you believe. She clouds your judgment and at times feeds into your ego, making you believe that you know everything there is to know about the grieving process. Frankly, I can't stand her. I know with certainty that I have done some of the things I've since learned are not at all helpful to a grieving person.

Sawyer has a T-shirt that reads revolutionary with the letters, "e-v-o-l" in bold. Look carefully. Do you see it? *Love* is spelled backward. Walking through grief often requires looking at love from a different angle. It takes time to become a rebel in this way—a heart that loves with abandon. Even though this isn't how I wished to earn my education in being revolutionary, today I can say that I am not the same person because of what our family has walked through. As much as grief gets on my last nerve, I have also learned life-changing lessons that led me to love like a rebel. Learning to see the world through God's eyes and learning to love with abandon were game changers for me.

So please take heart! If you are reading this book and feel that you, like me, have hurt a grieving person, forgive yourself. God has used this journey to teach our whole family much about forgiveness and being aware that you never know what burdens someone else is carrying. Stage your own revolt. Forgive, be kind, pray for someone, but most importantly, show up in life.

I have dreamed of being a writer for a few years, but just like I didn't want to join the club of grieving parents, I never wanted or intended to write a book about this subject. But God has better plans than I do—all the time.

This book was born out of a conversation with a local pastor's wife. As the dust settled in my whirlwind of chaos, she asked whether I would be willing to share what our community had done well to help my family heal. The conversation we shared that morning over coffee (okay, for those who know me personally, I had a sweet tea) laid the foundation for this book, which I believe was God's plan all along.

While this isn't what I dreamed for my life story, I am so thankful that God has given me vision to see his love—life-changing, grace-filled, healing, revolutionary love—overflowing from the people who have helped us along the way. It is to every person who has done something— actually anything—through God's prompting to love our family that I dedicate this book. You are truly an inspiration to us.

the redbird sings the song of hope

If I told you my story, you would hear hope *that wouldn't let go.*
—Big Daddy Weave

HOPE.

Four tiny letters strung together to form a relatively small word, but to me and my family, that one word is probably our saving grace. Throughout the journey we have endured since our darkest day, hope is the one thing that has held us all together. There were times in our lives before February 19, 2008, when clinging to hope was the only thing that made sense, like the time then eight-year-old Reed asked me why God would allow him to have an eye condition that could potentially cause him to go blind. I responded the only way I knew how. "We have to believe that God has a plan for your life, Reed, and we can have that hope through all of God's promises."

Words have always captivated my imagination. In the months and years following the bus crash, I often heard others describe me as strong and sometimes inspirational. I almost shuddered at the thought because neither of those words would have been the ones I would have chosen to describe the living nightmare we were experiencing. Better descriptors could have been exhausted, sleepless, emotionally drained, worried, and wounded. Every time I heard someone say, "I wish I had your strength," I would remind them I wasn't all that strong and that all of what they saw was simply faith.

I kept right on correcting people until my pastor told me, "Knock it off." Considering he was the one who finally bore the burden of telling me Reed was gone and I slugged him one good hit before he enveloped

13

me in the tightest hug imaginable, he's earned the right to tell it to me straight. As one of my husband's best friends, he had had enough of hearing me deflect comments about what other people saw in our family's story. His admonition centered on the fact that we had a choice in how we were going to respond to every hurdle and struggle we encountered. Pastor Don believed that we choose ways that brought us closer to God when perhaps others would have turned their backs on his promises.

Considering he spent almost a week with us in the hospital, including driving me there that awful night as Daniel flew in a helicopter with Sawyer, Don has seen it all and is probably a pretty good judge of our story. Even so, *I still had my doubts.*

My reasoning isn't all that remarkable. Maybe our choices were limited. We could choose to believe that everything God promised to us prior to 3:40 p.m. that frigid Tuesday was still valid when we laid our heads down in the sterile pediatric ICU that night, or we could abandon it all. Having previously placed high esteem on our intellect, maybe we discovered we weren't all that smart. Maybe we just didn't know any other way to be, to think, or to live. Giving us credit where perhaps credit wasn't due made me really uncomfortable.

But after my come-to-Jesus moment with Pastor Don, I realized that perhaps I was selling us short. I still don't believe that we are anything all that special, but I do know the one thing that kept us going and keeps us still going.

Hope.

They say it springs eternal, and in our story, it doesn't so much spring as flit around.

But before I get to that, I must share a moment that actually happened in that cold hospital room. After saying good-bye to Reed and waiting for Sawyer to return from multiple surgeries, we were eventually led to a small pediatric intensive care room. This would be Sawyer's home for the next eight days, which included his eleventh birthday. As monitors chimed the rhythm of life for Sawyer, I felt as if my heart was going to stop beating. *When am I going to wake up and see this was all a bad dream?* Sleep, however, was the farthest thing from my mind, which was racing from all the thoughts no mother should ever have to process.

We were told by the hospital we would be able to room with Sawyer, and the nurses converted the equivalent of a La-Z-Boy recliner into a bed. One look at that bed, and I knew that we both were not going to fit there for a restless night's sleep. I also knew of the two of us, Daniel was the only one who would be sleeping that night. Encouraging him to rest, I took the wooden rocking chair and sat next to my battered and bruised, still covered in bus glass and paint, little boy.

Much like the porch swings of my childhood, I did the only thing I knew to comfort myself at that time. I began to rock, crying out to God with one son fighting for his life next to me and the other one three floors below waiting to *give* the gift of life to so many others. When everything that once made sense in my life was stripped away, I was left with rocking and pleading with God, only I didn't even know what words to pray. *So I told God that.*

He and I both know I am no Bible scholar. I have read the Bible from cover to cover, but I am not always good at remembering where things are specifically found. I know certain promises are there and I had to rely on that.

Rocking and praying. Praying and rocking I told God, "I don't even know what to pray. I know somewhere it says that your Holy Spirit will pray on my behalf when all I have is moaning. God, this is all I have right now, so you're going to have to fill in the words."

As soon as the thought left my being, God responded in a way I never believed possible.

In a real and audible voice, which sounded remarkably like that of a pastor I met years later, I heard God's gentle voice calmly reminding me that He understood because his son died too.

I added crying to my rocking and praying, because the God of my morning met his daughter that night when she needed him most. The promises of the morning were still true that sleepless night. Those six words steeled my resolve. I didn't know how and I didn't know when, but I knew that we were going to be okay.

Six little words provided me hope, but what I didn't know was that God would provide a messenger of hope to our family from his vast creation.

When Sawyer was released from the hospital, he came home with a wheelchair and very little resemblance to his old life. In grief circles, the term "new normal" is mentioned often. As hard as life was for all of us, Sawyer and all he would endure physically for the rest of his life was excruciating, but nothing compared to the emotional scar of losing your best friend and hero. I will never forget his words when we told him two days later that Reed had not survived the bus crash. Through anguished tears, he cried out, "I don't know how to be Sawyer without Reed."

Deep was the bond of my two boys.

Exactly one month following the bus crash, we saw exactly how deep.

The night before that one-month milestone was anguishing. Sawyer, who had recently been cleared to begin using a walker for some small steps, slipped and fell. A trip to the emergency room and an X-ray revealed some major damage had been done. The fall caused the heads to be knocked off two of the screws attached to the metal plate holding his leg together.

One step forward led to twenty backward. Instead of getting the okay to continue moving ahead, our boy was told to sit for another month, allowing only adults to move him unless he was in the wheelchair. Heartbreaking news for us, devastating news for Sawyer.

The next day, March 19 was unseasonably warm. We opened a window to enjoy the world outside that we weren't getting to experience much those days. While my attention was needed in the laundry room downstairs, I left Sawyer to sit in the recliner to watch anything that was going on outside the large picture windows of our living room.

Our family has been enthusiastic bird watchers for years. We have numerous feeders throughout the yard, and we taught the birds' songs and calls to our children even when they were very little. Taking a page from my mom's book of greatest Christmas gifts ever, we decided to merge our love of birds to annual presents. Similar to my mom, who annually gives every one of us Hallmark ornaments, we decided we would give each of our children bird ornaments. Each has their favorite bird, and we search high and low to find a blue jay for Reed, a cardinal for Sawyer, a chickadee for Erin, and a goldfinch for Cloie.

With all those feeders in the yard over the years, we had been able to attract a lot of birds, and for my little ornithologists, all of their favorites, except the cardinal. No matter what we did, the cardinal was the elusive feathered friend who never made an appearance—not once in the ten years we had lived in our home at that point. No matter how we tried, we just couldn't get a cardinal to our backyard.

While I was busily folding towels, I heard Sawyer scream out my name. I have never been much of a runner, but fearing the worst, I bolted up the steps believing that my Boy Wonder had taken another spill and worried about how I would load him and his wheelchair and his baby sister for a second trip to the emergency room.

Instead of a boy on the floor, I found a tearful young man pointing out the window. Right at the level of his chair, sitting in the tree, was the most beautiful scarlet-red cardinal singing with all his glory. There was no earthly reason for the cardinal to be there. With what little energy we had to make it through those days, filling the bird feeders was not on our radar.

I was amazed, but it took the faith of a little boy to see the miracle unfolding before us. Sawyer recognized immediately that the redbird was a messenger straight from God (most likely at the request of our own redheaded wonder) to tell us Reed was doing just fine in Jesus's arms. Reed would have known exactly what bird to send to get our attention. We believe he would have also known how deeply hurt Sawyer was at this point in our healing journey and would know which bird of all God's birds Sawyer needed to see.

There is an old legend regarding the cardinal, known as the redbird to me as a little girl growing up in the South.

The cardinal is a beautiful bird with gorgeous red plumage and an equally inviting song. According to legend, the cardinal was once a white bird—as white as snow. The cardinal came to the cross on Calvary's hill and sang to Jesus at the base of his cross. The tiny bird sang with all its might to his maker and master. During his song, Jesus's blood dripped on his feathers, and henceforth, the male cardinal has been his brilliant red color.

Old legend or not, those red feathers captured our attention.

From that moment on, the redbird has appeared when we have needed a hope-filled moment. When we lost a dear friend, the cardinal sang right off the back deck of a neighbor. Our first vacation without Reed, there he was singing away. My personal favorite was the time we took the whole family to see a life-sized dinosaur exhibit at the

Minnesota Zoo. Reed loved anything and everything dinosaur. While we were enjoying a few exhibits close to the entrance, we began to be dive-bombed by a flash of red feathers. We quickly realized it was a redbird. We decided the cardinal had somewhere else he wanted us to be and started making our way toward the dinosaurs. Our thinking must have been correct because we were escorted by that beautiful redbird all the way to the entrance of the reptilian exhibit, where he perched and sang the most beautiful song.

For our family, cardinal spotting is simply a boost of love straight from heaven. God's tiny part of creation serves as a reminder of how much he loves us and Reed. The redbird will often sing the song of hope when we need it most. Some may look at our story and call it coincidence, but *we choose to believe in miracles!*

PART ONE
What Are You, a Bunch of Idiots?
In Nicer Terms: Things That Are Not Really Helpful

GOD'S ABILITY TO TRANSFORM PEOPLE IS SOMETHING THAT HUMBLES ME every time I experience it. I can honestly say losing Reed and our babies made me a gentler person. My transformation was a direct result of Jesus's spittle allowing me to see things I was blinded to before. My eyes were given a divine cleansing, and suddenly my quick-witted tongue realized I didn't always see the world the way Jesus does. I also recognized no one ever really knows how uncomfortable a neighbor's shoes might be. My transformation is only one story in my family. Sawyer's story is definitely another one.

He came into the world as a hothead. When he was little, just months old, he would get so mad that he would literally turn red, clench his little fists, and scream until he almost passed out. His temper flared up at times over the years, leading to him twice knocking people flat at school. One was to right a wrong because a sixth grader kept picking on a kindergartner. His third grade "truth and justice" meter laid the big kid out. Another time was when a classmate (who later became a close friend) would not stop pestering him. The eruption took place during gym class. In his first grade explanation, which sounded a lot like Popeye, he "took it 'til he couldn't stands it no more," but for the record, he told us he did warn the guy before popping him one.

My boys couldn't have been more different when it came to temperaments. Reed had a "water off a duck's back" personality while Sawyer was a "hit first; ask questions later" kind of guy. That difference between the two boys, who were inseparable, was crystal clear one day at the bus stop. Erin emerged from the bus and skipped over to the van, followed by the boys. Reed simply walked over and hopped into the seat next to me. Sawyer stomped to the side door with steam billowing out his ears. I didn't need my degree in advanced chemistry to figure out something was amiss. Like a lion roaring, Sawyer blurted out, "Reed, if you don't say something to those kids, I am going to knock them flat!" He had already twice proven he could and would, so I tried to intervene. Eventually I learned that kids were doing and saying awful things to Reed on the bus. All I could think was, *I am Momma Bear; hear me roar.* But Reed, who never should have been accustomed to this type of treatment, blew me away with his response to my aggravation. "Momma, don't say anything. They don't know Jesus." In my momma bear heart, knowing Jesus and giving people a "come to Jesus" moment are two vastly different approaches. In Sawyer's defense, the apple doesn't fall far from the tree.

My daddy's all-time favorite grandchild story involves Sawyer's temper and some training wheels. I don't recall the reason why only my dad came to visit, but while he was here, we decided to make a trip to our favorite ice cream place a few blocks away. With Erin in the stroller, the adults took to walking while the boys hopped on their tiny bikes. At the time, Reed was six, making Sawyer four and a half. As a sneaky way to encourage him to learn to balance and, thus, pedal on his own, Daniel rigged Sawyer's training wheels so only one could touch the ground at a time. In theory it was a good plan, but in practice, not so much. From behind the boys, all the grown-ups shouted encouragements, which only incited the bees—like the time my cousins John David and Hayden took to smacking Papa Noles's beehives with belts. I have no idea what in the mayonnaise would have possessed them to do that! Nonetheless, our words and suggestions only served to make our pint-sized pedaler angrier and angrier. Eventually the anger overtook him as he shouted back at us, much like those bees to my cousins, "I'm doing the best I can! What are you all, a bunch of idiots?" Even today, I almost crack up laughing about it.

Transformation can be painful, but the darkest day in our lives produced a gentler and kinder momma and son. If you didn't know these stories shared here, today you would never believe them. My boy wonder is a kind-hearted, gentle giant who would give you the shirt off his back, but he is still one who doesn't suffer fools lightly.

The crazy thing about grief and grief recovery is something that few people ever talk about. It is never pretty. It is never packaged up in a linear set of steps to be climbed one step at a time. Grief can and will drive you crazy, and even more puzzling, grief can bring out the worst in support players. Nowhere is this more apparent than in the book of Job. I am amazed at how supportive Job's friends were during his trials and tribulations. They sat by the outer wall with him for days, their physical presence bringing hope and encouragement. So supportive were these friends that they didn't leave his side day or night. Everyone needs at least one friend like that. (I have several.) But the character flaws for these friends were illuminated when they opened their mouths. We have all been those friends—the ones who say the wrong things at the wrong time. Although we only want our hurting loved ones to feel better, instead of bringing comfort, we make the pain sting more.

Take it from me, one of life's biggest idiots. In college, my roommate, Michelle, lost her grandpa—the man who helped raise her when she was little and who was the light of her life at that point. She was at a really low place, so we decided to go for a long drive in the country. At some point, our discussion turned to the merits of interment compared to cremation. We were twentysomethings and definitely thought we knew everything. I said something about burial that really hurt her. I have never forgotten that while we were having a friendly chat, I lost sight of the fact that her grandpa was recently buried. The words from this idiot's mouth really hurt her, and I still regret it. She is probably long over it, but I am a burden bearer. Hurting people lingers with me, and I strive, with God's help, not to repeat those mistakes.

The biggest problem with coming alongside a grieving person is that while most people genuinely want to help, when it comes right down to it, we don't know what to do. Often our words and actions come out all wrong—adding insult to injury.

Get a room full of grieving parents together for any length of time, and inevitably the conversation will turn to stories of hurt inflicted by well-meaning people. It is a safe crowd in which to vent, knowing every

21

other soul in the room understands what it is like to feel wounded. Like a fine mist settling over us, a few uncomfortable laughs tickle the air when we realize we don't stand alone.

One of the sweetest compliments I have ever received was "Kandy Noles Stevens, you are brave! You have taught this entire community how to grieve." The compliment bearer meant that I was open and honest with my grieving, which was not something she had witnessed often. I wasn't given a manual; I have simply been doing what God laid on my heart. I am by no means a grief expert, nor do I really wish to be. I am simply a momma whose story God is using to touch other people. I wouldn't call it courageous, but these are some things that I (and other bereaved friends) wish more people knew about how not to be an idiot when offering help to the grieving.

Feelings Are a Dime a Dozen

I HAVE HAD THE PLEASURE OF TEACHING WITH SOME AMAZING people over the years. Teachers are good people. I am not just saying that because I am one. It really is true. We show up with lessons planned and hearts ready to help children grow and reach new heights. I love sharing ideas and tools of the trade with other teachers, but my favorite part of the day is when real conversations flow at the lunch table. I have always been a collector of stories, and some of the best ones I have ever heard were at a table while God was knitting hearts together through the swapping of tales.

One of the finest women I have ever had the honor of teaching alongside shared a story one day that really made me appreciate her more. Most at the table knew her past. I was not one of them. She had left an abusive marriage, changed states, and worked two jobs—all to support her seven children. Before that day, I had thought her a little caustic—a good teacher but someone with just a little more of a biting sense of humor than I had. When I learned of her background, I never once passed on an opportunity to hear one of her stories, and I never thought of her as caustic again. She was simply a warrior with an armored exterior.

We were all complaining one day about the rising costs of groceries, which is a real challenge on a teacher's salary. She interjected with the times she would take all her kids to the market, spending most of the trip telling them, "No! We can't afford that!" Beaten down and weary, she would leave the market with an industrial-sized bag of rice and very little else. Without one hint of sadness, she referred to those days as *the rice years*.

23

By the time she came into my life, she had been remarried to a lovely gentleman, had another son, and was quite well off. The rice years were long forgotten. If I had missed the table talk, I would have never known how courageous this friend was. It is something that I have never forgotten, because it was the first time I really learned that you can never know someone's story without knowing the chapters preceding its intersection with yours.

While my family never experienced *the rice years* while I was growing up, we weren't too far off when my daddy decided to go back to graduate studies when I was in early elementary school. I remember, much like my husband's upbringing, we didn't know we were poor. Our parents just did the best they could at the time.

Back in those days, visiting family was the only kind of vacation we knew. That is, until my mom hit the big time, winning a thousand dollars in a supermarket extravaganza! I remember the tears running down her face as she realized she had won. A hi-fi stereo system and one family vacation later, we were walking in high cotton to be sure. That family vacation still involved visiting family, but it is what we did differently that made it so special.

I have been blessed with amazing kinfolk, and one of my favorite aunts and uncles lived just north of us in a rural area outside of Atlanta. Much like the Beverly Hillbillies, we loaded up the family and went to Hills of Hotlanta, minus one granny rocking away on top of the vehicle. We went to Six Flags, Animal Kingdom, and my personal favorite, an Atlanta Braves game. All of those things were ones we could never have afforded without that supermarket payday!

While we didn't have a lot of money, we did have a lot of love all those years. Every gathering with friends and family during baseball season, always—and I mean *always*—had a Braves game on the television. If we couldn't pick up the game on the TV, we'd find it on the radio. Being a Braves fan ran deep inside my veins. Granddaddy Cunningham, my great grandfather, used to go to bed at four in the afternoon, to be able to get up and watch or listen to the West Coast games before telecasting. My summers involved playing outside every day, sweet tea, and the Atlanta Braves.

When I was about eight years old, I remember visiting the old

Atlanta-Fulton County Stadium. When I arrived with my uncle, two cousins, Daddy, and my brother, I believed I was standing on sacred ground. Looking back now, I am so glad they didn't think I was too girly for the adventure. It was the Fourth of July, and it was the first time I ate ice cream in a little plastic helmet, a tradition I still treasure today. I don't recall who my Braves played, but I do know that they won the game. I cheered my little heart out and was ready to leave when the game was over. But Daddy and Uncle Rendell had purposely left out one detail. Not only was there a game that night, but a fireworks show followed!

Next to lightning bugs, fireworks are my favorite bling in the entire world. Both are way better than diamonds in my book. It was too much for my little self to contain. Too much! On the edge of my seat, I waited (probably not too patiently) for the show to begin. When it finally did, I was stupefied by its beauty. I remember that baseball game as the single best fireworks show I have ever experienced. After an amazing display of aerial launchings, the show ended with what was billed as the world's biggest wall of fire. It was a pyrotechnic wonder, strung from right field to left, and every inch of it glowed with blazing glory. After our optical rods and cones adjusted, somehow they illuminated the Braves logo on home plate (*home plate!*) as the piece de resistance! Even though it was about 110 degrees in the shade, the whole display gave me the chills.

Several years ago, our family was at a summer gathering. At some point, the conversation of the group shifted to baseball. I shared that we often take in the fireworks game of a local minor league team but that those games didn't shine a candle to my Fulton County stadium day. So special was that memory, I actually cried the day the stadium was demolished. A very special piece of my childhood was gone forever. Since my boys were so young on demolition day, I never had the opportunity to share that experience with them. Years later, that same uncle took my family, including the little boys, to a game at the newer Turner Field. Although not the stadium of my childhood, I was impressed by the design.

While swapping stories, I shared the joy of our experience. It was clearly a stadium where great lengths were taken to create a homey atmosphere, as well as having the air of a ballpark of years gone by. The best part was sharing the evening with my boys and my beloved uncle, just like I done many years ago. Before I finished speaking, someone jumped in and began to pick apart my whole experience. He stated that if I thought *that* was something, I should get box seats at that stadium, like his company did. He went on and on about his experience and how it was so much better than mine.

I hadn't meant it to be an apples-to-oranges conversation. It was simply a bunch of people who love the game of baseball sharing their experiences. It reminded me of something my boys' football coach always says. "Don't blow out someone else's candle to make yours burn brighter."

There is true wisdom in his words. The greatest lesson that grief has taught our family is that you never really know what someone else is going through. *Ever.* When someone says, "I know how you feel," it is meant to be empathetic, but in reality, the words sting.

My relationship with Reed was so unique and so intricately woven, that no one (not even my husband or my other kids) knows how I really feel. I realize that I am not the first momma to lose a child, and I certainly won't be the last. But unless you can crawl into my skin, my heart, and my memories, this isn't something that I can share with you. I am not certain you would want me to do so. Grief is a lingering ache. Empathy and sympathy and knowing about loss—those things I can share. Much like my feelings after sharing my baseball stadium story, my reaction to such statements was one of bewilderment, because it felt like it diminished my grief. At times, it was as if I didn't have a right to my own grief, because other people *knew how I felt.*

When your child dies, you join a club to which not a single person wants membership. The other members do understand, but they also have experienced the trauma of well-intentioned sentiments gone wrong. Thankfully, there were three mothers (club members) who had also lost children who came and comforted me. Not a single one said, "I know how you feel," even though they had lost a child too. The horror of losing a child is so enormous that there isn't an English word to describe the ones left behind. *Widow* or *widower* is used when a spouse passes away, and *orphan* when parents die, but there isn't a moniker for grieving parents. The loss is too deep, too profound, to be summed up in just one word.

When you experience the loss of a child, you realize how unique that particular pain can be. It isn't the right order of life. The example of listening and loving but not comparing, shown by all three moms, was one I appreciated then, and even more so now. In our story, Reed was not the only child who died that awful February day. Among our three families, we are all grieving the same crash, but we are definitely *not* grieving the same loss.

No one ever really is.

God's Plan for the Butterflies

SINCE OUR OLDER KIDS WERE LITTLE, WE'VE RAISED ALL SORTS of animals. It's an occupational hazard when the momma is a science teacher. Quite often our premium counter space is occupied by one experiment or another. One of our favorites is hatching creatures. We have had tadpoles, snails, ladybugs, fish eggs, and painted lady caterpillars, and we have watched in amazement as God's creations grew or transformed from one stage to another.

We were successful much of the time, but not always, as was the case with the caterpillars. Arriving in the mail, they were about the size of the head on a straight pin. Tiny! The miniscule larvae ate the supplied food source, and just like a family favorite, *The Very Hungry Caterpillar*, they grew and grew and *grew* until it was time for them to take a really big nap.

During this sleep (the chrysalis stage), our caterpillars followed God's divine plan of transformation. Our boys were amazed that if you lightly touched the chrysalis, the soon-to-be butterfly would wiggle inside. We didn't do it often, but just enough to prove that indeed the pupa stage creatures were alive and well.

The anticipation of their emergence was almost too much for our little ones. We waited and waited and then waited some more, which is agonizing when you are four and two. Every day the moment their feet hit the floor, it was a race to see if any butterflies had magically appeared. (Actually, that was Reed's plan, because Sawyer's first question of the day was always "Is it time for bweakfast yet?") Finally, we noticed a little red stain on the bottom of their enclosure. Butterfly day had arrived! Ironically, that day coincided with the day of my commencement for my master's degree in science education. Instead of doing what we really wanted to do (watch the butterflies emerge), we attended both the breakfast and later the commencement. Yet since I knew that I would be the third person to walk across the stage that day, I told my family and extended family to sit in the back and save themselves the torture of sitting through a three-hour program with two little ones. They took my advice and made an exit while I braved the heat, eight and a half months pregnant, in a steamy, black get-up resembling a ball gown for an orca whale. When I returned from the ceremony, three of our five butterflies had emerged. There was one struggling to make an appearance, and one hadn't changed at all.

We thought we were something else (something else!) when we pulled out the camcorder, set up the tripod, and hit record. Two hours later, there were still three butterflies and two chrysalises. One eventually emerged a few minutes after the tape ran out of room. So much for that plan! The final butterfly struggled, appearing to be stuck. Reed really wanted to help it out. He thought if he could just assist the straggler, it would be okay.

In life, there are moments when you get to see your children's hearts. This was one of them. The greatest educational achievement of my life was celebrated that day, but what I remember most is my little boy's heart. He loved animals so much, and for most of his life, we believe he was a real-life Dr. Doolittle. He could commune with nature in ways I have never seen before or since. He was the only child I have ever known who would lie flat on his belly to talk with animals at zoos. Somehow, all animals spoke his language too. At zoos, barns, and petting places, they followed him everywhere. If ever there was a time when Reed, the "Animal Whisperer," could do a good deed, it was to set a butterfly free.

Only, we wouldn't let him.

He cried for quite some time about how if we just helped the butterfly get out of that chrysalis all would be fine. *Why wouldn't we just let him try?* When he calmed down, we explained that God's plan for butterflies required them to do the work of getting through the chrysalis on their own. If we helped, the butterfly would die for sure. It was simply the way God made butterflies. We didn't have to like it, but that was his design. Sadly, his plan didn't include little redheaded "super boys" jumping in and monkeying with his plans, which sometimes means not all caterpillars become butterflies.

The same can be said when it comes to the lives of his children.

Several times after the crash, people would say things like "I know your pain hurts, but this was God's will." *Do what?* I had to muster up a weak smile to hide the biting of my tongue. I believe in a loving Heavenly Father. But what Father would wish this fate on his child? Even Disney villains don't go that far! In my heart of hearts, I can't ascribe this to being God's will. I do, however, believe God knew it was going to happen. He had Reed's days numbered in his book, and ultimately, God will use Reed's life *and* death as a part of his colossal love story for the world.

My job and life training has included education in chemistry, mathematics, teaching, Southern food and manners, and all thing momma. Please know I am definitely not a theologian, and I am certain those who are would love to take exception with my thoughts. This crash was not God's will! Yet in his plan, God gave us each a free will. Unfortunately, the woman who killed my child exercised her free will by making a series of bad choices that culminated in a tragic outcome for many families, including her own. Having given us this free will, God can't then run around like Superman cleaning up all the bad things we choose to do. In this case, that includes saving my son and the other three children from tragic deaths and many others from severe injuries.

Following the bus crash, we have had many people tell us Reed's testimony has changed their lives. Their stories remain a sweet, soothing balm to our souls. Isn't it amazing? Some words crushed our spirits, while other words boosted our souls.

One of the most amazing testimonies came from a cousin of ours. After a late night just hanging out, he and Daniel went for a long drive. During the drive, our cousin shared that he wanted my husband to know he was a changed man because of a twelve-year-old redheaded boy who loved God above everything else. He went on to explain how he sat at Reed's services expecting something completely different from a time of praising God for his presence in the storm. When he heard the pastors' stories (more words) about our little "preacher" boy's life, he knew that if Reed had that kind of faith, he wanted it too. He had attended church for years and loved God, but one little piece, being more than just a "fan" of God, was missing. With tears in his eyes, which were reflected back in my husband's watery ones, he said he was going to heaven because of Reed's life story. Even writing this, I tear up just knowing how proud Reed would be of our cousin's choice.

I find peace in the distinction between what people said and what they truly meant. While the word choice was "It was God's will," the heart song was saying, "God will use your child's life in a good, even *amazing*, way." God's will wasn't to kill my child, but his plan included using Reed's life and death to save someone else's. There is comfort in knowing that God is true to his promises in using everything (even tragedy) for his good, even if that means my boy caterpillar never became a butterfly on this side of heaven.

The Better Place

As a Southern transplant to the central plains states, there are some things I have had to become accustomed to. Rhubarb and lefse are a couple food items I had never encountered before moving north. Cold weather is an obvious one, but blizzards are something altogether more than a treat at the Dairy Queen, and I had never been to one of those either until my parents moved us to North Dakota.

One tradition I have grown to embrace is the annual Crazy Days sales that most towns host. This is so much more than a real-deal sidewalk sale as entire city streets are blocked off and all kinds of discounted and clearance wares are sold at incredible prices. There are pie socials, lemonade stands, meal deals, and in our town, my personal favorite: the kiddie parade. This annual event involves local children dressing up in the theme of their choice and marching down Main Street. Considering Crazy Days are held on the third Thursday in July, typically the costumes are lighter weight. Sadly, though, I have seen some poor babies roasting in this reverie in plush costumes.

Now, I love any reason to dress up and use my imagination. Apparently, I passed that particular gene on to my children as well. Over the years, my kiddos have participated and won the costume contest several times. When he was three, Reed dressed as an old-fashioned paperboy, complete with newsboy hat, knickers-style pants, and a mock newspaper. In his squeaky little voice, he proudly performed, "Get ya paper here! Get ya paper!" Since the parade is sponsored by the local newspaper, it was a slam dunk. Another year, the boys recruited some neighborhood friends. They pulled out Daniel's old army jackets, Papa's old police uniform shirts, and asked me to sew their sister a Statue of Liberty costume. They went as a 9/11 tribute. Their creativity knew no limits.

For years, we participated in this parade, until the event that broke our hearts. Erin had a Dorothy Gale, of *Wizard of Oz* fame, costume given to her as a hand-me-down (my favorite kind of clothes *and* costumes). She had used it the fall before, and we decided to go as the four main characters for the kiddie parade. Since it was July, we knew that there was no way our kids were going to be able to pull off full costumes (except Erin because hers was cotton). As luck would have it, one of their friends had participated in a local ice skating extravaganza as the Scarecrow. We were one child short of the four characters, so we asked Stephen to join us. As an only child, he was delighted to be part of the group. That left one Cowardly Lion and one Tin Man to create. I used felt to create cuffs for the lion's paws and tail. A little eyeliner worked for whiskers, and voila! Sawyer's chubby cheeks were transformed into the perfect timid lion. I bought a large oil funnel and some silver paint. Along with cuffs made from tin foil as well as a cardboard and tin foil axe, my little redhead transformed into the character who only wanted a heart.

The day of the parade was beautiful, if not particularly cool. As my merry foursome marched down the street, Daniel was videotaping them along the way. I walked alongside, just in case our youngest, at only three years old, became too tired. The kids didn't notice Daddy until we got to the point where he was standing behind the judges. On my honor, I promise we didn't plan this. He just happened to pause there between the crowds of people. When my spunky little girl spotted the hero of her life in the crowd, her whole personality changed. It wasn't just her ruby red slippers that were sparkling. She came alive, waving to everyone while tenderly balancing her basket with her little stuffed Toto. The judges were smitten. I know I am partial, but we were too!

When it came time to award the winners, my little gang was happily sitting on the edge of the curb eating their ice cream sandwiches provided by a local business. They didn't even realize they had won as the judges handed me the gift certificates and tried to walk away.

About that time, two ladies walked up asking who had won, because they were super proud of their group's costumes. For the record, they were adorable, but the judges chose the friends from Oz as the winners. Neither the judges nor I could have ever anticipated what happened next. The judge explained that my kids and their friend had won the group category.

Now, I am a sports mom, so I understand getting caught up in the moment. But never in my life have I harassed a child. (All the referees and umpires in this area are currently whispering behind their hands, "Yeah, but she sure has a few ideas on how we could improve!") As a teacher and a mom, I simply would not entertain the thought.

I wish I could say that is what happened on the corner of Third and Main. But instead of walking away, one of the two ladies got right down in my children's faces and screeched, "They're not so special!" Right before our eyes, she transformed into a modern day Miss Gulch. I was mortified. Messing with me is one thing, but messing with my kids is a totally different story. Instead of dignifying her outburst with a response, I hastily got the children up and marched to the pie social, where Stephen's momma was working that day. As I stomped off (believe me: it was a stomp, and according to the other mom, a steam as well), I overhead the ladies arguing with the judges over why they should have won.

In my heart of hearts, I don't believe those women truly meant the words they spoke that day. The damage, however, was done. I know they were proud of the hard work (and from what I overheard, it was hard work) they had put into their costumes. What they wanted was recognition for all the extra effort, but what came out instead was horrible. The joy for me was gone.

Early after the loss of a loved one, a commonly offered condolence is that the person who died is "in a better place." Deep in the recesses of my heart, I know this to be true. After doing some reading on heaven, I can only imagine that it is the most wonderful place ever. No suffering, no death, and no tears—surrounded by God's beauty, in God's presence. I look forward to the day when I join my children in heaven. This, however, does not imply that I'm looking to join them anytime soon.

No one plans for their child to die. It is not the typical order of life. We expect that our children will bury us. We *never* expect to outlive them. Immediately following the loss of a child, this is one sentiment a grieving person just doesn't want to hear.

They're not hollow words. Heaven *is* a better place. The disconnect comes when head knowledge and heart knowledge are not compatible. No matter what people think about grief, it is rarely rational.

In those early days, the thought that my child had been ripped away from my life and our home was almost too much to bear. So rather than receiving the "better place" analogy as a balm to my soul, my grieving heart heard that my home—my arms—wasn't such a great place after all.

Similar to the ladies after the kiddie parade, that is not at all what comforters were trying to imply. They wanted me to know that heaven is a great place, and if Reed (and the babies) couldn't be with me, the well-wishers were comforted knowing that he was at God's house. While I knew it to be true as well, that phrase wasn't the way I wanted to hear it, because for me, the better place would have been wrapped in my arms.

Time + My Heart Does Not Equal Healing

THE LOVE OF MATH IS IN MY GENETIC CODE. IT HAS BEEN PASSED down through generations on my daddy's side. One of our family treasures includes mathematics lesson plans from the early 1900s written by my great great great grandfather when he was a schoolteacher in North Carolina. All those figures written in perfect penmanship just make my Daddy and me smile. Of course, as true math teachers, we lament that the days of longhand figuring of problems are probably going by the wayside. My own children never stood a chance as the math genes have been amplified. Not only do my daddy and I have math degrees, so does my husband. That is a whole lot of love of numbers and operations to build a foundation upon. Although my kiddos do have other talents, they all share a love for numbers, just like I did when I was their age.

When I was in the fifth grade, my teacher announced an all-city mathematics competition would be taking place. We would be practicing and studying in his classroom for a test at our own school. The winners from each school would then move on to a central location for a day of competition and math fun. (Trust me: I know from the personal experiences of parent-teacher conferences that about half my readers just let out a collective groan. It is okay. I understand not everyone adores mathematics like I do.)

In school, there were many things I enjoyed, but math was my *thing*. Upon hearing the news of the great mathematics test, I set out to do everything possible to achieve my best score and be the one selected to represent our school. In my eyes, it was a huge honor, and I believed I had the stamina, fortitude, mathematics knowledge, and just enough

Southern sass to pull it off. Whenever I had free time in the classroom, I was poring over sample test questions, getting ready for the big day.

The day of the test finally arrived, and the anticipation was palpable among the bright scholars all gunning for the title of "Top Dog Math Student." (Okay, there really wasn't a title, but I know we were all hoping to win.) We all settled in with our crisply sharpened No. 2 pencils (as if there was any other choice), test question booklets, and answer papers with the neat rows and rows of ovals—ripe with possibility. Nerves were steadied, the sun was shining, destiny was about to be determined, and I was on a quest to be crowned queen of the math nerds!

It seemed like an agonizingly long time before the results were revealed. We waited and waited until a victor was named ...

Indeed! I came away with the top score on the All-City Mathematics Challenge. I was so excited. I practically flew home to tell my mom the good news. As a family, we were all pretty excited that night. We celebrated with a family supper, awaiting the next steps in the process. All the hard work, extra effort, and nerves of steel paid off. I was going to the Columbus, Georgia, Mathematics Extravaganza. I could not have been prouder.

At school the next morning, my teacher was waiting to talk to me. While he got the rest of the class busy doing geography worksheets, he quietly asked me to come visit with him at his desk at the back of the room. I remember happily floating back while looking out the bank of windows along one wall of our classroom. I remember the blooms on the giant magnolia tree, with the hint of sunshine peeking through the waxy green canopy. Hoping to learn more about the next steps in the competition, I was all ears, which was a lot for the ten-year-old version of me.

My teacher explained that he was so proud of my efforts and achievements on the test and how I had earned the honor. I should have seen what was coming next, because my children's truth-and-justice meter came from my gene pool, just like my love of all things mathematics. He continued to talk about how I was an excellent student with a kind heart and how I was going to have all kinds of opportunities in life. He explained that since my daddy was a college basketball coach, I had the chance to travel to exotic places like Augusta and Savannah, so I should consider myself one lucky little girl. Even after all this blathering, I still didn't see what was coming. Finally he got to the point of his little pep talk, which was basically that, while I had won fair and square, there was another little girl who should go instead, because I already had such a good life.

I just stood there staring at that magnolia tree with tears running down my face. My teacher made no effort to comfort me. Rather, he made a motion as if to wipe his hands clean of the conversation. I was so stunned I couldn't move. Every fiber in my being wanted to scream, to run away, and to tell him what I thought of his great plan. He truly didn't know how much earning that top score meant to me. In his mind, he was doing a greater good by allowing another student to attend instead of me. When he made the announcement to the class, I was mortified, feeling like I had been stripped of my crown of mathematics glory. Even now as I write this story, my heart hurts for that little girl.

Time has not healed that wound.

Reed's passing was a sudden death. In the world of grief counseling, it is considered a traumatic loss. Your body, including your brain, goes through physiological changes when you experience a trauma so great. It actually feels like someone picks you up and holds you upside down, because nothing in your world makes any sense at all.

I remember distinctly the first time I went to a store following the bus crash. It was the day after we buried Reed. We needed to stop on our drive back to Minnesota, and since Sawyer was in a wheelchair, we needed a place where we could stretch our legs. I walked into a Target store, thinking it would be a quick in-and-out maneuver. It ended up being nothing of the sort. I made it maybe ten feet into the store and just sort of crumbled. Gripping Sawyer's wheelchair for a reality check, I watched as if someone had sped up the people inside the store. I was standing still, barely upright, in the rushing wave of grief while every other person in the store zoomed past me. Just like that day at the math teacher's desk, I was rooted to the floor, but I wanted to scream, "Do you not know that I just buried my son today? He was the sunshine of my world. I don't know how I am supposed to keep on going. I don't know how to help myself, let alone comfort my grieving children." But not a word came from my mouth. I just stood there watching what appeared to be ants scurrying about, retail shopping. It was just one of many things my grief-laden brain could not put into a sweet, orderly fashion.

Another one of the things I felt I could no longer manage was time. Even making it minute by minute was a struggle. For someone to tell me that years from now it would hurt less was about as useful as if they were giving me instructions on how to perform surgery while speaking in Chinese. All I knew at that moment was that every cell in my body ached with pain, loss, and grief. My love for my son (for all my children) runs so deep there was no way I could comprehend a day in the future, distant or not, when I wouldn't hurt this badly. Previous reference points like money, meetings, commitments, and time become nonexistent when experiencing traumatic grief. They lose all value when your child dies.

So much in our culture is planned out, micromanaged busyness. How often do we say, "Oh, I wish I had just a few more hours in the day"? We planned on time being on our side. We saved for the future, including Reed's college accounts. Suddenly all our hopes and dreams for this child were gone in an instant, and because he was a child, we continue to endure the pain of watching his friends and classmates experience the things we dreamed for him. Using time as a reference point only reinforces that we no longer have time to spend with our child.

Early in the grieving journey, a mother whose son also died in a traumatic way told me, "One day this won't be the first thing you think of when you wake up." She also shared that it took a long time (many, many years) before this happened for her. I did take comfort in her words, because I knew how deep into the valley of grief she had walked. She was right. That day did come, but it was many years later.

I still don't believe that time heals all things, but the words we chose to put on the thank-you notes following Reed's services sum up my heart's definition of healing. Little did I know when searching for quotes the history behind the words we ended up choosing. Irish songwriter Thomas Moore was a gifted and talented musician and lyricist. Yet his life too was plagued by loss. Over the years, he lost all five of his children. His penned words "Earth hath no sorrow that heaven cannot heal" spoke to my heart. He understood that it wasn't time but the love of God meeting us in quiet places (over a long course of time) that would someday allow us to begin to heal.

"Call Me" Was Once a Hit Song

ONE OF THE MOST COMMON PHRASES GRIEVING PEOPLE HEAR IS "If you need something, please call me." I get it. Many people want to help but don't know what would actually be helpful following a loss or tragedy. It is a really sweet gesture, but let me tell you a little secret. Most grieving people don't even *know* enough about what they need to be able to ask someone else to help meet those needs. In my case, I was so run down and weary, half the time I didn't even know my name. Calling someone was not even on my radar.

The sentiment behind the words is genuine. Comforters are offering to help, and later in this book, I will give some amazing examples of how people did amazing things to bring us help. But asking us to lead the charge was just not in the realm of possibilities for me.

When I was a little girl, the Life cereal commercials featuring Mikey were often on television. "Give it to Mikey; he'll eat anything" was the tagline. For most of my life, I have been the female Mikey when it comes to getting things done, so to shift from a lifelong habit of being a doer to asking for help was a huge (and at times insurmountable) hurdle for me. My mother can attest to the fact that this definitely describes my behavior habits and not my personal taste buds, as I was a pretty picky eater growing up. If you have enough time to chat, she will tell you all about how I once caught them putting store-brand mustard into the bottle of my favorite brand because I refused to eat anything other than one brand.

Anyways, my palate matured, and my natural instincts to jump in and lead tasks and projects only grew stronger over time as well. "Need something done? Ask Kandy to do it." "Kan do" became my life's mantra.

More than once, I have had good friends say when I continually resist the help of others that I am not allowing them to use their talents from God. One dear friend explained my reluctance to ask for help equated robbing the giver of bestowing a blessing. I tried. I promise I really did, but most of the time I simply didn't think to ask. When the rug of a simple life was yanked out from under us, my initial response was to circle the wagons to simply survive through the minutes. I didn't know what I needed other than to help my children and my husband. Everything (and I mean *everything*) else became inconsequential. When I needed help the most, I had no experience in asking.

Thankfully, my world is full of long-suffering people who knew we would need every kind of assistance. The floodgates of help were open wide, and many friends and family members stepped up to help us and the other families involved. Thankfully, many of those who loved us watched us with attentive eyes and saw our needs before we could even verbalize them. But there were many whose parting words were the infamous "Call me for anything, anything at all."

Back at home after Reed's services, a dear neighbor stopped over just to see how we were faring. Her visit was simply to hug us and leave, but while she was there, it took the courage of our son to help me get over the hurdle of asking for help. I have always been the go-to girl. "I've got this!" was my battle cry.

Ticking off a mental checklist in her good-byes (yes, I said good-byes; it is one of those Minnesota things people must complete at least three times before departing), she inquired if our people were fed, if our animals were being cared for, and if our snow was being removed. We assured her all was the best it could be under the circumstances. On that final stanza of the Minnesota good-bye song, she asked if there was anything we needed. Just as I was about to say, "No, we're okay," a very worn and broken-hearted little boy piped up from the recliner that had recently been donated to him by a local furniture store.

His request was simple. "I could use a Dr. Pepper." With tears in her eyes because she couldn't stand to see him hurt, she dashed out the door with a "Then a Dr. Pepper you shall have." Ten minutes later, the Boy Wonder won the Dr. Pepper lottery when she returned with bottles and cans of assorted sizes packed under her loving arms.

It took that moment for me to realize the only way we were going to survive all of this was to let my defenses down and let others in to help. Many others had tried to break the impenetrable defense before her, but it was the innocent request of a little boy and the joy in our friend's eyes that finally broke through. I didn't transform overnight, but I was able to articulate needs a little easier after that one small moment on a frigid evening in March.

Fast-forward eight months. We were once again tackling a first that none of us really wanted to tackle. Much like the offers of help, we resisted until we were finally worn down by requests. The night before we were to report to court for the sentencing of the woman who caused the crash, we found ourselves donning number 75 jerseys, which was Reed's football number, for our family portrait for the church directory. *How do you take a family picture when one of the family isn't and will never be there?* When I finally agreed our family would participate, like most things, I did it on my terms. We would include Reed in some way. Our sweet and kind school athletic director had given us all the number 75 junior high jerseys he could find at the school. Reed was buried in one, one hangs on our living room wall, and one was turned into curtains in the boys' bedroom.

The photographer didn't quite know what to do when I very swiftly and most emphatically announced I would not be purchasing any portrait settings. It was too soon to even consider it. She tried for quite some time to guilt me into buying pictures for my other kids, until I looked her in the eye and said, "Lady, I don't even want to be here." My lack of interest was only compounded by the fact that the pictures were running behind.

One of my friends has a saying when her cell phone gets a lot of calls and texts, especially from the same person repeatedly. In her Kentucky accent, she always tells the story about how someone "was blowing up my phone." About the time I finally convinced the photographer to just get the whole thing over with and we secured a way to hang Reed's jersey in the picture, both Daniel and my phones were "blowing up." We didn't answer them, but we noticed all the calls were from family in North Dakota.

Momentarily, we were buoyed because we mistakenly believed these were messages telling us that they were coming to be with us at court the next day. Oh, I wish with every fiber in my being that was what the messages were really saying. But the actual news, the death of a very young cousin who we saw more as a nephew, rocked us to our core. I would have purchased a million pictures if it would have changed the events of that day. Suddenly, going to court didn't seem so important, as all we wanted to do was get to our family as quickly as possible.

If I had a magic wand, I would completely erase 2008 from ever existing. In that year, we lost eight people: Reed, Jesse, Hunter, Emilee, a beloved uncle who happened to be the grandfather of the cousin we were mourning, an adopted grandmother, a beloved youth pastor (who was like a big brother to our kids), and finally our cousin.

Although it came as a big shock to our friend, it really didn't surprise me when she caught our littlest "playing" funeral. You can about imagine my friend's heart and how sad it was for her to tell us that news. But for our tiny curly-headed three-year-old, a third of her life had been dominated by funerals and grieving. For that whole year, it was all she knew.

After court the next day, we were whisked away to a safe place to be with the other two families, the Olsons and the Javens, to simply recover from the roller coaster we all wanted to get off, only to discover we had purchased lifelong passes. We needed an environment where we could begin to heal and where no one else was watching. Eventually, we picked up our kids and traveled to attend our cousin's services.

We arrived late and stayed with other cousins, who lived nearby, and the next day was the first time we were able to simply hug the immediate family and cry. Their year wasn't much different from ours. They lost a brother/son, a father/grandfather, and Reed, who happened to be their godson. That first embrace said it all. We quietly joined the ranks of our very large extended family to file in for the services in a beautiful cathedral in Grand Forks.

It was all too much.

I remember sitting in the service and just wanting to get up and run and keep running. This was an unusual feeling for me, as another one of my mottos is "I don't run, even if it's a good sale." All I wanted to do was get up and run away from everything sad, because every corner in my world was hurting. Our family (immediate and extended) was hurting. Our church was hurting from the loss of Reed and our youth pastor. Our school was hurting, not only because of the children killed and injured but because of the innocence of many others being eroded. I had to use all my willpower to not bolt out of the pew. It took much more work than I ever thought possible. Inside, I felt like a caged animal, but somewhere in my spirit I decided to pray, asking God to first help me stay put and second to help us all find peace in this moment. The praying worked much better than my willpower.

I calmed down enough to hear the words the priest was sharing about our cousin. Then, if willpower kept me from running down the street, not wanting to embarrass my family is what kept me in my seat when he said, "I've heard a lot of people say to the family, 'If you need anything, call me.' To that, I say, 'Baloney!' Don't be that person! They are never going to call you. Instead, you should stop by the house and offer whatever kindness you can. But don't ask a grieving person to call you. It's just plain ridiculous."

My Southern Baptist roots were starting to show as I wanted to shout out, "Preach on, Brother!" I had to settle for a nice hand squeeze from one of the aunties, who has her own grief story, seated next to me. Her hushed reassurance echoed the feelings of my heart: *truer words were never spoken.* I wanted to jump up and down, giving this priest a rousing ovation, because he breathed marching orders of true comfort into the entire community present. It was a beautiful reminder that we truly can provide comfort to others, because for the grieving, "Call Me" should be just a song on the radio.

The Question

WHEN I WAS LITTLE, WE OFTEN GATHERED FOR FAMILY DINNERS at both of my grandparents' homes. At Nannie and Granddaddy's house, all of us cousins played outside and then were transported to the streets of Paris come mealtime. It was our little secret when we were relegated to the kids' table to eat. While the adults were sitting in the kitchen back in plain ol' Pensacola, all of us kids were chatting away at the best Parisian restaurant in the carport turned dining room. Mostly we spent our time just talking, swapping the stories of our lives. Although I wasn't as close with my cousins from Alabama, the same scene played out when all the Noles gathered at Mama and Papa's house. While the food brought us to the table, it was the conversations that knit our hearts together. As much as I love both grandmothers' signature styles of Southern cooking, it was the telling and retelling of tales that really drew me to the table.

Sadly, my children are growing up in a world where sit-down, look-you-in-the-eye conversations are rare. *My heart breaks for them.* Even though my dad was a college basketball coach during my growing up years, family dinners were something my parents tried very hard to make a ritual. It was a challenge during the hoops season, but somehow we managed. Daniel's family had to work equally as hard to make family mealtime work since they owned and operated a small business. This time of togetherness is a tradition we have continued with our own children. Just recently, we banned all technology from our table. (I wish I could lay all the blame on my kids and their generation here, but all too often I have replied to a text during a meal.)

Erin recently told me about the rule at one of her friend's grandfather's house. His rule is simple: leave your phone in the box by the door when you enter his house. He desires to cultivate real relationships with his guests—especially his grandchildren. I admire his efforts.

We (including me) are so saturated with online relationships that we sometimes forget to engage with the people and surroundings right in front of our nose. How many times are we snapping away pictures of that great sunset rather than just sitting back and enjoying it? Over the last Christmas season, I chose to be present, embracing whatever was before me rather than worrying about checking the next thing off of my long to-do list. Refreshing is the best word I can choose for how the Advent season was for me because of that one simple choice.

In the early days of a grief journey, people offer to help in all kinds of amazing ways. But many times, in an effort to be as helpful as possible, comforters will ask a "million" questions to clarify specific needs. Dealing with all these questions can be overwhelming.

Although most of my years of being an educator have been at the junior high, senior high, or collegiate levels, I have held a few positions as an elementary teacher. After my first day teaching second grade, I came home beleaguered and weary, announcing to my family, "Do not ask me anything!" When my sweet husband attempted to ask about my day, I explained that I loved junior high students but second graders might be the death of me. Having worked with kids for more than twenty years, I thought I was ready to help out when I was asked to take over this classroom, but I had never been asked so many questions in one day. Frankly, it was exhausting. Add to that their propensity for tattling, and I was a woman under siege. While it got better with time, I did have to pull a few tricks out of my teaching sleeve.

So it was with the onslaught of questions we fielded following our darkest day. Like the song lyrics "Signs, signs, everywhere there's signs," questions seemed to come at us at a rapid-fire pace. One question which never really made a lot of sense to me, and still really doesn't, is "How are you doing?"

It is a question asked all the time, but do any of us really mean it? In our hubbub of busyness and our chaotic, frenetic pace of life, how many of us ask that question by looking someone in the eye and genuinely hope that they will get real with us and give us an honest answer? We ask it in the grocery store (when we know we don't have time to listen to the answer), and the sad truth is most of us ask it because we lack something better to say. So easy is it to send a witty reply (or sometimes snarky retort) as fast as our fingertips can fly on social media that the art of genuine and sincere conversation is becoming an antiquated relic.

Then my child dies, my other children are severely injured, and people ask me that question. "How are you doing?" For the first few months, I know I looked at them dumbfounded. I would think, *Are you serious? Do you really want to know? Honestly, it stinks to be us right now. How are we supposed to be doing?* But out of my lips came "We're hanging in there." I could no longer look at people and give my typical answers of "We're fine," because it didn't apply any more, or "We're busy," because that would be the understatement of the century.

I didn't really want to get into how I was really feeling or how we were coping because it was too terrible to say the words aloud. Hearing how awful we were doing only magnified the desperation of our situation. Sadly, I once heard that my response to that question had people in some circles saying, "Kandy really isn't taking this well." Apparently I missed the class on how best to deal with profound loss and sadness. But instead of getting angry, I chose to show revolutionary love. I reminded myself they didn't have a clue as to how it felt to be in our shoes and moved on.

For years afterward, that question continued to stop my husband in his tracks. I think deep down he would have loved to tell someone how awful he felt, but in our society, as the dad, he would look weak and vulnerable. I don't know many men who want that image, so I am certain he gave some pat answer and went on with whatever he was doing. Thankfully, some real men who cry and listen have supported my sweet man from the first moment they learned of our sadness.

I don't know if it was exhaustion, not taking it well, or insanity, but one day about four months after the crash, someone in the grocery store asked me this particular question. Without one bit of sass or attitude, my reply was honest and heartfelt. "Is this the kind of question that you want a simple answer to, or would you really like to know how we're doing? If it's the latter, I will be happy to spend some time telling you, but if you want to just get a one word sound bite and move on, there will be no judgment here." Now before you judge this person, understand that

I gave them an out and they took it. Frankly, I was proud of them for being real in the moment. I didn't feel any less loved because they were courageously honest about where they were in life at the moment.

As I watched her wheel away down aisle 6, I secretly wished that a point would come when I would not be consumed by the overwhelming circumstances we found ourselves in. In time and with the peace that can only originate with God, that did happen—even if there was a bunch of "How are you doing?" in between.

Prime Real Estate

WHEN I WAS IN HIGH SCHOOL, ALL SCHOOLS IN THE STATE OF Florida offered a course pertaining to life skills that was required for graduation. Along with mandated state testing each year, we were required to learn how to plan a budget, balance a checkbook, plan a menu, and live within the budget we had planned. Additionally, we tackled larger projects like planning a wedding (which, I have to tell you, bore absolutely no resemblance to my actual wedding) and having a tough conversation with our parents regarding their end-of-life wishes. As the oldest child in my family, I always knew that someday I would need to shoulder this responsibility, but I was in no way prepared to have this conversation with my parents.

There was one glaring reason for this lack of preparedness. My whole life I was terrified by death. As far back as I can remember, I would wake up at night, trembling because I was afraid to die. At four years old, I doubt I understood the spiritual implications of my fears, but my real and soul-searching concerns were twofold. I loved (and still love) life, and I was paralyzed by all the unknowns.

For much of my life, I was fixated on death, which really made no sense whatsoever as I hadn't experienced much loss in life. Many times my parents would tuck me into bed at night, only to have me come out crying much later because I was afraid to die. My sweet daddy would cradle me and comfort me, telling me I didn't need to worry about dying. Eventually, I would fall back asleep, but the tentacles of death—or rather the fear of death—would come sneaking in again at some unexpected moment. This fear had a stranglehold on my life, until the moment my child died.

Some people outgrow their fears. I did not. These stifling moments continued well into my adulthood. Even after my children were born, I would often wake up in sweats because my mind had been dreaming about death. This fear had a stranglehold on my life, until the moment my child died.

In that moment, fear lost its grip on me.

Some of my metamorphosis came about because this time the stakes were higher. I had never held my miscarried babies, but Reed had been a big part of my life. Because of him, my name changed to Momma. Now that he was there instead of being a place of endless mystery, heaven became a place I really wanted to be. Only I would have to die to get there. The fears that haunted me all my life weren't controlling me anymore.

The crazy thing about fear is it keeps you from truly living. The truth about debilitating fear is that it *never* comes from God. He would never want something to prevent us from truly living. Like a bird with the cage door left open, I never looked back. The prison of fear no longer held me captive. The shackles of mistrust, the true underlying issue for my fears, were broken. Death is a part of God's story. His own son had to die for me to truly live, and on the day my son died, I realized that I hadn't truly ever lived.

My transformation from fearful to free could best be described by the first puppy I ever loved. When my parents drove us to the pet store just down the road from Knead-Um-Donuts, we had no idea we would be going home with an adorable puppy that day. I was about five years old, and my brother was a little more than two. Only in Florida in the seventies could you find a pet store teeming with most of God's creation, including birds of all kinds and, yes, alligators. The reason for our visit, though, was a pen in the middle of the store filled with poodle-cross puppies. There were precocious puppies, bright eyed, yipping, and filled with energy. On the edge of the pen sat a tiny, curly-haired one who could be summed up in one word: pathetic. She looked sickly and pitiful. Her brothers and sisters did nothing to encourage her and spent every moment they could picking on her and knocking her down, to the point where she didn't even move at all. The other puppies treated her horribly because she was tiny and different.

To this day, my brother and I are still big fans of the underdog, and I have to believe this is where it originated. Of course, we chose her. Our parents, however, were a little reluctant, despite the owner's insistence she was going to be a great dog. Mom and Daddy didn't want to tell us we couldn't have the puppy we had chosen, but unbeknownst to us, they had asked the owner if they could have their money back if she didn't make it. She was literally that pitiful looking, but all four of us felt sorry for her. The moment my dad picked her up, her whole demeanor changed. Overcome with disbelief, she was shocked at the positive attention. Right before our eyes, Gemima transformed into a spunky little puppy who ran around and around the pet store so excited to have been picked. As we took her home that day, she only grew peppier and became the most loving dog ever.

More than not living, I had believed the lies of the one who is the author of fear. Even at four years old, instead of bringing me closer to God, my fears had driven me far away from his peace. Like the tiny puppy who wouldn't even lift her head, my fear of death kept me from focusing my eyes on my loving Father. A wedge of lies and unknowns prevented me from experiencing a full relationship with the one who loves me the most. The tentacles no longer had a stronghold on my life, and even though I had lost a child, I gained a freedom I had never experienced before.

Like Gemima, I have kept on running right into his love.

Although I still didn't know all my answers of what heaven will be like, I ran headlong into the security of knowing that while Reed was there, more importantly, God and his Son were there too. More times than I can count, I have heard the song "I Can Only Imagine" by Mercy Me. When fear ruled my days, imagining that moment was incomprehensible to me. But now, I feel fairly confident that the first thing I will want to do is hug them both and then hug all of my people.

Back in high school, as we interviewed our parents for the mandatory class, we were all required to use the same questionnaire. I don't recall all the questions, but the one that completely shocked me is one that ended up causing quite a divide in my family. When asked about their future wishes on internment or cremation, my parents unanimously chose cremation. It was absolutely too much for my teenage self to comprehend. They gave their honest and heartfelt reasons for their choices, even explaining where they would like their ashes to be returned to God's creation. I was utterly unprepared for their answer because I had never attended a funeral in my life. In my parents' defense, they probably didn't want to subject me to my biggest fear. Despite having a big family, I had only had one member to whom I was close, Aunt Martha, pass away in my childhood. I don't know if it is good genes or plain old stubbornness, but my family tends to lead long lives. I had visited plenty of cemeteries, especially for Decoration Day, but I did not attend my first funeral until I was a sophomore in college.

During graduate school while living with my paternal grandparents, we chose one day to tend to the gravesites of some of our people. It was during the car ride between locations that the great divide first appeared. At the family plot in the local cemetery, Mama showed me where she and Papa would be laid to rest, along with my other Alabamian aunts and uncles. Then she pointed to these two extra spots and explained that those could be for my momma and daddy. In hindsight, I should have just smiled and nodded. Instead, what innocently came out of my mouth was "I don't think that will be necessary because my parents want to be cremated." Remember "What are you, an idiot?" Never before have I seen Mama that upset, as I am pretty sure she wanted to snatch me bald-headed. Under her breath, I heard her say, "Well, they better not die before I do, because I will fight you on that one."

On television and through stories, including the one about my maternal great grandmother's passing, I learned that tension and strained relationships can cause a lot of friction during the funeral-planning process. At this point, I still had only attended the one funeral in college, one for Daniel's aunt, and later his dad, so I still led a fairly insulated life from that type of bizarre behavior. I had no idea the firestorm of critique we were about to walk through when our son died.

I know that our friends and family protected us from most of the craziness. While we were in the hospital for all those days with Sawyer, news teams were camped out in our neighborhood. Our front door was plastered with business cards, which were perfunctorily removed and discarded by our neighbor each day.

Almost like an out-of-body experience, I watched our lives and our privacy be sucked away. One morning, a friend and I were trying to set up a CaringBridge account so we could control what was being disseminated about our family. The computers available for families were outside of the locked children's wing and before we could finish our account setup, hospital security swarmed around us like the one time my family somehow ended up in the middle of the manhunt for a fugitive on the interstate. More questions came flying in, asking if we had agreed to hold a press conference at the hospital. The bewilderment on our faces was all the answer the staff needed.

Flanked on all sides, we were escorted back to the locked-down unit and told the whole story. Apparently a rather convincing reporter had told the hospital administrators I had requested an interview and was expecting him. Due to HIPPA regulations, the hospital had obvious concerns. Upon realizing that I had done no such thing, the hospital did their very best to insulate us from the outside world. So too did our church, our friends, and our family.

We did not grieve in a vacuum. Everyone who loved Reed was hurting too. Sadly, we could not protect everyone any more than they could protect us. They too had to develop tougher skin and a keep-your-chin-up attitude. But on one occasion, a chink in the armor of our inner circle was exposed. My sweet friend had gone back home after spending days with us at the hospital. She needed to pick up some items at a local store and while on one side of the aisle, she overheard employees talking about how they wished "that Stevens family would just get their act together and tell people when that kid's funeral is going to be."

Much like the missing scale in the dragon Smaug, the weak spot was exposed. *How dare you kick my friend when she is down?* My barely five-foot friend flew around the aisle and exclaimed, "Did you ever stop and think that maybe they have other children fighting for their lives?" The unrepentant reply broke my friend's heart.

While wanting to protect us, our friends did tell us this story because they wanted us to know that when we left the isolated hospital wing, the world had changed for us, aside from the obvious reasons. Suddenly, instead of being just a grieving family, we were a big news story and some people felt entitled to more answers than they had been given.

Even at the time of Reed's death, I had been to fewer funerals than I have fingers on one hand. The thought never crossed my mind that I should question someone's decisions on how they chose to remember their loved one. Each person is a beautifully unique creation of our Lord, as is the grief of the people left behind. So I was stupefied when we were asked over and over again, "Why North Dakota?"

This inquiry was perhaps the most hurtful and the most bizarre at the same time. We live in southwestern Minnesota, but we chose to bury our son in north central North Dakota. Where Reed is buried was a deliberate choice on our part and a decision that we did not take lightly. We didn't understand what compelled people to feel that they were entitled to weigh in on our choice. When asked that question, my heart heard that we were not capable of making a good choice as to the final resting place for our son. Up until the day that decision was made, we had made every decision to help guide and nurture this child—the child we prayed for, adored, and were proud to call our own. He was our sunshine, the living embodiment of a dream I had wished for my entire life.

I simply could not understand why anyone would question our decision. Nor do I feel that I am compelled to share our decision-making with anyone today. Just like our services were a unique reflection of who Reed was and who we are as children of God, Reed's final resting place was a choice made by our entire family.

If I had charged a dollar for every time we were asked that question, our family would have never struggled to pay all of the medical bills that ensued for years following the crash. I will be very honest and say that I "stomached" this question up until about the two hundredth time it was asked. At that point, I lost it and said something along these lines: "Why North Dakota? You know what? How about you give me Reed back and we kill your kid? Then you can bury him wherever you want and I won't question you about it."

I promised I would be real and raw in the writing of this book. Certainly I am not proud of that little outburst, but the ridiculous nature of the question finally broke me. I think my tantrum spread like wildfire because no one asked me that particular question ever again.

One of my favorite quotes is by the late Robin Williams, who said regarding Glacier National Park, "If God doesn't live here, he's certainly nearby." For any North Dakotan reading, you know, as we do, God *definitely* must live close to the prime real estate under those big blue skies where our beautiful boy lies next to his grandpa.

What Happens in Aisle 4

THE FLIP SIDE TO QUESTIONS IS COMPLETE SILENCE. THIS IS another piece of that puzzle where things simply do not make sense. Again, no one plans of their child dying. So for some people, we (grieving parents) are a painful reminder that your child could die too. It is like a blinking neon sign announcing to the world that things can and do go wrong. I had several people in my life who couldn't look at me at all and others who could only look at me and cry for about six months. I know that these were sincere emotions, and I realize that Reed's death impacted more than just myself and my family.

I have been this person. You know, the one that sees someone who has gone through something devastating and who quickly goes down a different aisle at the grocery store? Why did I pull that stealthy move in aisle 4? The answer is simple. I didn't know what to say. (Okay, there are also those times when I have avoided people who get on my last nerve just by being themselves. This says more about me than them, but I am all for being real.) I was at such a loss for words that it was easier for me to run and hide. The key words in that sentence are "easier for me." What I didn't know at the time was that I was hurting the already hurting person in a new and different way.

We all know these people. Some look at the floor, some actually cross the street, some avoid eye contact altogether, and some duck and hide in the grocery store. They avoid returning phone calls and e-mails, simply because they don't know what to say or how to say it. On the receiving end, I have more than once wondered what I could have done or said to elicit this lack of response or interaction.

Recently, a friend of mine sent me a news article on being mindful.

57

The article was on how to deal with stress by being mindful—in other words, fully present—in small ways, thereby reaping stress-inhibiting benefits. The article listed all sorts of research studies documenting proof of the rewards of mindfulness and concluded with some small ways to put this simple act of slowing down into practice. My friend, who experienced a tragic loss that year, chose her words carefully. "I think you'll really like this article." I responded to her after reading it and stated I did indeed agree with the article's suggestions. She replied that I already had one—"Hug mindfully!"—mastered. Tears fell across my cheeks as we exchanged quick comments.

To the dismay of many, I hugged every single person who came through the lines at Reed's memorial and celebration of life services. Sadly, both days that same friend was the cut-off point, never getting close enough for one of my hugs. Hugging is soothing to me. Daniel often warns people, "Watch out! She's a hugger!" This may be hard for people who truly know me to believe, but there are many times when I am at a loss for words. Hugging someone is the most natural way for me to convey that my heart hears the hurt of another person's heart.

Last year, our church began a new tradition of having the parents of that year's high school graduates come up and share a few stories about their child along with a dedication for them as the young scholars prepare to embark on the next step in their journeys of life. One mom said about three words before she burst into tears. Her graduating son was her baby, the youngest of four, and she could not get the words out. My heart hurt for hers as she was the first one to speak that day. I knew it was going to be a long service, and I knew I would want to hug them all. Daniel knew it too. When that first momma burst into tears, he whispered in my ear, "Don't even think about it. I know you want to jump out of this pew and hug her. Do not even entertain the thought."

When I was a little girl, there was a ritual that happened every day whenever I was at Nannie and Granddaddy's home. Their humble home went through several additions before it was completely finished. Their original three-bedroom home with one and a half bathrooms (which wowed my mom and siblings when they first moved in), living room, and kitchen had an attached carport. Over time, the carport was closed in to create a den, and my grandparents built a greenhouse, the livelihood for their nursery business, off the back of the former carport, now den. As their business grew, they needed more greenhouse space, tearing down the one greenhouse and building two farther back on their lot. They also extended the den to the empty greenhouse. The larger space housed a more formal dining area along with a large gathering place for family. The end result created a perfect track for kids to walk a complete lap of the house, moving from room to room. Granddaddy's television viewing chair was directly next to that indoor walking path, and this is where the ritual came into existence. Every time we would make a lap, he would stick out his gigantic, arthritic-riddled hand, palm up, and exclaim, "Hey, Granddaughter!" Every single time, I would give him five and say, "Hey, Granddaddy!" right back. Of all the things I miss about my grandfather, this is what I miss the most. The verbal exchange was important, but the slight clasping of our hands reverberating the love between us is one I longingly wait to repeat in heaven.

Silence and not knowing what to say are completely normal and, I daresay, challenging to overcome in our culture, where death is not spoken about openly like it is in other parts of the world. If you don't know what to say, say exactly that. "I simply don't know what to say. I am so sorry for your loss." Believe me: it goes a long way. Simply acknowledging someone's hurt is another one of those revolutionary acts of love. "We're praying for you and your family" also conveys the words that we want to say but just don't know how to express. If you are a hugger like me, physical touch, including pats on the shoulder or hand, goes a long way as well. Take it from me and Granddaddy.

Don't Come See Me When I'm Gone

TWICE IN MY LIFE, I HAVE HAD THE PRIVILEGE OF LIVING WITH both sets of my grandparents for reasons very different from most people I know. Several of my friends were raised by grandparents or lived with them because of extenuating family circumstances, such as job loss, divorce, or a death in the family. I jokingly refer to my parents as nomads. Between military service and later coaching college basketball (where tenures are not always guaranteed), my dad's occupations kept us on the move when I was young. In all my school years, the impact of being the new kid was wearing, but never so much as when I entered my senior year of high school. My dad accepted a teaching and coaching position in North Dakota, and my family relocated once again. Not desiring to be the new kid, I elected to stay and finish my senior year at good old Wm. J. Woodham High School in Pensacola, graduating exactly twenty years after my mom at the same school. During that year, I lived with my maternal grandparents, Nannie and Granddaddy, preparing for my next year as a college freshman.

About the most trouble Nannie and I whipped up while I lived with them was purchasing a shih-poo puppy, Susu, whom Granddaddy swore could not live in the house and could never eat from the table. The first person to break those rules was Granddaddy himself. Who were we to argue with him? His famous trick was to engage you in a deep conversation at dinnertime, locking your gaze with his while simultaneously taking tiny pieces of pork chop and slipping them under the table to the tiny black ball of fur at his feet.

When I was a little girl, my granddaddy, Ernest Campbell, was my hero and my best buddy. Have "Delta Dawn" come on the radio, and I am transported back to the tiny three-year-old version of myself riding shotgun with Granddaddy on every sort of mission. For a while, my family lived across the street from my grandparents so I went everywhere with him. The only place I wasn't thrilled about going was Joe Patti's Seafood in downtown Pensacola. I still remember all those freshly caught fish staring at me from their bed of ice, all those glassy eyeballs looking straight at me! At three years old, it freaked me out. Even today, one step and one whiff inside that iconic fish market and I remember all the trips I made with him to pick up shrimp for supper.

But it didn't matter where we went, there was always one thing that was a perennial favorite at each of our stops. "Sing for them, baby." No spotlight was needed, as I stepped right up and belted out every word of "Delta Dawn," Granddaddy beaming with pride in the corner, his larger-than-life hands applauding louder than anyone else. As the oldest grandchild, and for many years the only granddaughter, I enjoyed being his little buddy.

Although I missed my family, I thoroughly enjoyed that year getting to know my grandparents as the people they were rather than simply being my ancestors. My relationship with my paternal grandparents was a different beast altogether. Don't get me wrong! I loved Mama and Papa, but we didn't spend as much time with them as we did Nannie and Granddaddy growing up. Mama and Papa were hardworking, salt-of-the-earth kind of people without any flair for pizazz. Nannie epitomized bling and sparkle. As a child, I loved them all. Mama was always in the kitchen making some scrumptious Southern meal. Breakfasts with her signature patted-down biscuits were always my favorite. Papa, David Reed Noles Sr. (who went by Reed), was always a firm, my-way-or-the-highway man who had a variety of jobs over the years but for most of my life was a police officer at Auburn University. Despite his stern demeanor, he was an amazing storyteller, and his tales drew me in time and again.

I found myself needing a place to stay when I became terribly homesick in graduate school. I was attending Auburn University and Mama and Papa offered for me to live with them. This was one of the best decisions of my life. I really got to know them as individuals, and like the relationship with my other grandparents, I only grew to love them more.

Of course, things got off to a rocky start. At twenty-one years old, I was on top of the world and basically knew everything, which you can about imagine went over really well with Papa. Sadly, the beginnings of his dementia had started to take hold, and there were moments of confusion interspersed in our daily routine. One of the saddest things is to watch a person you love slowly slip away from you because their mind struggles to remember who they are.

I've never considered myself much of a feminist, but I am all about treating everyone with respect. At one of my first meals with them, Papa and I began to butt heads over a little thing Aretha and I like to call R-E-S-P-E-C-T.

We had a fabulous supper, prepared like always by Mama. The previous fall, she had thrown some sweet potato peelings out the back door, only to find out they landed in a large pot that had previously held some plant or another. Lo and behold, the sweet potato peelings planted themselves and took off without any assistance. We harvested the planter full of tiny sweet potatoes, which became our dessert that evening by way of a delectable pie.

Our dinner had been a lovely time of visiting about classes and other things, but dessert was altogether more like the witching hour for dementia patients. Papa began questioning my grandmother about how she made the pie.

"Did you put shortening in this pie?"

"Yes, Reed, I did."

"Did you put cinnamon in this pie?"

"Yes, Reed, I did."

"Did you put nutmeg in this pie?"

"Yes, Reed, I did."

This back-and-forth banter continued for just about every ingredient a decent cook would consider putting into a sweet potato pie or its crust. Although patient with every inquiry, I could tell he was getting on her last nerve. Then it happened.

"Did you put mustard in this sweet potato pie?"

"Why Reed, nobody puts mustard in sweet potato pies! Harrumph!"

Turning to me, looking quite smug, he announced, "See, Gal? I knew something was wrong with this pie."

Her last nerve was nothing compared to my righteous indignation. We girls have to stick together. I had never before defied my grandfather, but he had gone too far—too far, I tell you. Rather than just laying into him, I chose my words carefully—very carefully.

"From the way I see it, you must be one amazing cook. Since we have supper every night at 5:30, Mama and I will be happy to see what you put together tomorrow night. We'll stay out of your way, looking forward to your shining moment."

I do not know who was more shocked sitting at that round table in our swivel chairs, with their pit bull, Sassy, who happened to be the sweetest dog ever, lying at our feet. Once the words were out, I could not believe I had just stood up to the man I had never—I mean not once in my life—spoken to like this before. Mama, mouth agape, could not even get out one word, but Papa's face was priceless, clearly indicating that *no one* talked to him like that. Even though *Wheel of Fortune* and *Matlock* played on the television, the rest of the night was filled with stony silence.

The next day was more of the same. Evening rolled around and, true to form, Mama made another amazing meal. The vow of steely silence was broken when the meal was over. Looking me directly in the eyes, he said, "Of all the cooks I know, Mama is the best one." It was the closest to an apology he would ever muster.

There were many exchanges like that one, but over time, they became the glue that solidified our relationship. I was the girl who dared to challenge him, and he, in turn, loved the challenge—even though he would never admit it. This was never more obvious than when I decided to move away. My dad came to help me pack up my things to accept a teaching position back in North Dakota. While my dad and I were hooking up the topper on my first vehicle, a little Ford Ranger pickup truck, Papa came out to offer his advice on our lack of packing prowess. He bossed us around like we didn't have one lick of sense in our heads. This went on for about twenty minutes or so. It was hot. We were tired. Not used to being told how every single thing I was doing was wrong, I lost it.

"It must be tough being you, knowing everything about everything" was all I said.

He stormed off, muttering that he knew about packing because he had once worked for a moving company and if we didn't want his expertise then he had better ways to spend his time. For the record, he *did* work for a moving company—for one day. There is a famous bridge in Opelika which does not have standard clearance. Coming from the south, it is one height, while coming from the north, it's another. Papa forgot that fact when he worked for the moving company. When he returned on the side with the lower clearance, he knocked the top off the moving truck. He didn't know I knew that story.

As Papa walked away, continuing to talk about our utter lack of respect for his expertise, my daddy and I took a much-needed break. With a sheepish smile creeping across his face, my dad said one of the most poignantly real things he has ever said to me. "Kandy Noles, you might be the only person on earth who gets along with that man. But you get away with a *whole* lot more than any of the rest of us *ever* would!"

He was right, and I knew it. I had an extraordinary relationship with Papa. During the time I was living with them, we had many frank and honest conversations. One of those conversations centered on people who should have a part of your life but choose not to. During this time, Papa told me to spend my life being the person I was, not somebody else's version of me or who they wanted me to be. It was some of the best advice I have ever received. Whenever we parted, he never said good-bye, instead always sending me with the marching orders of "Be particular," which was always good advice. As we talked about how to be the person God wants you to be, he asked me to do something that completely floored me, and that's saying a lot now that you've gotten to know him a little bit.

He had one person in his life who disappointed him time and time again. He asked me to call that person when he died and relay this message: "You didn't bother to come see me while I was alive, so don't bother to come see me now that I'm dead." This was one of his more lucid moments, and he made me vow that I would keep my end of that deal. I promised him I would do my very best to keep his wishes.

Papa wasn't about pretense or putting on airs, and he felt reverently about funerals and paying last respects. So to him, it was a huge disgrace that someone didn't think enough of him to come see him until after he died.

When Papa went home to Jesus, I called Mama and asked if I was still obligated to keep that pledge. Something deep inside me really wanted to, because I have experienced exactly what he was talking about. She laughingly told me that it probably wouldn't matter either way. (True to his wisdom, the one person he didn't want there showed up!)

I really don't know many families or friendships that don't encounter struggles. Earth is not heaven, and perfection really isn't possible, even though we use that word to describe so many things in our ordinary days. Just like Papa's prophetic prediction earlier, there were people who came to Reed's services that brought little comfort, and in some cases brought more hurt. In the months preceding his death, there were relationships that had been tested and broken.

Healing broken relationships is hard to do, and even more challenging when you are hurting with profound grief. At the time, I could not understand how someone could say really hurtful things to or about my child and then show up when he died as if nothing had happened to strain our friendship.

I think that was exactly what Papa was trying to prepare my heart for all those years earlier. Thankfully, my heavenly ancestry laid a way for forgiveness for the hurts I have perpetrated upon people and, more importantly, upon God himself. Revolutionary love paves a way for forgiveness, even when our hearts are not ready. Thankfully, Jesus's death modeled that we can do extraordinarily tough things, including loving others when it hurts.

Take Me Out to the Ball Game

SIX MONTHS TO THE DAY FOLLOWING REED'S DEATH, OUR FAMILY had the opportunity to visit a wonderful grief retreat. Meeting other grieving families revealed some universal truths that were previously unknown to me. Seeing a grieving person and having an overwhelming desire to help can at times lead people to say the most bizarre things. I think every grieving family I have met has a story about a situation like this, where someone walks up and makes a completely absurd declaration on the best way for the family to heal. In defense of people who really want to bring comfort, again, this is a replay of not knowing what to say.

No one likes to see their friends hurt. It is quite possibly the worst thing in the world to sit on the sidelines and watch as your friend or relative has to battle a war in which there is very little you can do to help. Watching not only my grandfather, but also the father of a dear friend, slowly drift away due to dementia and Alzheimer's was excruciatingly painful to endure. Hearing your friend's child has cancer, with a questionable prognosis, felt like someone punched me in the gut. Reading remarks on social media about milestone days for a friend with whom I had recently connected caused my knees to buckle when I realized that his son had passed away too.

I am a doer. I hate sitting on the bench of life and not being able to do anything. One of the metamorphoses I have made since our darkest day was to accept that sometimes God orchestrates the waiting places so we will be drawn back to him, the One who is ultimately in control. Instead of being frustrated at not seeing any progress or, worse yet, at the realization that numbered days are passing by, I have learned these waiting times are best spent kneeling before God's throne while asking him to show me his presence in all of it. Even though I was a great student, I am not the quickest to remember that when I am waiting, prayer is the best way to pass the time.

A few years back, my mom clipped out a newspaper cartoon and later found a cross-stitch pattern of the same clipping. The sentiment displayed was "If I am a mom, why is my time always spent in the car?" A big part of the chaos that defines my life is running my kids everywhere, often in multiple directions on the same day. Despite the fact that I have completed a triathlon, my favorite joke to tell about myself is "I hate to run. I don't run—even if they have a good sale." Running, on my feet or in my minivan, is equally unenjoyable to me.

To preserve my sanity, I took up knitting and crocheting. Neither my shoulder nor my chiropractor appreciates this practice, but I go nowhere without a yarn project, a good book, my Bible, and paper to fill the times in between the hurry-up-and-get-there moments. Mama always says if she has something to keep her hands busy, then her mind is occupied. I get her. I totally get her. When relaxation is needed more than mind enrichment, I have even succumbed to bringing a pillow and blanket and taking a nap in the backseat, especially on those days before the Boy Wonder could drive and we needed to leave by 5:00 a.m. to make it to early morning football practice. *A mom has to do what a mom has to do to survive.*

We often reenact the *Saturday Night Live* sketch about living in a van down by the river, but to tell the truth, I could probably successfully do that, as some days I spend more time in my van than I do my house. I know my mom did a bunch of running with us kids, yet I don't recall being as involved in activities as my kids are today. My mother may have a completely different viewpoint on my memories.

One thing is exactly the same between my childhood and that of my children. We all grew up about as country as a turnip seed and as American as the old truck commercial of my youth. We like baseball, hot dogs, apple pie, and Chevrolet. Although I grew up as an Atlanta Braves fan, my kiddos are true blue hometown fans of the Minnesota Twins. Win or lose, we still love them. We have pictures of all four dressed in fan gear when our baby attended her first game at six months old! We love the hometown team so much that our basement family room is dedicated to Minnesota sports teams, with the majority of the decorations being Twins memorabilia. When we were remodeling the downstairs, I was ecstatic when I discovered Major League Baseball carpet designs. Imagine my dismay when my sweetie was adamant he was not putting in Minnesota Twins carpet now or ever, insinuating that I had gone too far on that selection. (He later also vetoed Astroturf when we redid the boys room in a football theme.) Talk about dream crushing!

Reed loved the Twins and everything about baseball. He didn't miss a chance to make a "Circle Me Bert" sign whenever we made it to the ballpark. A month before his passing, we attended the Twins Caravan followed a few days later by TwinsFest at the old Hubert H. Humphrey Metrodome. Reed ran into Bert Blyleven in both places, and he was downright giddy when Bert said to him, "Hey! Didn't I just see you a couple days ago?" The moment was so monumental to him that on the trip home, he convinced us to not make a trip to Cooperstown, New York—home of the Baseball Hall of Fame—until Bert or Roger Maris was finally inducted. When that moment finally came for Bert in 2011, I had to smile, knowing one redheaded boy who would have been proud.

Our shared love for America's pastime is pretty well-known amongst our circle, as we often choose to spend our wedding anniversary at one ballpark or another. Attending sporting events is what Team Stevens does. It is who we are as a family, and I have to say that my husband is pretty lucky to have a girl who loves sports as much, if not more, than him. We may be sports fanatics, but our shared love for our favorite sports teams pales in comparison for our love for Jesus and, second to that, our love for our kiddos.

Still, it came as quite a shock when, about a month after Reed had passed, someone who was trying to help suggested what we really needed was to go to a Twins game. *What I need right now is to go to a Twins game? Really? Because what I think I need right now is my child back.*

No amount of diversionary tactics was going to change the singular focus of my mind—wishing my child back to life—even when I knew that wasn't a possibility. Their intentions were good, but my grieving brain was struggling to process what one minute was like without my child, let alone thinking about doing things that child loved without him.

Television on in the background while I worked in the kitchen recently, I heard an actor quip in a family comedy about it being too soon for a Pearl Harbor joke. At first I didn't understand the reference, but when I stopped to think about it, seventy-plus years later is still too soon for that type of humor. After the death of a loved one, the line of "too soon" is a difficult one to draw. I know this suggestion was coming from a heart wanting to make the hurting stop, even if only for the stretch of nine innings, but my heart wasn't ready.

My Latin professor in college always said, "nihil in excessu," which translates to "nothing in excess." His feisty spirit was often applying that to the amount of drinking that took place on campus, but his words apply here as well. Even when trying to help, "too much, too soon" can be a hindrance and not a helpmate. At the right time, returning to life and revisiting things the loved one enjoyed are wonderful things to do, but not necessarily right away. It works for some families, but for others that day never comes. The hole is so large, the void so vast without their loved one, the time never comes to revisit whatever beloved activity they previously enjoyed.

Your reality, your whole existence, after losing a child comes down not to one day or one hour, but quite literally one second and one breath at a time. The future becomes a foreign entity. You have to learn how to exist with the new normal of today before you can even begin to think about a future, with or without all the things you loved together.

I have been guilty of rushing way ahead of God's plans in so many facets of my life. When I recognize a hurt or see a need, my organizer mind hatches a plan all too quickly. More times than I wish to reveal, I rush in full steam ahead without so much as asking God what he thinks. As many times as my ideas and plans are fruitful, just as often they fall far below what I would measure as successful. With a mixed bag of good intentions, especially when I want to alleviate someone else's suffering, I have learned that I need to slow down and wait for the intersection of "hands out" and "heart up" to coincide with what God has planned for the need or hurt he knew long before I did. When I have had the foresight to pray first and act second, the resultant blessings (even the times when I was forced to wait) were better than I could have ever imagined. Thankfully, God is in all those places—the ones of helping, the ones of waiting, and even the ones in between—giving the broken-hearted and the comforter the peace and confidence that he will bring them together at just the right time.

The Antics of Joe the Bear

THE VERY FIRST NIGHT OF OUR GRIEF STORY WAS A CLEAR indicator of the long nights that would be in store for us for quite a long while. We were not all together in one physical location until close to nine o'clock that night. Our girls had been picked up by friends earlier in the afternoon. Daniel refused to come to school, choosing to go the scene and later to the hospital where we knew Sawyer had been taken originally, later riding with him in the helicopter and ambulance to Sioux Falls. Surrounded first by mostly strangers and acquaintances, my pastor and other close friends were with me when I was given the news I desperately did not want to hear. Two teaching friends, my pastor, and his wife escorted me to the hospital, where the rest of my family was already waiting. It was one of the longest drives of my life.

Upon arrival at the medical center, I wanted nothing more than to see my sweet boy, the one we called *our sunshine*, but the staff of the hospital was adamant that wasn't going to happen. Having not spoken to Daniel, we both were keeping a secret—about our worst news—to protect the other one. I had only been told Sawyer had a broken leg. When I was whisked into his room, I realized very quickly my knowledge of the Boy Wonder's injuries had been woefully lacking. The nurse quietly and reverently said she would retrieve the doctor so that we could make some decisions. At this moment, I realized this was worse, way worse, than I had even imagined. After making decisions on what needed to be done for Sawyer, we were taken to see Reed.

In what I can only ascribe to God's loving providence, our boys were taken to the same hospital and were in rooms right next door to each other. Considering all the hospitals in the area, the fact that my boys, inseparable in life, spent their last minutes on earth together side by side was the first in a string of blessings we would need to make it through the coming days. The room, so quiet, cold, and sterile, was completely antithetical to the warm, caring, and loving energy that was our sweet boy. It was just too much for me to bear. I could not stay in the room for long, although later in the evening, Daniel and Pastor returned to be with him.

Meeting with paramedics from Reed's helicopter, doctors, and nurses, we were able to ask questions and receive the only peace we could at that moment. After expressing our wishes, we were given a phone so we could make arrangements to keep a promise to our redheaded sunshine—a vow I never anticipated we would have to keep.

I believe that little boys come in two major categories: those who love cars and those who love superheroes. Reed (and Sawyer) fell in the latter group. They never were much into cars, but superheroes were something altogether different. They would battle pretend bad guys for hours on end. When Reed learned about his great uncle Donnie's (my daddy's brother) choice to be an organ donor on a trip to Mama's house, he had a lot of questions (and if you knew Reed, "a lot" is an understatement when it came to questions). Mama and I tried to answer those questions the best we could. Gathered around the table that night, Reed learned all kinds of grown-up things ranging from social security to the gift of life known as organ and tissue donation.

That night, after my routine of reading to the kids, singing each their favorite song, and tucking them in, Reed quietly called me to the sofa sleeper where he and Sawyer were sleeping. "Mom, I want to be a donor." He became quite agitated when I lauded his decision as brave and courageous. "No, Mom. Promise me that you will do that for me." To calm his nine-year-old emotions, I agreed if I ever needed to do so, I would honor his wishes.

I never dreamed I would need to.

Carrying a portable phone throughout the hospital and escorted by hospital security, we were taken to the surgical waiting center. The staff at that area took one look at our little girls, realizing it was going to be a long night, and brought blankets and pillows to create a makeshift camp out. Flanked by our friends and pastors, we settled in for the long night. My nerves were too on edge to even think about eating, but the thought never crossed my mind that our entourage had forsaken eating as well. Learning that the surgeries would most likely take the better part of three hours, our insulating circle excused themselves to go to the cafeteria.

Without their physical presence and comforting prayers encircling us, for the first time that day I felt agonizingly alone, even though Daniel and the girls were right there too. The realization of how challenging nights were soon to become was awakened. I didn't realize it until later, but the hospital staff physically separated us from the other bus families by placing us in different waiting areas. Across the divide were the families of children who were very severely injured and also having surgery. Only one family crossed the divide to simply hug us, as word of our loss as well as that of the other two families had already spread.

It was bedtime and I did the only thing I knew to do: continue being momma to my girls. We curled up together on the waiting room floor in our makeshift bed and I attempted to help them get to sleep. Despite my best efforts, sleep would not come for them or us until much later in the evening. Our group checked into the hotel adjoining the hospital, while Daniel and I stayed with Sawyer in the pediatric intensive care unit for that evening.

Our old routine of reading books, singing songs, saying our prayers, and tucking our children into their own beds went out the window. Of that whole list, only prayer remained. For the next six months, Sawyer's injuries and much-needed medications necessitated some very creative sleeping arrangements. Once home, we had a boys' room and a girls' room. Our nights were filled with night terrors, tears, medications, therapies, and very little sleep. We were barely functioning.

Daniel took the brunt of Sawyer's care, while I did my very best to try to insulate the girls from the terror going on in the room next door. Like clockwork, as bedtime grew closer, so did the edginess in our demeanor. Girls who had previously gone right to sleep now became balls of energy, literally bouncing off the walls. None of what was going on in our lives was the fault of my little girls, but one night, my patience began to wear thin. Out of the corner of my eye, I spotted a bear which had been given to Cloie by some friends.

Instead of yelling at my babies, I picked up "Joe the Bear" and politely asked him to keep the party down. At first my girls, who were three and eight at the time, exchanged glances that easily said, "I think Momma has finally lost it." But when they saw my smirk, they knew I was, at least partially, still with it. For the next hour, Joe the Bear completed all kinds of partying antics, the sillier the better. His shenanigans were my saving grace at bedtime. He danced, he shimmied and shook, he tickled toes, he would try to read books (even though he didn't know how to read yet), and he would sing songs; his creativity knew no boundaries. Replayed every night, he would party with gusto, every action followed by belly-chuckling giggles. Normal bedtime was eight o'clock, but Joe would party on until at least ten.

After his hijinks began to settle down, so too did my littlest ones. Somehow, the energy spent in creating elaborate scenes of ridiculousness magically sucked all the sadness out of the night for those two, at least for a little while. They would settle down into deep sleep. Sadly, though, sleep for me and the boys came in fits and spurts, and it would continue that way for many months.

Like I have said before, I am a doer who likes to stay busy. More than once in my life my friends have declared that I exhaust them once I get on a whirlwind of activity. I don't mean to have that effect on people, but I simply don't know how to exist any other way. When asked how I can get so much done in a day, I reply honestly about the secret to my success. "I take naps."

In our grief story, only Daniel and Erin returned to normal routines of work and school in the wake of returning from the hospital the first time. Sawyer's pain was so intense he spent the better part of the first six weeks screaming. Add to that a toddler who didn't go to daycare, and naps weren't just my anti-kryptonite; they were a lifeline. No sleep at night meant naps were a necessity to simply function.

But every time we tried to nap, the phone would ring. Eventually we came up with plan B, mainly because we were so sleep deprived. I have high sleep needs, and until my senior year of college, I was in bed by nine or ten o'clock most nights. Daniel and I were barely functioning on the few short hours we were sleeping at night, and enough was enough.

While we always appreciated the support, we knew we could not continue at that rate and be of any help to our children. Finally, the kids and I brought blankets and pillows into the living room, after burying every phone under the covers from our bed behind a closed door. We would shut all the blinds and lock all the doors (because we often seemed to get visitors at that time of day as well). If I could have figured out how to disconnect the doorbell, I would have done it.

Grief changes everything. *Everything.* No facet of life is left untouched. In addition to dealing with emotional needs, physiological ones must be met too. Sleeping, eating, and meeting other basic needs became a challenge for our family in the aftermath of the crash. So while we cherished the support each call or visit brought, we had to claim a few hours of the day for ourselves. Once we explained (and many times apologized) for our reason for not answering, most friends confessed they hadn't realized how bad things were and wanted nothing more than to tell us they were thinking of us.

We needed every call, every prayer, and every visit. The words of encouragement were lifelines to help us keep going, knowing God had prompted the outpouring of love. This is definitely not a missive urging comforters not to call or stop over unexpectedly. Far from it. Without the constant pool of overflowing support, we would have been lost. Instead, this is a gentle reminder to prayerfully consider the rituals of the family involved. Nap times and mealtimes might be the hours held very tenderly by families who need a whole lot of grace with a smattering of peace and quiet too, especially if they live with a bear named Joe.

Love My Tupperware

I AM SIMPLY NOT A STUFF PERSON. OH, DON'T GET ME WRONG! I have plenty of it, but there are times when I wish that God would call me into the mission field far away so I would be forced to donate or sell most of my belongings. Just like Don Quixote battled the windmill, I wage war on material goods. I despise clutter, and it seems I daily do battle with too much stuff. Although accumulating goods is something that we seem to be champions in, taking the plunge to "let it go" is much more difficult for my family.

Growing up, I remember Sundays very distinctly. We would worship at our church home, go out to eat at my parents' favorite diner, and then oftentimes walk the mall. Shopping is in my genes, although I don't excel at it. Most times, mall walking was just to stretch our legs, although my mother may as well have held several PhDs in bargain shopping and hunting for just the right object. Even today, if I need an obscure item, I reach out and dial 1-800-ASK-GRAM. About 99.75 percent of the time, she is successful in *the hunt*. I sometimes imagine her performing a little celebratory dance akin to an end-zone-spike-the-ball-shuffle right there in the aisles of the Bealls, Belk's, or whatever little place she completes her quest. My mother has great genes for decorating, which were passed down to my sister. It's not that I don't have those genes, but my need for less clutter dominates my desire for my house to look like the pages of *Southern Living*.

But if I was asked to part with my earthly goods, there are some to which I would cling tightly. They are simply that precious. In my battle with clutter, I have read very sage words over the years regarding what to keep and what to let go. One day while having lunch with a momma friend, we started a very philosophical discussion about clearing out clutter. I admire this friend, because she ruthlessly purged many nonessential items from her home. She took pictures of items her girls were hesitant to part with but then found new homes for all of them. Her life was much more peaceful, and secretly I was jealous. I asked her what motivated her to finally take the plunge. She shared about a heart-wrenching conversation she had with an aunt on this very subject *after* she lamented about how she was sick of picking up all evening long. (I hung on her every word because when I had three babies under the age of four, I was guilty of cleaning for the cleaning lady.) This dear wise woman asked my friend tough questions, but one in particular left us both speechless. She asked, "If there was a fire, what would you grab?"

As we sat eating our Chinese food on Main Street, tears welled in her eyes as she told me her answer. "I can't believe I am tearing up over this again, but when my aunt asked me that question, it hit me hard. I looked her in the eyes and choked out, 'Those two little girls and my wedding ring.' It wasn't so hard to let someone else love the extras in my home after all." It was a tender and heartfelt moment. A lesson that not only gave me some gentle reminders of how much stuff actually matters, but also of how much we truly don't need to be happy.

Among the things that I hold near and dear to my heart is something that I never thought I would own. One year while visiting my husband's family for Thanksgiving, my other mom asked for help. (I've been in this family for well over twenty years and threw the in-law moniker out the window years ago.) She quietly suggested over breakfast she would like my help with clearing out the china cabinet after we finished our banana bread. I was ecstatic to help because my other mom is a fiercely independent woman who will literally kick you out of "her corner" in the kitchen if you get in her way. Tenderly and gingerly we began to wrap up and box the china belonging to her mother, who had passed away many years ago.

I wasn't really sure what the purpose of our mission was, but if Mom needed help, I was a willing worker bee. Finally, we had all the beautiful silver and cream pieces packaged safely and securely. Then, as if someone from Publisher's Clearinghouse knocked on the door while simultaneously juggling a ridiculously large check and bunch of balloons, she whispered some of the most shocking news of my life. "When it is time for you to go home, I want you to put Grandma's china in your car." Still clueless, I inquired where I was supposed to take it. Her answer was gentle but firm. "Your house." Giant crocodile tears pooled in my eyes, and my throat constricted from the lump which formed. I argued that I simply could not. *Would not!* I reasoned, used my best logic, and then sobbed. I am only the daughter-in-law. (Okay, I can use the term when I am trying to be deductive.) "You have three daughters. It's too precious of a gift!"

I wouldn't say Mom is a softie, but it was clear as we stood our ground in the dining room that she wasn't budging. It was hers to give. She had made peace with her daughters (who unbeknownst to me had agreed I was the one who would appreciate it the most), and now she intended for me to take it. It is lucky she lived past that moment, because I nearly squeezed the stuffing out of her, loving her like she has always sang to my babies, "a bushel and peck and a hug around the neck." That, my friends, is a precious gift, and one I will treasure always.

I have other things ("pretties" as one friend says, some of which are so ugly only a mother could love them) I would have a hard time releasing. But for the most part, if I own it and you could use it, I share because I feel that is what God would want me to do.

Our family's willingness to share with our friends hasn't always ended with positive results. There have been a few mishaps over the years, but nothing so large that God's grace couldn't cover it.

The proverbial mixed blessing is how I would describe all the wonderful ways people (both friends and strangers) pitched in to help our family. From the moment we walked in the door the night before Reed's services to today, because—I will be honest—the generous giving from loving hearts still continues, on a smaller scale.

So many people came with so many gifts, our heads swirled for months. Keeping track of the sheer volume of blessings became a logistical nightmare. We actually joked sometimes; thank goodness it was winter and we could use our Minnesota refrigerator, also known as the garage.

I will shout it from the mountaintops. *This outpouring of support gave our family hope when we needed it most.* Our nightmare began on February

19, and I didn't prepare a meal for my family until June 19. I am not exaggerating. I made one meal for Easter dinner in those four months, but that was it! With the aftermath of hospitalizations, appointments with doctors, and therapy visits for our other children, it took four months before I was capable of making a meal for our family.

Love and support so generous was both humbling and amazing. We are and will be eternally grateful, but there were times when it was a little frustrating as well. When strings are attached, it simply isn't helpful. Frankly, it is extremely stressful. A few times folks dropped off a meal and said, "This is my best pot, so I need to know when and how I'm getting it back." I couldn't tell you what day of the week it was, much less when you would get your pot back. There were also offers of movies and books that came with strings attached. Those items sat in our house, causing us to worry about damaging or misplacing them. We finally had to gather up all the things folks wanted returned and give them back in one day. In the pit of grief, keeping track of these little details is a real challenge.

One of my best friends at this point will be saying, "Preach on, sista!" because I know her story is similar to mine. Humbly I will admit I, too, have learned a valuable lesson about gift giving and loans from this experience. I understand having a heart of hospitality and the desire to not bring a gift in tin foil (I do have some of those decorating genes after all) while also wanting the recipient to know love and thought went into the blessing.

A few years after the bus crash, a friend from church was battling leukemia. When asked if we could bring his family a meal, I was happy to comfort in the ways we had been comforted. I made a big batch of soup, homemade bread, and some sort of treat to accompany the meal. Not wanting to deliver the soup in a pot (I had none that I would write home about anyway), I placed it in a beautiful white soup tureen. When we arrived at our friends' home, I could see the haggard look of worry in his wife's face. I'd been there. Immediately I knew what the issue was— the tureen. I assured her I had bought it at a thrift store, it already had a chip in it, and if it didn't make it back to my house via *the river* (the description we use with some of our best friends for the flow of items between homes), I would not care one hoot. And I meant it. I wanted them to know they were loved and treasured much more than my stuff.

80

Balancing between wanting to serve and knowing what to give can be as tough as balancing between our tendencies to be a Mary or a Martha—or, for that matter, Martha Stewart. Love God; love others. It is really that simple. If no one has ever done this for you, I am whipping out the red pen from my teaching days and writing you a pass. When giving from your heart, it is okay to leave your best stuff at home. I won't be sending Grandma's china out anytime soon. Trust me: no one will ever know the difference.

On Cats and Kittens

ONE OF MY ALL-TIME FAVORITE TELEVISION SHOWS IS *DESIGNING Women*. While I might look like Ouiser Beaudreaux (from *Steel Magnolias*) out in my garden, my heart is every bit as refined, cultured, and sassy as Miss Julia Sugarbaker. Although we have already established my decorating style wouldn't cut it at the interior design firm, my ability to grow some beautiful tomatoes would definitely impress them. My quintessential favorite scene is when Bernice's niece is trying to have her committed because "she is crazy." While trying to solicit the ladies of the design team to join her quest to get her hands on the eccentric Bernice's dough, Julia produces one of her signature monologues on how we Southerners don't hide away our crazy people. We parade them right on out in the living room. She further states that no one in the South asks if you have crazy people; it's just assumed that you do. When questioned on which side of the family her crazy people hail from, she proudly states, "Both!" Now, before anyone gets their feathers ruffled, this is certainly not meant to be disparaging to any mental health issues. The kind of crazy I'm talking about could also be called eccentric quirkiness.

My love of animals is a part of my crazy, which like Miss Julia's shook down from both sides of my family tree. Nannie Campbell and Papa Noles rubbed off on me something fierce. I have battled ravens taking hairless baby bunnies out of their nests, have wanted to rescue an otter that I desperately attempted to avoid hitting with my car, and have driven frog-fensively when it is "raining frogs" in a Minnesota downpour. Crazy, I know! And proud of it!

Over the years, Nannie has been a trendsetter in all kinds of crazy when it comes to animals. My mother often regales us with stories of her kitten-breeding days. My redheaded granny raised the most beautiful Persian kittens. I'm not sure if many of them were sold or where they all went; it was long before my time. My questioning of their destination will make more sense in a couple of sentences.

My earliest recollection of Nannie's house came from the fish decade. What? Your grandmother didn't have decades devoted to God's species like they were years from the Chinese calendar? Well, mine sure did! When I was knee-high to grasshopper, Nannie and Granddaddy's family room had an entire wall dedicated to fish aquariums. Looking back now, we should have seen the writing on that same wall someday she would become a hoarder extraordinaire. Anyways, if a fish could be bought on the market, she had it on display in the room where every Saturday night we kids would watch all-star wrestling and Lawrence Welk (in that order) with her daddy and my great grandfather: Papa.

Like the song "1970-something," the dawning of a new decade produced a new fetish. Scales and fins went out as feathers and beaks came into vogue. The wall of water became lined with cages of all species of birds. Her prized one was a cockatiel named Ern. Not sure what Granddaddy thought about a bird named after him, but much like Mama Noles and my sweet hubby, I think he just resigned himself to the idea that loving someone includes embracing their kind of crazy. Topping the previous ten years, the decade of the bird raised the bar to an all-new height. Not only were there birds all over the house, but next to the banana tree outside was a huge aviary where every type of finch imaginable gaily lived out its days. I loved my Nannie with every fiber of my being, but even this animal-loving girl recognized her way of raising creatures was odd.

Papa bred a different kind of crazy for animals. A policeman for Auburn University, he befriended the campus animal and plant scientists over the years. Auburn, the land grant school for Alabama, offers many different degrees in animal sciences. Over the years, Papa brought many of the studied animals home. Donkeys, horses, goats, chickens (more on them in a minute), ducks, and bees were all a part of his little farm. Papa Noles had a farm, E-I-E-I-O.

I find it interesting that most marriages I know that have one crazy animal lover are almost always tempered by one more rational thinker. Which explains how after being stung coming in and out of the front gate numerous times, Mama calmly explained Papa had a choice to make. Either the bees or she had to go. They were married over sixty years, so of course it was good-bye, farm-fresh honey!

Papa loved his dogs and adored his farm animals, but it was the chickens that truly stole his heart.

I am probably one of the few people in the world who have had the chance and choice to live with her grandparents for a year. When attending my first year of graduate school at Auburn, I chose to live with Mama and Papa. This is where the chickens come in. I was very serious about my studies in chemistry, so dating wasn't really on my horizon until one day my cousin Gregg's friend asked me out for supper. Just like I would insist (and I mean *insist*) upon for my girls, this young man came to the door and visited with my grandparents before I would dream of stepping foot outside. (Remember Papa was a police officer.)

Well, during our visit, Mama was fit to be tied and her normally genteel ways went out the window while Papa, who was in the beginning stages of Alzheimer's, had a captive audience. He knew I wasn't leaving until he finished, so I sat back for the ride. The boy, on the other hand, didn't see the one-two punch of stories coming until Papa finally paused long enough to take a breath and a drink of water from a Mason jar. My grandfather was a fantastic storyteller, and that day's tale involved him and his chickens. Papa shared how his chickens were trained like dogs (I am *not* making this up!), how they followed him everywhere, and how their favorite part of the day was when he sat in the porch swing. While swinging away, those chickens would come and sit on his shoulders and at his feet to talk to him. He went on talking about their conversations right before that aptly placed pause in the story. Mama, ten shades of embarrassed, seized her moment, coming out of nowhere with the zinger of the night. She looked that boy in the face and without batting an eyelash declared, "I bet you didn't know that Kandy's papa spoke fluent chicken."

I knew he would never be the boy for me when he didn't pick up on her sarcasm. Fluent chicken is my kind of crazy!

Now, I hope you understand my love for all of God's creatures isn't some passing fad; it is programmed into my genetic code which was handed down to some of my kids. Reed and Huck's relationship would be a good example. We knew that it wouldn't have been right to have Reed's services without Huckleberry (a boy's best friend) as a pallbearer. I don't know this for certain, but our funeral director must have understood my crazy because he didn't once try to talk us out of that plan. Huck sat or stood silently next to his boy the entire service. If my people are animal crazy, our dog was boy crazy. It is a hurt he has never gotten over.

Loving your animals or pets is something I truly understand. My sister-in-law, Mary, and I have exchanged more than once an e-mail that explains if you don't like our dogs to kindly remember you are a guest in our home and that we would gladly pick our animals' company over that of many people. Yet as much as we both love our dogs, they will never take the place of our children.

Once again, I understand what people say and what they mean are sometimes two different things, but when a sweet little lady hugged us and explained that she understood what we were going through because her beloved kitty had just passed away, Daniel and I exchanged a couple of perplexed eyebrow raises and later a good belly chuckle about that analogy. *What do you say to something so ridiculous?* My friend Amy, who also has some "Sugarbaker" sass, has a saying that tickles me to pieces. When somebody says something ridiculous, she quick-wittedly retorts, "Just to let you know, you did say that out loud." This would be one of the occasions where that would have fit, but Mama would have snatched me bald-headed if I had.

Again, grace won out and I said nothing other than thanking her for coming. She wasn't trying to equate Reed's existence to that of a pet's, but she wanted us to know that a void was present in her life like the one we were feeling.

I truly love animals, just like the lyrics of my favorite childhood hymn, written by Cecil Alexander:

> All things bright and beautiful,
> All creatures great and small,
> All things wise and wonderful,
> The Lord God made them all.

In my heart, however, he made my kids just a little more special than Huck and all the other animals my crazy people have loved.

These Stones Hurt

FROM THE MOMENT HE ENTERED THE WORLD, SAWYER WAS A big kid. Upon first meeting him, one of his godmothers looked at him and then looked at me astonished. Compared to Reed, who was always tiny, Sawyer was a big boy. For years, we would dress them in matching outfits. Bouncing along in a side-by-side stroller, we were asked, more than once, if they were twins. Eyebrows raised, I always looked at the person asking as if they were playing a joke on me. One of them is talking in full sentences and naming dinosaurs, and the other one can barely sit upright. *No, they're brothers but not twins.* Every time (by which I mean every single well-baby visit), we would hear, "Well, his growth milestones are almost off the chart." Like I said, he was a big kid.

I have always felt a little sorry for him, because I think people expected him to be older, and as such, they were disappointed when he didn't "act his age." He was just being himself, which was a full twenty months younger than his same-sized brother. Other than the training wheel experience, he handled it with grace and dignity. Yet for every milestone that Reed hit, Sawyer wasn't far behind him.

Twenty-eight months behind Sawyer, along came Erin, affectionately known as Sister to all of us. Once she was big enough to move, all she desired was to keep up with those growing boys. She followed them everywhere. When we would go through their clothes, putting aside all the ones they had outgrown, Sister would be circling around us like a vulture waiting to swoop in, all the while cawing, "Can I have it? Can I have it?" She loved her ReedSawyer. (No, that isn't a typo, because to her it was one word.)

Try as she might, there were some ways in which she just could not catch up. Shooting hoops was one of them. Sawyer had asked for a basketball hoop for his sixth birthday. Since basketball runs in our genes, we invested in a portable and adjustable-height hoop that would last most (if not all) of their childhoods and has been used in our neighborhood for years. When it arrived, the boys would shoot buckets for hours, but no matter how hard Sister tried, she could never quite get the ball up high enough, never reaching the rim even at the lowest setting. All she wanted to do was play ball with her boys. Daniel and I would encourage her to just keep trying, sometimes lifting her high in the air to dunk one.

The summer before kindergarten, almost singularly focused, she was determined to improve her basketball skills. Even in the heat of the day, she would be out in the driveway trying her best. One day, her efforts paid off. Being four months pregnant, the hot August sun was not very inviting to me so I sat at my craft table, scrapbooking and watching her through the picture window. Observing her closely, I saw a ritual unfolding that involved some stepping and what appeared to be personal words of motivation. Ball in hand, she would start at the edge of the driveway, take one step, and mutter something that I couldn't quite make out by reading her lips. Another step and more mouthed words. Dribbling was completely optional at this point in her schooling. One more step and one more word, then shoot.

This went on for a long time, and then it happened—nothing but net! The smile was priceless! Instead of excessive celebration, she kept repeating the routine over and over with success. At some point, she looked up and was a little surprised to find me watching through the window with tears in my eyes. Even as an educator, persistence and determination are not traits I can teach my children. Sister tore through the front door, almost breathless, asking, "Momma, did you see? I did it! I really did it! Do you want to come and watch?"

Not even pausing to find my shoes, I was out the door and ready to witness the joy that had just unfolded in my driveway. Like an Olympic runner stepping into the blocks, she backed up to her starting point, took that first step, and said, "Laura!" A second step was followed by "Mary!" The third and final step was proclaimed to be "Carrie," and then she shot!

"I knew it would work, Momma! It just had to!"

That summer, my little girl born on the prairie was enamored with all things *Little House*. When you live just forty-five miles from Walnut Grove, it's hard not to be. So with the help of three prairie sisters, my Sister learned to make her first buckets. It was a milestone to remember.

Outside of rites of passage that the world celebrates, I believe families have ones uniquely their own. Of course there are all the firsts written in the baby books. (Okay, let's be honest, that probably only happens for firstborns consistently, and good luck to the rest of you.) Learning to ride a bike without training wheels, losing teeth, and tying shoelaces are other indicators that you are growing up, but unlike those universal examples, a time-honored Team Stevens tradition of growing is getting your very own library card. I adore books and am a firm believer that a library card is a responsibility, not a right. I feel when a child checks out a book, it is a treasure to be cherished. Hidden in those pages are adventures untold, and if the reader was too careless with the treasure, the journey within would be lost for other brave explorers. Even though most of their friends had library cards when they were much younger, my children were not allowed to get theirs until they could legibly and consistently write their name—first *and* last. Instead of me signing their name on the library patron contract, they were able to do it themselves. We made a big hoopla out of the whole thing, complete with paparazzi-style photography and fanatical cheering, replete with high fives. (Seriously, we celebrate the little stuff!)

Reed reached this milestone toward the end of kindergarten, while Sawyer and Cloie were somewhere in the middle of that same grade when they signed the dotted line. But the one who surprised us was Erin. The second week of kindergarten, she came bouncing down to my classroom (because at that time I still taught at the same school my children attended) and announced quite proudly, "We can go get my library card today!" Knowing the boys were nowhere close to being able to spell Stevens legibly at this point, I asked her to prove her proclamation. Imagine if you will the look of sheer determination on her face, biting her tongue in concentration, chubby little fingers gripping the pencil, as she scrawled, "Erin Stevens," in childlike writing. I was completely shocked because we hadn't been working on this at home, and I knew they hadn't even gotten to the letter S yet in the kindergarten room. I asked her how in the world she knew how to do that!

To be completely honest, this is one of the few moments I remember with clarity of her kindergarten year. It is that baby book syndrome for the middle children all over again. But hey! I had a baby that year, and other than the fact that Sister was completely steamed when she had to "pull a card," indicating her behavior went from great (green card) to not-so-good (yellow card) when she got out of her seat because boys were trying to cut her hair (this is *still* a thorn in her side), the library card moment was monumental in kindergarten year. I had to laugh when she shared the secret to her early writing success.

"You have to promise not to get mad," she told me. Assurances secured, she continued. "Well, I don't really sleep during nap time. I move my sleeping mat to the cubbies where my name is written. Instead of sleeping, I have been memorizing my name!" That's my girl! Persistent and determined! I could hardly contain my giggles. We rushed right over to the library on our way home.

All of those little moments are ones we choose to celebrate. Truly, these are some of the happiest moments of my kiddos' childhoods. But as happy and precious as they are, in the corners of my heart, I feel a longing for the ones that did not come to pass for the three babies we lost. I don't think I ever truly understood the meaning of the word *bittersweet* until I went through some of my life's greatest heartbreaks. My heart soared with each celebrated moment but at the same time mourned the absences of the ones that never came to be. In those moments, I was almost tongue-tied, unable to articulate what my heart felt, imaging all the big and little moments that we would never experience together.

The absence of reaching milestones became profoundly significant when Reed died. In the grief world, there are many firsts that must be endured when a loved one passes. The first birthday (which sadly coincided with Father's Day for us), the first day of school, the first Christmas, the first snowfall (which is when we bake cookies and make cocoa), and all those other firsts were gut-wrenchingly painful. For me, the second year was harder because, while we knew the firsts were coming, in the second year we were forced to come to terms with the hard truth that Reed's absence was always going to be felt in those moments. This is the kind of hard stuff that can keep you in bed all day.

Not every family watches the last sunset of the year as a tradition, but most families of young teenagers anticipate attending their graduations. Reed was in the seventh grade when he and the other children died. Our children attend a school that houses preschool through grade twelve in the same building. When I was still teaching there, the principal created a celebration (akin to a graduation minus caps and gowns) for the eighth grade class. It was always such a wonderful event, celebrating how far our young scholars had come and recognizing each one of them for their unique gifts and talents. Our family as well as the Javens family had been invited to attend the graduation.

I really just wanted to stay in bed that day. Please don't misunderstand me. I was and still am proud of the boys' classmates, but knowing my son wasn't going to be there was too much to bear. I was equally happy for my friends, who are those classmates' parents, but I wasn't going to be bringing home a certificate to hang on the refrigerator. Even more heartbreaking was the fact that I couldn't hug my son at the conclusion of the ceremony. We attended with very broken hearts simply to honor the children who were working very diligently to help us with Reed's Run and the Reed Stevens Memorial Scholarship.

We live in a neighboring community to our school, and in our hometown, sadly, there have been many children who have passed away in recent years. When I walked into the auditorium that day, I was expecting the type of recognition for deceased students that I know had been done in our community in the past.

I couldn't have been more wrong.

The greatest fear grieving parents have played right out before our eyes. We found a seat toward the back and opened our programs. Scanning through the list of names, there was absolutely no mention of Reed or Jesse. Tears welled in my eyes as I tried to avoid eye contact with anyone in the vicinity. Fortunately, the dimmed lights were a good cover as I began to fall apart. All my grieving mind could think was *He is being erased* as I forced my stomach contents to stay down. I felt like a caged animal as my eyes darted around the room, looking for the quickest escape. The program included a special recognition where both families were given a figurine, which was a nice gift (that I do sincerely appreciate), but all I wanted was to see his name in the program. I didn't want to go on stage for a gift or for any reason. I just wanted my son (and his classmate) remembered.

We didn't stay for the reception afterward, rather heading to our van and sobbing in the parking lot. I don't believe anyone intended to hurt us in any way. The people in the community are much too amazing to do anything of the sort. But the omission ripped the scab off the wounds of our hearts, and our grief flooded out.

Three and a half years later, we received an e-mail from the principal regarding the class's upcoming high school commencement. From the junior high experience, I knew I did not want to be blindsided and expressed my thoughts on what I hoped would happen. My requests were few: their names in the program and perhaps a gown and rose in the chair where they would have sat. I had visited with Jesse's mom about what I was going to say, because in no way did I want my request to be one that would hurt her.

I wish I could say it was as simple as all of that. It was not. Our suggestions were met with much resistance, even the idea that our families needed to consider what might make other families uncomfortable. *Are you kidding me?* My son died on a school bus coming home from this school, and somehow it was my responsibility to make everyone else feel better about that? I was devastated. I felt betrayed. And I kept thinking, *I thought Reed's name missing from the program was bad.* This was much, much worse, and I sobbed for three days, rarely leaving my bed.

Eventually, I did the only thing I knew to do, which was to pray. Daniel and I resolved if Reed would not be remembered, we would not be attending the graduation. Every year, I (because it is just too hard for my husband) attend the school's senior banquet to award Reed's scholarship. On the drive there for what would have been Reed and Jesse's senior banquet, I called one of my friends, Brenda, who knew of our dilemma with commencement, and said, "I can't do this. I simply can't do it. We have worked so hard for five years to raise money to help kids at this school, and I just feel cheated. I can't do this." Even though she was just getting comfortable at home, all she said was "I'm on my way." She drove to the school, held my hand, and basically held me upright to get through the banquet.

We didn't stay for the pictures and hugs afterward. We simply sat in the van and cried. A week before graduation, we received a call informing us that the few wishes we had requested would be granted. I was thankful and appreciative, but knowing how hard it was to watch his classmates earn scholarships and hear of their future plans, I wasn't sure how we were going to make it through.

I sent a message to a grieving mom friend whose son died in our town when he was a freshman. I was at his graduation ceremony, where they received a bronze plaque commemorating his membership in the class. I bawled with them as they accepted the award in front of all those people. My message was simple: *I don't know how to do this.* Her encouraging reply acknowledged that she didn't either, but they had gone to honor their son. She and her husband were invited to attend the parties and open houses of several of his closest friends. They didn't want to attend, but when they did, each family had created a special tribute to her son. Their kindnesses touched her in a long-lasting way.

We did attend graduation, flanked by Brenda's family. On the drive there, we discovered the Olson family had decorated the cross memorializing the four children at the crash site with balloons. It was a gift we could have never imagined! Much to my surprise, and I am guessing to the surprise of Jesse's mom, several graduates chose to honor us with roses, along with giving them to their own mothers. Two little roses went a very long way toward boosting the spirits of some very sad people. We did exit before the recessional, which was our plan all along, because we never wanted the day to be about us.

My feelings and thoughts on those difficult days are entirely my own. Some of the best advice I have ever received is "Don't apologize for being your child's momma." Graduations are difficult for some parents, even when their children are living. I know. I am struggling with one coming very soon. Graduation means a change in a family's life and dynamic.

This was probably the hardest chapter of this entire book to write. From their first day of kindergarten until graduation day, we dream of what our children are going to do and what impact they will have in this world. To have it all gone in an instant is almost unbearable. Reed loved school. He loved learning, and my grieving heart only wanted that recognized. No matter what happened that day, the school staff and administration would not have been able to take away the pain. I am truly thankful for what the school has done over the years for our family, but when it comes to reaching missed milestones, I needed (and will continue) to be my child's momma first.

It's All in How You Look at It

I LOVE WORDS. I KEEP FOLDERS OF CLIPPED QUOTES AND notebooks full of words that have touched me in one way or another. One of my recent favorites was painted beautifully on old barn wood. "Grace isn't simply a little prayer you say before a meal. It's a way of life." I have limited wall space so I didn't buy the décor, but I did snap a picture of it with my phone to save for another day.

Amazing grace is more than a song for my family as well, but when it comes to mealtime we do have a ritual of blessing our food, thanking God for both its sustenance and for the hands who provided it. Every family has their "thang," as one of my friends says. In our family, we had to create a schedule of who would bless the food on what night. "Why would this even be necessary?" you might ask. Well, simply, when they were little, our kids loved to pray and mealtimes would turn into arguments over who said the blessing last. The new system had every day covered but Sunday. Each one of us would bless the food on the night of the week that corresponded with the day of the week we were born. Since Reed and I are both Thursday's children, I graciously offered to take Friday so he could have his day. My children have always called it "blessing the food." The words penned on the rustic barn wood were simply the way we lived, not what we have ever called the meal prayer.

My mom has always lovingly called her grandchildren "those little short people." Of course, for my children, that description only lasted until fifth grade, when most of them passed her in height, but the moniker has stuck around for longer. On one occasion, when she, my dad, and Nannie were visiting, we were preparing to sit down and eat. At the time, our table was too small to accommodate that many guests, so my children were relegated to the infamous kids' table. My mother was aware of our mealtime routine, and she asked, "Could a little short person over there say grace?" This was met with our three oldest children enthusiastically, almost as if on cue, raising their right fists to the air as if they were offering a fist bump to Jesus, shouting in unison, "Grace!"

Mealtimes are always special when you can share the table with those you love. I love my mom, and she has an amazing sense of humor. She doesn't, however, tolerate sassiness too well. And she was not amused at their antics. Before the lecture of the century began, I cut in and explained to the kids that she was asking for them to say the blessing. After quickly calculating the day of the week, they agreed it was Wednesday, which was Erin's day to pray.

My dad tells the story of how he lost out on being the valedictorian because he was a bad speller. He and another student were neck and neck, but because of his spelling ineptitude, his competitor won the coveted position of first in the class. He and I have joked more than once about a T-shirt we once saw boldly emblazoned with "Bad spellers of the world: UNTIE!"

As a classroom teacher and a momma, I know the struggle is real for some with spelling, but I also know that with a little eye for detail, some common errors can be avoided. For a long time, I glossed over the word *angel* spelled as *angle*, but the more frequently it happened, the more I noticed it. I began to wonder, in the way only a math teacher would, *If Reed is an* angle, *is he obtuse or acute?* Without getting into the theology of various faiths on this topic, there is one thing I know for certain. My son did not transcend this life and become two lines diverging from a common endpoint. He did not leave earth and become an angle. But sometimes the ability to deal with life's little moments is all in how you look at them. I finally decided that he was a right angle. Right in the glow of the radiance of Jesus Christ! Right in the land with no tears and no suffering and, for him, no blindness! Right in God's loving arms, where he would be until we could join him again!

You Can Always Have Another

I AM REALLY NOT A GRIEF EXPERT, AND I DON'T PLAY ONE ON TV either. One of the very things I always hoped I would never do is hurt someone else while they were grieving. That was a great plan, until I did. About six months after the bus crash, I received a phone call from an acquaintance, telling me she had a teddy bear she wanted to show me. This sweet woman knew of a gal who had started a ministry of sorts by taking the clothing of loved ones and turning it into teddy bears.

We still had all of Reed's clothing. In fact, the day we returned home from the hospital right before Reed's services, the first thing I wanted to do was fuss at him for not putting his clothes away. When we got home, I needed to grab something for Sawyer from their room, and there sat all of Reed's laundry on his bed. I wanted to yell and scream and tell him to clean it up but instead composed myself because we were meeting with the funeral director a few minutes later.

When I received this unexpected phone call, I was intrigued, because aside from doing the laundry chores for him, I simply didn't know what to do with his clothes. As soon as she stopped over and visited on the front deck, I knew she had brought me a gem of a gift—the knowledge of what we would do. I have seen memory bears since, but they are nothing like these bears. The bear she brought was the work of one incredibly talented seamstress who didn't just use the material but kept the integrity of the item when making the bear. If it was a collared shirt, the bear would have a tinier version of the collar. Similarly, a pair of pajama pants would have the waistband on the bear. This seamstress, who is now my friend, has no lack of creativity or talent.

After holding a family meeting, we decided that we would take some

97

of Reed's clothes and have bears made for every set of grandparents, aunts/uncles, and cousins, which we would use as Christmas presents for that first one without him. As a family, we went through the painstaking process of choosing. Just like jury selection, anyone could veto an item for any reason whatsoever if it was too painful to let go. When the gigantic box of bears arrived, it was like opening a big box of hugs. With every bear revealed, we all traveled down memory lane, savoring the last time he wore each item. These were his favorite jammy pants! Oh, his shirt from Nannie he wore on the first day of school! His hunting jacket! "Look, Momma. This is the shirt he wore when he walked me down the aisle when you and Daddy renewed your marriage vows!"

We loved our bears, and our family members loved theirs as much as we did. To date, Cloie has loved hers so much that we may have to send him for a rehabilitative session with Cindy the seamstress. Many a time, we have cuddled with our bears to just feel closer to him. They have brought us such peace and comfort we have probably since become her biggest clients. Whenever someone passes *and* we feel a bear would be comforting, we send an order form and an enclosed check for the family to send away.

Last year, one of my best friends lost her father very unexpectedly. As will happen over the years of friendship and raising children, her parents somehow assimilated my kids into their lives as well. I could not imagine what my friend was going through, while at the same time I grieved losing someone who brought such joy to my kiddos' lives. There were lots of little ways that we helped in the aftermath, but I wanted to let a little time pass before I sent the bear form and check.

What I had hoped to be a sweet gift and gesture for her and her children was instead one that brought pain to my friend's world. The family had chosen to donate her father's clothing to a local charity, and there were no pieces left with which to make a bear. We could have bought something to use, but it wouldn't have been one that "Grandpa" had worn. There I went being an idiot again.

Although I have admitted to not having much experience with grief and loss prior to college, my life after marriage has been filled with many losses. After rereading that, I feel I should apologize to my husband. Marriage did not cause me grief, and thankfully, we had each other to rely upon when facing our greatest losses. Since our wedding day, we have lost one parent, numerous aunts and uncles, a few friends, three of my grandparents, several "adopted" grandparents, Reed and the other children who died that day, and three of our own babies to miscarriage.

My whole life I only wanted two things: to be a teacher and a momma. But never meeting three of my children this side of heaven wasn't in my plans. Having been mostly successful at whatever I set my mind to, for years I felt like a cosmic failure because of my seven children, three went to live with Jesus without taking a single breath on earth. Never once did I hold their hands, stroke their tiny heads, or sing them lullabies.

Over the years, little moments catch me off guard, like the time I broke into hysterical tears at church when I realized one of my sweet babies should be up there with the other children receiving his first Bible.

I have been stunned over the years by the insensitivity of some people who have suggested, "Well, at least you can have more children." *Really? Because the one I want is the one I cannot have!* I can't replace them any more than I could go and find a redheaded boy at the grocery store and have him suddenly assume Reed's identity. The thought process is ludicrous.

After our first loss, the doctors were optimistic the dream of having more children could be true, but they weren't absolutely certain. For some, another baby or even a first baby will never be a part of their story. In most cases, the grieving is done in silence because pregnancy loss is rarely recognized. It is also why Mother's Day services can be extremely painful to some families. For some reason, losing a baby the parents didn't "know" yet isn't acknowledged as grief worthy, suggesting that no attachment could have formed. I have never met the baby we named Timothy, but that didn't matter to my heart when I sat in the foyer of the church and sobbed and sobbed for a Bible he would never hold.

For two of our sweet babies, we held very private services grieving their loss. On one of those occasions, our pastor was away on a sabbatical. In his absence, a dear friend and his wife came to remember and pray with us. I still have the card he handwrote, expressing his own grief and acknowledging our loss. It says, "We grieve the hands we do not hold." Eight little words conveyed a lifetime of love. Having their own pregnancy-loss stories, their comfort came from a deep place of understanding.

We lost our first baby during Daniel's last year of college studies when he worked as a tutor for the academic lab. After a long wait, we finally learned that the troubles I was experiencing meant we were losing our baby. Daniel's boss, who was the sweetest lady, sent us a note that simply read, "I understand your pain." It was a loss we had never known existed in her life, but again, her four little handwritten words were penned from firsthand knowledge.

Teddy bears made from old shirts are indeed a far cry from newborn babies. My intention for wanting to give my friend something to hold through the grieving process was very similar to the comfort that friends gave in simple words when I didn't have a baby to hold. But in both cases, a replacement would never be sufficient—no matter how many shirts we could buy or babies we may or may not be able to birth.

Waited Sixty Years to Do That

WHEN I WAS IN GRADUATE SCHOOL LIVING WITH MAMA AND Papa, I had one week that was grueling in every sense of the word. Midterm grades were due for the hundreds of students in the laboratory course where I was the teaching assistant, which meant hours upon hours of grading chemistry lab reports. Then I had my own midterm examinations in biochemistry and organic chemistry. The latter class was quite a step up from my college course work, and I was spending late night hours (something I had never really needed to do before) preparing for the exam. Papers graded and tests taken by Friday afternoon, I practically floated out of my office in the old chemistry building at Auburn as I prepared for a weekend of much-needed rest and relaxation. Or so I thought.

Planning to sleep in for quite some time, I was deep in dream mode on that Saturday morning when Mama came in before the rooster even thought about waking. She lightly tapped me on the leg and said, "Get up and get dressed, Shug. Papa wants to show you something." I sat right up in bed, eyes wide open, mouth about to protest, but when my vision cleared, the look on her face said I should get ready to go.

Before the Alzheimer's (I hate that wretched disease), Papa loved to go riding and visiting. We traveled all over the state visiting sites and family and, of course, people we didn't even know. That particular morning, he wanted to show me some fine Alabama history. We drove on up the road from Opelika, heading to the Valley, where we would stop and get us a biscuit at the Hardee's. They had been eating biscuits every day for fifty years, so why would that Saturday have been any different? "If it ain't broke, don't fix it" was my grandparents' motto.

Traveling took on a whole new meaning that year I lived with my grandfather. Even with temperatures reaching one hundred in the shade and humidity around 90 percent, he had no qualms about leaving Mama and me in the car while he stepped into the gas station for an RC Cola for all of us. By the time he finished visiting with every single person—*every single one of them*—we were ready to be poked with a fork and turned over. The lukewarm drinks he brought back did nothing to improve our spirits. I would have sworn he knew every person in the entire state of Alabama.

My grandparents used to have a lake cabin on up the road from Valley, Alabama, known in our family as "the Valley," and we would make this same stop if we were planning to head up there for a day or weekend. Once, Papa made this trip in his old 1980 green Ford pickup truck, only instead of eating in the Hardee's, he went through the drive-thru and took his breakfast to a field where he loved to wait for the sunrise. After enjoying his breakfast and the unfolding beauty of God's creation, he continued his drive on down to the lake. He parked the truck to unlock the gate to the cabin's property and received the surprise of his life. Out from under the hood of the truck popped one of his roosters. My animal-loving grandfather never had the heart to put that chicken through such an ordeal again, and he lived out the rest of his days down by the lake. Well played, rooster! What a tough gig—retirement at the lake.

But on this particular Saturday morning, Papa decided we needed to get out and "stretch a bit," which was code for "I want to visit with all my friends in the Hardee's, even if they don't know they're my friends." Mama and I ate our biscuits. She enjoyed her coffee while I needed something stronger than orange juice and opted for a Coke, heavy on the ice. It was going to be a long day since it was only six in the morning and we had already driven for about a half hour.

As we sat in the booth with our breakfast, a sweet little old lady looked over at us and smiled. We instantly knew this was the smile of someone who got us. She understood the hardship we were suffering, because her husband was chatting it up with just about everyone in the diner as well. Eventually he and Papa sat down at a table as if they had planned for years to meet there on that weekend morning.

She quietly slipped over to our booth and complimented Mama on her beautiful white hair. She wistfully commented that if she could have hair as gorgeous as Mama's, she would stop dying hers altogether. "Whatever is your secret?" she asked.

I come by my sass genetically, although at that point in my life, I was only just discovering that fact about my ancestry. Mama leaned in as if she was giving away the secret recipe to Bush's Baked Beans. She whispered with dramatic flair, "I will let you in on my formula. I get up in the morning, I wash it, and then I dry it." Her stage whisper was followed by a theatrical wiping of her hands. The poor woman's face was a cross between being duped and flat-out jealous of Mama's luck in the hair gene pool. I really wanted to laugh out loud, but Mama's pinching fingers were within reach so I refrained.

Eventually, the two old men finished up their conversations with a "Y'all come see us sometime," and off we went to see whatever was pressing enough to pull me away from my warm and toasty slumber.

The driving went on and on for what seemed like hours, and I tried my best to stay awake in the backseat. Eventually, we ended up in a field. A field! We had gotten up at the crack of dawn (No! Before dawn!) for this? Papa proceeded to start school with a lecture.

"Gal, do you know what they used to do in this field?"

Um, grow stuff?

Well, that might have happened there too, but I was soon to learn that for many years, a tent was set up right on that land, where tent revivals took place underneath its canopy. On this very ground, hundreds, maybe even thousands, of people came to know the Lord. While I was thankful that all those sinning souls had gotten right in their walks with God, all my eyes saw was a bunch of knee-high grass and weeds. I just nodded and smiled, not exactly sure what type of reverence I should bestow upon that hallowed ground. With a sweeping motion, he pointed across the road to what looked like a dilapidated stump of wood. Upon closer inspection, I could see it was a carved structure of some kind. Papa went on to explain the rundown statue was an inspirational. (If you are familiar at all with Foghorn Leghorn, imagine one of his speeches right here). "Inspirational," I say. "This is no ordinary statue. This is Kaw-liga. You know Kaw-liga, don't you, gal? This here is the same wooden Indian—I mean the very wooden Indian—ol' Hank Williams wrote that song about."

I could hardly contain my excitement. I sat there stone faced, looking at that sorry old thing and, completely nonplussed, muttered, "I can see why he called him poor ol' Kaw-liga."

This did nothing to improve grandfather-granddaughter relations, because for the next half hour, I was forced to listen to a lecture on how he was trying to teach me some history and apparently I cared nothing about my Alabama heritage. "Trying to teach you something, and you don't even appreciate it." I didn't protest, but if I thought I was getting up for something exciting, this was not what I had in mind.

Papa eventually cooled off and we kept on driving, eventually ending up in Alexander City, home to a huge Russell Athletics mill. We drove around, taking in the sights of the town and the Russell franchise. Close to suppertime, we decided to start making our way back to Opelika. This Alabama history tour was kicking my tail and I was beginning to doze (a safe plan) in the backseat. As we were heading south out of town, Mama nonchalantly inquired as to whether I would be interested in seeing where Papa and his first wife once lived.

Do what? I was awake now as this was the first I had ever heard of Papa having had another wife. I went from dozer to inquisitor, leaning over the front seat in two seconds flat.

"Why have I never heard of this? What was her name? Why did you live up here?"

Eventually, my grandmother answered all of my questions. Papa and his first wife, Rhode, were only married briefly before the marriage was annulled. At one point, my grandmother and her sister-in-law traveled to Tuskegee to see this lady because they caught wind Rhode was working at a café there. Curiosity satisfied, Mama never spoke about this part of Papa's past until this particular Saturday.

All of my questions and my grandmother's ease of answering did not sit well with Papa. He took my barrage of inquiries until he couldn't take it anymore. He pulled the car over to the side of the road and told us to get out. While standing on the side of the road, I was still trying to piece it all together. We didn't stand there for long before he finally composed his thoughts. "I've heard all I am going to hear on that woman. Now, if the two of you can stop your chatter about all that history" (which I found more than ironic, considering the mission of the day), "you can get back into this car. If you can't, it's a long walk to Opelika."

We were hungry and I was still pretty tired, so we agreed to his terms. The remainder of the drive was completely silent. Once we got home, Mama followed me to my bedroom, where she plopped down on my bed and laughed like I had never seen.

"I've waited sixty years to do that" was all she said before we fell into a pile of giggles.

Other than learning of a heretofore unknown chapter in Papa's history, what I most learned that afternoon was that there are some things in life you simply don't get over. These things may lay dormant for years, but their emotional entanglements weave webs in our hearts. I don't know why I was completely blindsided when months (mere months!) after the bus crash, kids and adults started to insinuate that my children should be "over it." Some even went so far as to suggest that they weren't that close with Reed in the first place, so they should have been able to just move on without any struggles whatsoever. My children, who were still dealing with the very real and physical scars of riding on the same bus, had absolutely no idea how to handle these "suggestions." As parents, we tried to equip them with the knowledge that unless someone had walked in their shoes, they really didn't know what our kids were feeling.

Perhaps I should have taken my own advice. Annually, our school has a wonderful tradition known as Track-N-Field Day. While other schools have similar days, I love how our day operates like a mini Olympics, complete with opening ceremony. Parents take the day off work to come and cheer on their delegation. Before the completion of the new school and new track, the opening ceremony march took place down Main Street, while the activities took place at the former football field. In 2008, Sawyer was released from the hospital for the final five days of school, one of which was Field Day. He was still in a wheelchair but participated in some of the events.

The next year, our elementary students participated in a fundraiser for the school and the company in charge of the fundraising wanted to make a donation to the Not4gotten Foundation, started by the three families who lost children on bus number 5 to help support other grieving parents. That decision was purely altruistic on the part of the company, as we never solicited funds from them. The company asked to present a check at Track-N-Field Day when all three moms would be present. After the ceremonial presentation, I walked back over to a group of moms. Once again, I was completely blown away to hear (did I mention I am a teacher with supersonic hearing?) someone mutter under their breath, "Aren't they over that yet?"

No! As a matter of fact, we are not. We are never going to be. You close on houses and businesses deals, but you will never, not now, not ever, close on your children. You know what, lady? I was just thinking about your children the other day, and the conclusion I came to was just how forgettable they are.

Doesn't sound so pretty, does it? I know my thoughts are not gentle, but they are real, expressing how much anguish the question evoked. Asking a grieving parent to be "over it" is essentially saying that there was nothing worth remembering about the child who passed away. There seems to be a pervasive need in the world for grieving families to "get over it." Those who ask the question have most likely never experienced a deep loss. I honestly believe this sentiment isn't for the grieving family as much as it is an attempt to make everyone else feel better. If we (the grieving) are perceived as being "over it," then everyone else can be happy too. The problem with this line of thinking is that we will never be over it.

Although my thinking earned me a whole lot of attention that I never intended, I liken our grief journey to the real-life struggles facing those who battle alcoholism. I used this analogy when we were given an opportunity in court to address the woman who killed our son and hurt our other children. I shared that we would *never* (this side of heaven) be over it, that we would always be recovering mourners. Imagine my shock later that evening when, while watching the ten o'clock news, a reporter reworded my message, suggesting I likened my grief to my own personal battle with alcoholism. Addictions are not laughing matters—period. But after such a stress-filled day, all I could do was laugh, because I do not have, nor have I ever had, such an affliction.

I will, however, have a lifetime longing to see my son, to wish he could be with us, to see the dreams we shared unfold, and to simply get one of those amazing hugs he was so good at sharing. We waited almost ten months to finally meet in the beginning, praying every day for his safe arrival. Those prayers, and the love that went along with being his momma, never left us when he was here, and they don't diminish now that he isn't. There is no cure for missing your child. With the love and support of others, determination to live out our faith, and God's grace, we will rejoice here on earth. We will get through it, but until we reach heaven, we will never be over it.

PART TWO
One Size Fits Most—
Things That Might Be Helpful

MY ELEMENTARY YEARS WERE SPENT IN THE ARMY BASE TOWN OF Columbus, Georgia. My dad was done with his military career, and we moved there for him to pursue his dream of teaching and coaching. As a former Columbus College alum, his college coach welcomed him on staff, and the rest was history in my family. As a citywide district, Columbus really promoted the arts. It was a blessed place to attend school in my formative years. Each year we were exposed to field trips ranging from ballet and symphony orchestras to musicals and art museums.

During the latter, I learned about more than just art. I have to give it to the teachers, who had to take classrooms full of young children on these outings. Inevitably, there would be the painting with the nearly naked ladies. Pretty scandalous for children being raised in the Southern Bible belt, where wooden white churches and football stadiums were our religion. Although for those of us who occasionally watched the Dallas Cowboys, we had already seen about that much skin on a cheerleader.

While the teachers blathered on about elements of painting like line and light, my eyes were always—and I mean *always*—drawn to the bellies of these barely clad ladies. As a sprite of a thing, I vowed that what I saw in those paintings would never—*never*—happen to me. Until, of course, gravity (that awful hussy) cast her spell. I am certain enjoying my food, having six pregnancies, and having days where I am lucky to get out of my pajamas has had nothing to do with it. (It is all gravity's fault, and we are barely on speaking terms.)

109

Just the other day, our little Cloie, affectionately known as Sally Gal, wanted a clarification on what it takes to be a Southern belle. I gave her some examples, ending with perfect hair and nails to go with the perfect suit. I neglected the part on firm tummies, because frankly, who needs that much disappointment in elementary school?

I am certain that not every woman ends up looking like the women in those oil paintings from the age of Enlightenment, but many of us have discovered that art sometimes really does imitate life. I am equally sure that marsupial-like abdomens were not what captured the attention of all my classmates, but we all left the museum a little more enlightened, one way or another.

The same can be said about grief. Grief will inevitably come to visit all of us, but what our souls are drawn to is about as individualized as creating the ideal sundae at a build-your-own ice cream shop. What works for some does not work for others. What debilitates one person is barely a blip on the radar for the next one. What encourages one saddens another. While gravity might be annoying, grief is just plain nails on a chalkboard irritating.

This past summer, my daughter and I were looking for leggings to go with a tunic. We have a couple of fun boutiques in our town, and we went first to the one where she works to see if we could find what our hearts desired. After hitting three other stores, we finally landed upon a possible solution for our legging needs. Picking up something that could fit inside an envelope, the saleslady said, "These should work. They're one-size-fits-most."

I was skeptical yet thankful. Breathing a deep sigh of relief, I realized she had the decency not to notice my Enlightenment-era abs. Then she said to my daughter, "They should fit you too!"

Honestly, I didn't know whether to laugh or cry. Laugh that I could consider this a moderate success. Cry that she thought I could pull off clothes that would work on a teenager who is five inches taller than me. Cry for my daughter being lumped into the clothing category with her mom. As a mixed bag of emotions, I headed to the dressing room, deciding they would work, even if they were not exactly what I was looking for.

The suggestions in this section are much the same. Loving grieving people takes work. Sometimes that work includes doing your homework. I know that can be exhausting, but trust me: your extra effort is well worth it when you know that your intention was received with the best of you wrapped inside. Even though I wore those leggings, I never really believed the one-size-fits-most claim because each one of us is unique, and so are our grief stories.

I Hate Chicken Nuggets

THE MORNING FOLLOWING THE BUS CRASH, A KITCHEN AIDE from the hospital walked in with two trays of food. My bewildered look was met compassionately by the tray bearer, explaining that since Sawyer was in pediatric intensive care, meals were provided for both the parents and the child. I could not tell you what was offered to eat, but I can tell you I didn't want to eat it. It was not the quality of the food in question but the ability of my stomach to keep it down.

For the next nine days, the pattern was repeated for every meal. A tray arrived for me, and I couldn't eat it. Once my family arrived from Florida, I asked my daddy if he could simply get me a gallon of sweet tea, which will not surprise anyone who knows me. Family and friends tried to tempt me with a few morsels here and there, but I simply couldn't eat.

The crash was on a Tuesday, and by Saturday night, my parents couldn't stand it anymore. They had my brother and sister and their significant others take us out to eat, assuring us they would stay behind with Sawyer and the girls. Saturday night in Sioux Falls, South Dakota, must be date night. We drove from restaurant to restaurant only to be met with long lines wherever we went. Neither Daniel nor I was ready to interact with people outside of the seclusion of the locked hospital floor. Their efforts were heartwarming, despite the frigid temperatures outside. Despite their begging and pleading to go somewhere nice, we finally settled on the privacy afforded by eating at the local Sonic Drive-In. There we were, the six of us, in our van.

Uncomfortable small talk filled our tight quarters as we waited for our food to be delivered. When it finally arrived, I realized I really was hungry after going four days without eating much of anything. But two

113

bites into my cheeseburger, I broke down. I felt guilty eating at one of Reed's favorite restaurants, when he would never eat a burger again. The uncomfortable chatter turned into a van full of sobbing people. I never did eat more than those two bites.

The next day at the hospital, I started to notice a pattern in the parent trays. Every day, the same meal appeared on the noon and evening dining trays: chicken nuggets. I am old enough to remember when nuggets first hit McDonald's. Having been a huge fan of H.R. Pufnstuf, the McNugget Buddies and all the other characters of McDonaldland were pretty cool in my junior high thinking. But when push came to shove, I always enjoyed a hamburger much more than chicken nuggets.

I know my grief brain wasn't thinking logically during our early days in the hospital, but for the life of me, I could not figure out why my parent tray was like reliving a food version of the movie *Groundhog Day*. If laughter would have come easily, it would have been almost comical. Every meal, the same foods appeared. I got to the point where I loathed seeing the bun, little strips of chicken, and mashed potatoes under the warming hood, but the meal, and my disdain for it, were the least of my troubles so I never said a thing. The staff, at every level, was so incredibly kind to our family, complaining just seemed rude. I did begin to wonder what in my character suggested that a foodie like me was a "chicken nugget super fan," but again, my palate's reputation was the least of my worries. Rather than wasting the food, more than once I gave the meal to others. I just kept my glass full of sweet tea and forged ahead.

After six days in the hospital, we were running out of time on handling Reed's services because of an old law in Minnesota. The hospital, despite their ideal wishes, allowed Sawyer to be discharged because there was no way we would hold Reed's memorial and celebration of life services without his best friend. Our extended family and friends went on ahead of us to start making preparations while we learned what the future held for Sawyer. We began the slow and tedious process of packing up our limited belongings along with all the medications and medical equipment required for healing. Daniel made several trips to the van with everything we needed for discharge. A nurse came and helped Sawyer into a wheelchair and picked up a bag of last-minute items. As we were leaving the room, my eyes caught a stack of papers left behind. Curious as to what further instructions might be explained on the paperwork, I picked them up to read, just in case I needed to ask questions. Instead of a list of explanations, I found a daily menu order form for the parental trays. Yep, exactly nine pages of order forms—one for each day we were in the hospital. The fine print explained the default meal was none other than chicken nuggets.

Comfort food is the one thing that, like me, crossed the Mason-Dixon Line and connects the home of my childhood to my home today. The foods originating from both places are night and day different, however. And for the record, like Sam I Am, I would not eat chicken nuggets here or there. No matter the region, whether the South or the Midwest, food is a large part of how we identify ourselves and our culture. Food is a bond that holds together families, communities, and churches. In our region of Minnesota, we even have community festivals dedicated to one type of food in several little towns. Folks around here joke about which church serves the best hotdish (casserole for my Southern friends), organizes the best fish fry, or brews the best pot of coffee. So when tragedy strikes, we whip out the crockpots and freezer containers and get to work.

The night of the bus crash, we met with a representative of the Red Cross who was a huge blessing. She assisted us with hotel rooms and other immediate needs. As she waited with us outside the pharmacy, she quipped, "I can about imagine every crockpot in Cottonwood is working overtime tonight." Even though we weren't there, I am certain her words were spot on. In small-town America, we feed the soul by nourishing the body. We do this with Olympic talent and hearts the size of Lake Superior.

In the stories of the days and weeks following the crash, this gargantuan love was shown repeatedly by little old men hauling boxes, cake pans, and cookie sheets full of cupcakes to the school. Word got around that all three families were choosing to serve cupcakes following the services of the four children. In what has been described to me as a never-ending line of gentlemen donning parkas and winter boots, they filed into the school delivering every kind of cupcake imaginable. Everyone wanted to help, and this one small thing was a way to offer their love and support. To this day, cupcakes equal love to me.

If food can be described as bringing comfort and offering love and support, why in the world would I have it listed in a section devoted to things that *might* be helpful? The simplest way to answer is it depends on the family. A dear friend recently shared her loss experience with food. She was diagnosed with breast cancer and was going to need surgery almost immediately. So like good Midwesterners, the calls from friends and neighbors started ringing in for offers to make meals. She turned them down and in one case had to defend her reasoning. Mealtimes to her family were sacred. It is through the preparing, cooking, and serving that her family bonds and decompresses from a busy day. She was already losing so much of her own personal identity, having someone else cook for her family felt like she would be losing touch points (cooking and bonding) in her world.

I cannot speak for the other families, but in our experience, food was a great help. Aside from Easter dinner, I didn't make my first meal until June 19, a full four months following the crash. The meals that people brought us relieved such a tremendous burden. During the day, I was wife, mom, nurse, therapist, counselor, and so many other things that I didn't have time to take care of my basic needs, let alone think about planning or cooking a meal. For our family, meals were simply manna from God.

We were so worn down and exhausted that every bite was delicious. I will admit that three meals still stand out in my mind. Along with our pastor, Daniel and I have become facilitators of a grief recovery group at our church that utilizes GriefShare. In one of the videos, a widower explains that his family began to express to some comforters that they didn't have any food allergies but had somehow developed an allergy to lasagna. Honestly, all the meals were so lovingly prepared that I could not believe how amazing our friends and neighbors truly were to us. After learning those endless hospital trays of chicken nuggets were completely my fault, I came home to a meal of prime rib and potatoes made by the father of a dear friend. Friends who share our Irish heritage made us an authentic meal from the land of the leprechauns for St. Patrick's Day, and a group of mom friends from our church made us walking tacos, which my kiddos thought were the best things ever.

I often joke that if our friends hadn't fed us, we would have subsisted on pocket lint. That was about how much energy I had left to expend on making meals, let alone shopping for the necessary ingredients. We never did develop an allergy to a hotdish, because we were just plain thankful for the kindness of others. If feeding others is your gift, there are definitely families that will find it helpful. Mine would be one of them. But please, whatever you do, don't bring chicken nuggets.

In the Pages of a Good Book

DOWN ON THE BOOKSHELVES IN THE BASEMENT, I HAVE A BOOK from my childhood. *All about Me* by Dr. Seuss and (stealing a line from Miss Piggy) *moi* that tells all about my life as a first grader living in a plantation home in Georgia. On the page depicting what I want to be when I grow up, you will find that I briefly had another career path in mind. Like a few of my own children, I must have chiseled with pencil so that the erased word of "nurse" is still legible but replaced by the word "teacher."

Over the years as an educator, I have loved hosting practicing teachers in my classroom. On one such occasion, I was asked to be interviewed as part of a student teacher's assignment. Knowing this was routine, I readily agreed, and we quickly progressed through her set of questions. But one question really gave me a moment of pause. "You are a science teacher, but not everyone loves science. What do you wish to impart to all your students?" After taking a moment to really digest the question, I answered that I hoped to provide a passion for learning whatever subjects spark their hearts and to model the quest of lifelong learning.

I once had a young man in my eighth grade class who every day would tell me about a book he was reading during our school's required reading time. His animated explanations made me smile. This young man was one of the kindest students I have ever taught. For a while, he would arrive early to regale me with the latest antics of the characters in the book and to explain a little bit more of the mystery they were solving. As a teacher, there is no greater bliss than watching a student actively engaged in sharing what they are learning. After one of our quick before-the-bell gab sessions, I was so taken in by the story I said that I would love to read the book someday.

A few weeks later, he came to class announcing that he had finished reading the book but still had the book in hand. I asked him if the copy was his or if it belonged to the school's library. In this case, the book was indeed one from the school. I told him to let me know when he was returning it so I could check it out. What happened next is what I refer to as one of the "best moments in teaching."

"Oh, Miss Stevens, you don't need to worry about that. I knew you wanted to read this book, so this morning I returned the book and checked it out again in your name."

I am a softie who cries over most Hallmark commercials. My husband says he rates movies based on the volume of tears I shed while watching them. Not ashamed to admit it, but the corners of my eyes watered up as my student handed a copy of *Chasing Vermeer* to me. In case you were wondering, the story was as good as he said, and Blue Balliett has since become one of my family's favorite children's authors.

Even though I am a science and math teacher, I love words. Whenever I go to a home décor store, it is the items with words that draw me in, especially words that convey a feeling of inspiration or encouragement. After overcoming a battle with reading when I was younger, I have since become a voracious reader. (A very special thank-you to Beverly Cleary for writing books that helped achieve that goal.) I shared many adventures with characters and attempted to pass that spirit on to my children. I sincerely believe three of the greatest gifts we have imparted to our children (outside of our love for them) have been the love of Jesus, the joy of imagination, and the adventures found in a good book.

All of my children enjoy reading, but Reed most epitomized my love of books. His penchant for getting lost in a good story was something we included in his obituary. It was common to hear his brother, Sawyer, tell him, "Reed, get your nose out of a book." Just like Reed, reading is not just a hobby for me. If reading qualified as an Olympic sport, I would be a medal contender hands down, although I would earn the silver compared to Reed's gold. Yet not everyone shares our love of reading— just like not all of my students loved science.

One of my children struggles with academic reading, so for her, like countless other people in the world, the gift of a book might not become a treasured possession. If you aren't sure if a family or individual likes to read, a book might not be the best option for providing comfort.

I do offer an exception to that rule. As with our family, many families have surviving children who are experiencing the grieving process. There are some absolute fabulous books that explain the grief experience to children in their language, with their developmental stage in mind. Those books were incredible ways to begin conversations in our home, especially for our three-year-old who simply wanted her brother to come home now!

Books, though, like aged cheese, take time to be appreciated. I remember one of the books given to our children in our early grieving days. I read the book and thought it was absolutely horrible. My heart had not traveled far enough on its grief journey to appreciate the wisdom in the words. I wanted to throw it away because I thought it was just that stupid. But I didn't. Three years later, I picked up the book at the behest of my littlest, and snuggled into her bed for naptime, we read it. That day, our pillowcases were stained with tears as the tender words spoke to a heart that was ready to receive them.

There are many wonderful books that provide real insights into the grieving process. However, just like all things in this world, not everything you read is good. Some of the books we were given early on, we wanted to pour ourselves into. When a loved one dies, you want reassurances that you are not alone, that you are not crazy, and that you will get through this. Books provided our family with an outlet to heal through reassuring stories of the lives and survival of other mourners.

Unfortunately, not all of the books we were given provided messages of hope and healing. Some of the books we received focused on comparisons, as if your child dying could be compared to a bad day at work. Reading something like that can be traumatizing, in the way it makes you want to smack the author. Some books focused on anger and hate toward the person who killed the author's child. We were looking for solace, not revenge. The grieving process is so intensely personal and, for many, is tied to a belief system. Some books promoting alternate life messages (and we got a couple) were extremely uncomfortable. We received several books via the mail from strangers with dramatically different beliefs from ours, and we were shocked at how the loss of our son prompted some to consider it an appropriate time to convert us.

Because of Sawyer's medical needs, we sadly didn't have a lot of contact initially with the other families who lost children. One of our first gatherings where all three families were together was when our school brought in a grief counselor to work with all the families from bus number 5. The counseling times were divided into two groups: those who lost children and those whose children were injured (even if it was a loss of innocence from such a horrific life event). While one group met with the counselor (who resembled the mascot from Notre Dame), the other group ate the meal provided. When the families who had lost children were eating, we had our first opportunity to really talk all together. I remember thinking, *We just heard that more than two-thirds of all marriages of bereaved parents end in divorce. Are some of us going to end up that way?* Rather than focus on that whopping statistic, we all sat down and tried to catch up as best we could. We were tables full of broken people still tending the wounds of feeling like we had been sucker-punched.

Eventually, we began to swap tales about what people were doing to help our individual families. The subject of books came up. We all agreed that we were astounded at the number of books that existed on the topic of grief. We all lamented that we weren't sure we would be able to get through them all. I am certain the other bus families thought we had lost it when uproarious laughter came bursting forth from the lunchroom. The reason for our laughter was that every book the Olsons and our family received, it seemed the Javens received in duplicate, having lost two sons that day.

Looking back, it probably wasn't all that funny, but from a group of people who weren't given "*the* manual" on how to grieve the loss of your child, it was hilarious. Just like getting captivated by a good book, sometimes the first step to healing is when you forget you are hurting and lose yourself in a really good laugh.

Too Much of a Good Thing

I LOVE TO COOK AND TRY NEW RECIPES. LET'S FACE IT: I REALLY enjoy food. However, when it comes to restaurants, I tend to go with the tried and true. My husband peruses the menu and decides what looks the most scrumptious at the time. Eventually, he will peek over the top of his menu and say, "Let me guess. You are having the _____." What goes in the blank depends on the café or restaurant in which we find ourselves dining. Nine times out of ten his assumption is correct.

My lack of culinary adventures has less to do with my taste buds and more to do with the balance in our checking account. I am not bragging here (well, okay maybe just a little), but I am a really good cook. There is nothing worse than venturing out of my known favorites and experiencing a palatal disaster. The joy of dining would be ruined, and to make matters much worse, I would be disappointed I just wasted money on something I did not enjoy.

At new dining establishments with all sorts of untried dishes, I am often paralyzed by the fear of choice. I often quip that I was a "great school lunch girl." My friends and fellow teachers in the teachers' lounge always raise an eyebrow or two at that assessment. I explain how at school lunch we were only given one choice (well, two, if not eating is considered an option). Rather than go hungry, I ate what was placed on my tray. No, I didn't like all the lunches, but going hungry was never (and still isn't) a fun idea to me.

In the last few years, we remodeled our home one floor at a time. The basement was first, followed by the upstairs the next year. I don't intend to do that again anytime soon because the amount of choices we had to make are plain aggravating. Don't get me wrong. Having a new look was amazing, but looking at cabinet hardware for six hours (and I am *not* exaggerating here) left me wanting to offer to cut off a limb if it would expedite the process. Remodeling was almost the death of me. Every detail had to be researched and analyzed. At the store, every item had to be inspected to make sure it met our standards. I seriously think less vetting goes into the choice for vice presidential candidates. The mere mention of heading to the hardware stores sent me into an almost catatonic state.

Prior to the invention of the Internet, one of the perks of living in a rural town was the limited number of retail choices available. In the town my husband grew up in, the owner of the hardware store (who is a beloved family friend) had a motto for his store. "If we don't have it, you don't need it!" Those are words to live by! This, however, was not my experience growing up living in larger cities. If it existed, it could most likely be found somewhere—unless, of course, you wanted the action figure Ben Frakle.

One holiday, my brother wrote out his Christmas wish list and gave it to my mom. My family had moved thousands of miles away from home in Florida to North Dakota. Also, my family had gone from living on the wages of a graduate student and assistant to stepping in high cotton. My mom really wanted to make it a great year of presents. She went through the list containing mostly items related to his love that year: GI Joe. She quickly snatched up the various soldiers and Cobra characters that she could find. I have already shared that my mom could hold a PhD in shopping and if something exists, she is going to find it. Well, she met her match in Ben Frakle. She searched high. She searched low. She traveled from store to store, perusing the toy aisles in search of the elusive Frakle. He was nowhere to be found—anywhere! A lot of mothers would just admit defeat and move on. Not my mom! She finally resorted to using the ace up her sleeve by talking not only to the store manager but directly to the owner of the town's hobby, hardware, and home goods store. She explained her dilemma, asking if he would order more Ben Frakles because they must have sold out immediately. The sweet elderly gentleman understood her predicament and vowed if any were still available they would order more in. Rather than sending her on her way, he invited her back to his office and they pulled out the catalog to place another order.

The quest for Frakle was too much. It consumed her thoughts like an unsolved puzzle or the desire to eat the last ice cream bar in the spot you hid it from your kids in the chest freezer. (Okay, maybe I am the only one who does that.) I wasn't there, but I can picture the two of them, heads bent over the catalog reading through each name carefully before he picked up the phone. They read the list. Then they reread it, slower the second time. Eventually my mom had to raise the white flag of surrender. Even in the GI Joe catalog, Ben Frakle was AWOL.

I wonder how many days passed between the moment of defeat and Christmas morning. For a woman who can find anything (like if you want to give your child's whole class moon pies for his birthday because they go along with the book he is bringing, she will ask you what flavor and what size), this had to be a huge letdown. We celebrated baby Jesus's arrival at church on Christmas Eve and opened presents the next morning. After all the gifts were opened, my heartbroken mom explained to my brother how sorry she was that she could not find all the guys on his list. Still donning a bed head, he looked at her like she was crazy. "Mom, I got all the guys on my list." She gently reminded him, "No. I'm sorry. You didn't get Ben Frakle. I tried. I really tried, but not one store had him."

From the couch, my dad and I watched this exchange, as intrigued as both the participants. "Mom, I have never heard of Ben Frakle. I didn't have him on my list," my brother stated again. This news was almost too much for her to bear, after spending months searching for the action figure. She finally could stand it no more and went to retrieve his list from her bedroom. With her finger, she pointed to his writing on the paper. Plain as day, "Ben Frakle" was written in his elementary penmanship. "Oh, I'm sorry, Mom. That isn't a guy. I was just trying to help you. If you didn't know where to get GI Joes, I wanted you to know they had them at the Ben Franklin store."

Sometimes, fewer choices are much better!

In the weeks following the bus crash, the requests and offers of help and support came like a bombardment at a military practice base. Coupled with the multitude of medications and therapies added to our

125

routine to aid in Sawyer's recovery, we were overwhelmed with where to begin, let alone what to do next. Thankfully a friend saw how the inundation of details was wearing us down. Like the hardware store of Daniel's youth, she boldly stepped up and took charge by limiting some of our choices. This amazing (and filled with grace) friend happens to be a nurse and often provided a much-needed sounding board for us as we dealt with our surviving children's injuries as well as our physical and emotional needs. She was and is also an amazing prayer warrior.

One night she called to check on how things were going, and I relayed how overwhelmed with household tasks I felt. She told me it might be therapeutic to make a list of all the things that needed to be done. At the close of our conversation, she reminded to make the list because she was going to call in the morning to check.

That was it. The conversation was over. At first, I thought, *Is she kidding?* but I knew her well enough to know that she would follow up on this. I didn't want to make that list. It was too painful, too personal, and incredibly difficult to honestly assess. Where would I begin? There was so much that wasn't getting done. Prior to the crash, this friend and I would often meet at the gym and walk (me)/run (her) next to each other on treadmills. This same sweet friend would wait in the dark for me when I said I wanted to get back to exercising, only to never show up because I was too exhausted. She never criticized or complained. She loved me enough to just show up.

If she would stand outside in the dark waiting for me, I knew she would call in the morning. Even though the task was daunting, before I went to bed that night, I grabbed a pencil and jotted down the list.

Bright and early the next morning, I received a call from her asking me how I was going to spend the day. My first thought was *Surviving* and after that *Who knows?* As the conversation went on, she eventually inquired about the task she had asked me to complete the night before. When I shared I had indeed completed the list, she asked which task seemed the most insurmountable, the most challenging that day. I confided, not too proudly, it was the bed linens. When I explained that it had been a month since the crash and we hadn't been able to wash the sheets, she said, "You've got exactly ten minutes." *To do what? Go crazy? Honey, I don't think I need ten minutes for that!*

126

At that point, she gave me some pretty clear instructions (and no choices either, God bless her heart!). She gave me ten minutes to strip every bed in the house, placing my biggest impossibility into garbage bags to be deposited by the front door. In what was probably eleven minutes exactly, she swung by to retrieve the bedding, which she took home and laundered.

It was an amazing gift.

Tears. All I had were tears. Tears and ten minutes. She, too, is an amazing, creative, talented wife and momma, and ten minutes meant ten minutes. When those sheets arrived home later that afternoon, our beds never smelled so fresh. When we fell into bed that night, we weren't just wrapped in clean sheets; we were cloaked in the best kind of love: selfless, sacrificial love.

Angela and I attend the same church. Our kids are friends. Our husbands worked together. She had my number, knowing that even if it killed me, I would attempt to get it all done because typically I am that girl. She knew well enough to know that had she given me the chance, I would have said I could do it or it would get done or something along that line. My friend was in the mood and the spirit to bless me, and she wasn't going to let me stand in her way.

Admitting that you are vulnerable and that you don't have it all together is difficult for anyone, especially for someone who one of Reed's friends dubbed with the title "Super Mom." On the day of the list, my tights and cape were probably in as rough shape as the bed sheets, and allowing myself to relinquish the image of superhero strength was incredibly difficult. Thankfully, all my friend saw was an opportunity to love me by doing something as mundane as washing my family's linens. She stood her ground and did not afford me the opportunity to let my own stubborn pride stand in the way of receiving a huge blessing.

Thankfully, she didn't ask me if I wanted them line or tumble dried, because that might have been one choice too many.

All About Those Chips

A WHILE BACK, I TOOK A SPIRITUAL GIFTING ASSESSMENT. Thankfully, it wasn't one of the very long and detailed inventories but a quick one. The reason for my gratitude was the end result shared that my strongest gift is hospitality. This revelation was not shocking.

Not that long ago, my pastor jokingly suggested we should paint our front door red, referring to the color red signifying a place of refuge in some cultures. Behind the painted crimson door, the lost, the weary, the traveler, or the stranded could find hope.

I distinctly remember when Daniel and I met with the grief counselor before we told Sawyer about Reed's passing. One of the toughest decisions we made that day was that our home would continue to be a place where people would find comfort. Trust me: that is indeed a choice that took enormous effort and work on our part, but we did want our home to once again be a happy place. Even though our hearts were broken and shattered, I did not want our place of refuge to be filled with sadness or bitterness

Many, many years ago, we were planning to have dinner on a Saturday night with some of our best friends. Between the two families, we had seven children, so the evening promised to be one of games and great food. Early in the afternoon, I received a frantic phone call, asking if we would have room for two extra little guys because our friends had a date night planned and the babysitter bailed on them. My answer was an unequivocal "Absolutely!" I never mentioned the dinner party because I knew the other family would be okay with it, as we were all from the same church family. A few hours later, another family called with the exact same scenario. I gave the same response without any extra embellishment. When the extra two families arrived to drop off children, both were aghast I had agreed to host an additional three children for the evening when we were having company for supper. The teachers among us will understand my mentality. Four, seven, or ten—it really doesn't matter when everyone is loved, fed, and entertained. To be honest, it wasn't stressful at all, as all the kids got along fabulously and were busy the entire evening.

Summers would find our backyard swarmed with kids, my own as well as friends and neighbors. Typically, I would make lunch for the masses production-line style, delegating the oldest ones to slather peanut butter on a piece of bread and pass it to the next kid in line until the troops were fed. I keep the freezers full of popsicles (a trick I learned from my other mother, who I swear is the only woman I know who packs half her suitcase with suckers when visiting grandchildren), my bathroom stocked with extra toothbrushes, my cupboards filled with extra ingredient for just about every recipe, and my heart prepared to dish out as many hugs as a child would ever need.

We do impromptu well. "Family dinners" are somewhat of a misnomer, as what I am actually referring to are the times when we get together with one set of friends. These friends, like us, are transplants from communities far, far away. Since three of us hail from the South, we often commiserate together by making meals dripping in southern fried goodness and spiced deliciousness. The unusual thing about these meals is that we often plan them in exactly eleven minutes. What often happens is we bump into each other at the grocery store and the snowball effect takes place. We decide we are in dire needs of a good ol' fashioned shrimp boil with hush puppies, and a mad dash through the store ensues. The food pales in comparison to the stories we swap while we share each other's company, passing plates and the roots of our childhoods.

Unexpected visitors and family dinners are things I cherish. They are the heartbeat of the story of our typical day. Every once in a while, the smooth rhythm of our ordinary days is punctuated with the staccato presence of a big shindig. I adore parties. When we celebrate, we really live it up with dazzling decorations, hearty homemade deliciousness, and lively conversation. Easter includes egg hunts and resurrection rolls. The Fourth of July means American flag toenail-painting parties for all the little girls in the neighborhood. Old-fashioned fun with games and family time and a garden-harvested meal of festival proportions are a must for Halloween. Christmas parties have taken many forms over the years. Everything from progressive parties to appetizer open houses, from remembering lost loved ones to giving to others in need all over the world have been a part of remembering Jesus's birthday.

In my early years of keeping house, as Mama would put it, being much more like Martha than Mary by nature, I did everything from the food to the decorations for all my holiday entertaining. I loved every minute of it, but my husband did not. Frankly, he thought it was much ado about nothing, especially when the hostess would be flat-out exhausted after the soiree. For a while, he put his foot down. *No more parties, period!* He acquiesced after I agreed to ask for help with food and games for children. I hate to admit when he is right, but I did enjoy myself much more at the parties when I didn't have to run around tending to every detail. Okay, so he was totally right. Just don't tell him. I enjoyed myself immensely when I wasn't stuck in the kitchen or craft room and was able to mingle among the guests.

My Martha planning style decided on a party trick that would work for me and my super detailed brain, simply asking guests to bring something within a certain category. Unlike our outdoor movie nights, where snacks are the treat du jour, our parties tend to be full meals, and I do not desire to serve all desserts to other people's children. (Although I confess that sometimes we do have ice cream for supper around here.) So when I send the invitations, I include a little note asking the guests to please provide a veggie tray, a dessert, a dish of fruit, or a cheese platter. I have never gone so far as to include recipes, but trust me: the thought has crossed my mind. This method has been successful 99.9 percent of the time, but there was that one occasion that still has me shaking my head.

The request I had made to one family was for a bowl of fresh fruit. I got a call from the mom in this family, who let me know she was bringing chips instead. I was completely baffled because this mom was kind of a health nut who more than once chided me on allowing my kids to eat Pop-Tarts for breakfast. Listen. When I had three kids under the age of four, I would feed them anything if it meant I got to sit down to a warm (yes, I would have settled for warm) meal. Anyways, she completely caught me off guard. I am all for grace, so I agreed to her suggestion of chips even though I had already bought enough bags for the party and now needed to go back to the store uphill both ways in the snow (Okay not really. I live on the prairie. But the snow part is real.) to buy fresh fruit. I hate to admit it, but the next time she had a party and she asked for a dessert, a little part of me wanted to bring a rutabaga instead. I didn't, of course, but the thought was there.

Many people realized fairly early in our grief journey that we were literally drowning in a sea of well wishes. A few years after the crash, I was afraid we might be considered potential candidates for the TV show *Hoarders*. Thankfully, these people dropped by and saw all the loving kindness spread around the house and decided to remember Reed in other ways.

When your child passes, the thought of a day coming when no one says his name is a real and tangible fear. We began to receive notices and letters stating donations had been made in memory of our son. The charitable gifts given to places which remembered things Reed loved were the ones that truly touched us the most. Friends and family supported hospitals, zoos, Boy Scouts, 4-H, and the library as a way of honoring the various interests he had. In the early hours, as the news of his passing rippled across the country, friends started a scholarship in Reed's name, which was a huge blessing to us because he absolutely loved learning! Supporting causes that mattered to Reed also became a focus for our family as a way of keeping his spirit and memory alive and as a way to begin our own personal healing.

So how in the world could donating in memory of a passed loved one be in the category of things which *might be* helpful? It depends upon the intention behind the gift. We received a few notices telling us that donations had been made to extremely political or divisive organizations, which had no reflection on Reed's life. I am certain the intentions were well meaning, giving to groups that reflected the giver's heart. It wasn't that we didn't appreciate the remembrances, but these were not places where we (as the keepers of Reed's legacy) would have attached his memory. This isn't necessarily a bad thing, but some people have very strong feelings about what they hold dear and about the causes in which they could take 'em or leave 'em (leaning more likely toward leave 'em).

If donations are something you would like to do, do it! But take your time; don't make your decision on a whim. Think about what things the honoree loved or the places where they spent their time. What a wonderful feeling to see Reed's name on a scholarship at a school he didn't attend one year and to see his name on a donation of Legos at the local library. Learning and Legos: those were things that really reflected his heart! Irish to the core, Reed loved everything about Ireland, including potatoes. He had a favorite kind of chips too, but for the love of all the zucchini, if I ask you to bring fruit to the next party, please don't bring them!

I Knew We Were in the Right Place

EVEN THOUGH I HAVE BEEN AN EDUCATOR FOR MANY YEARS, I avoid commencements unless one of my family members is graduating. My personal avoidance has less to do with the obvious fact that graduation ceremonies tend to be long affairs and more to do with the fact that I am a crier. Hallmark commercials, the underdog winning the game, a kind gesture, a special memory, and sometimes simply the beauty in God's creation will start the tears forming in the corners of my eyes. I am so proud of my students and their accomplishments, rich with anticipation for their futures, I bawl through the whole thing. I am also a lot like Daniel's Uncle Ted, who hated good-byes. When it was time to leave family gatherings, he would simply slip out the back door. Saying good-bye to students whom I have had the joy of teaching is sometimes just too much for my emotions.

As a mom of four children, I know I will get my fair share of commencement addresses and renditions of "Pomp and Circumstance." At the conclusion of his junior year, I began to have heart palpitations just thinking about Sawyer walking across that stage. To be honest, I wanted to crawl in a blanket fort and pretend all my kiddos were little enough to want to join me in there. Time marches on and waits for no momma to be ready for her babies to grow up. Even though I still wanted to relocate to Peter Pan's Neverland, we began the preparations that for some reason take almost a whole year to accomplish to prepare for graduation day. One of those tasks was taking senior portraits.

We have several amazing friends who are professional photographers, so picking one (here we go again with all those choices) was almost too much for me. Once the decision was made, we needed to explain that we wanted to do some rather untraditional shots. When we explained we wanted to do a "Clark Kent morphs into Superman" shoot four hours away at the St. Paul Union Depot, our photographer, Steph, was giddy at the thought, because she had taken a workshop in that very location. How is that for God sending you the perfect message that things are going to be just fine, momma?

We had photo shoots at various locations close to home and arranged a weekend to travel to the Twin Cities for the shoot at the beautifully restored train station. When the day arrived, we were all set, having chosen various spots in and around the historic building. Finally the time came for the transformational shots. Since there was not a vintage phone booth (wouldn't that have been precious?), the ornate vintage elevator was chosen as a suitable substitution.

Union Depot is not just a train station anymore due to its meticulous renovation. It holds all types of banquets and events as well as being home to a group of upscale lofts. The day of the portraits, a wedding reception was being held there. Just as Sawyer and Cloie (who was hiding in the corner of the elevator holding the "Door Open" button) were ready to get started, the bell system activated, alerting those in the elevator that the valet had guests ready to ascend to the second-floor dining area. Steph waited in the wings while Sawyer stood outside the elevator in his suit with his arms folded. The elevator vanished to the floor below while we secretly hoped we could finish the pictures before the good lighting was gone for the day. As the roomy cabled carriage arrived with the wedding guests, there stood Sawyer to greet them. Most in the elevator car were elderly ladies, along with one gentleman and a few moms with young children. It was immediately clear the partygoers had no idea where they were supposed to go. Almost instantly, they began asking my Boy Wonder for directions. Since we had already been at the station for a few hours, he politely explained that they should please exit the elevator to their right, continue to the foyer, and enter through the double doors. He even went so far as to explain that the maître d' would seat them once they were inside. I just smiled, but our photographer was overcome with giggles which soon turned into a bellyful of laughter. The benign chuckles morphed after one sweet little white-haired lady, who resembled a tiny Barbara Bush, walked right over to my boy, patted him on the cheek tenderly with her tiny wrinkled hand, and said, "I knew we were in the right place the moment I saw you." It would have been a precious picture to capture if fits of laughter hadn't been about to burst out of all of us. The laughter only came bubbling forth more when Sawyer responded by taking the sweet octogenarian's hand in his and replying, "That's what I'm here for."

Of all the wonderful things that happened at the station that day, I will always remember my seventeen-year-old taking time that was meant to be focused on him and helping a little old lady instead. For those who know my son, the way he handled this encounter won't be a surprise. He never wants to draw attention to himself but would rather serve others every day.

There are a lot of times I have doubted myself as a momma, wondering if I was really meant to do this job, because I have learned more about life from my children than I ever feel I have passed on to them. But serving others is something that brings me great joy in life, and my boy's kindness that day was one of those times that I could see my influence in his world. This is a skill that has been honed through generations in my family, and although we grew up literally at opposite ends of the United States, my sweet husband's family has the exact same gene amplified in their DNA.

My husband is always amazed how I can be in the grocery store, checking things off my list one minute and the next showing someone where to find the cough drops. Your child needs a kind word after a meltdown? I'm your girl. Lost animals and lost kids are my specialty. You move to the neighborhood and look overwhelmed? I will make you food and organize someone to mow your lawn.

When asked what we have done to heal from our darkest day, I answer unapologetically with two things: clinging to my faith and serving others.

The ability to step up and help others has been a joy in our lives and on the recipient end, a blessing beyond measure. In the strangest of circumstances, we were able to experience both almost simultaneously.

Almost a month before the bus crash, some of our dear church friends, whose daughter was one of Reed's best friends, lost their home in a devastating fire. Our church has loved many people through tragedies and has developed an incredible system of locating a touch-point person to assist the family. When difficult times arise, this person helps funnel offers of help in a way that doesn't overwhelm the family and attempts to get the immediate needs met before tackling some of the secondary ones. After learning of the fire, I was asked by my church to be the touch-point person for our friends. I did not organize every detail of help, but if calls were placed to our church, my phone number was given to explain what was needed and to coordinate efforts of picking up donations. I returned phone calls and fielded e-mails, with the hopes of alleviating some stress for our friends. Throughout that next month, I met many wonderful people in our community who gave in many generous ways. I considered it a joy to take my little girl and go visit with families who called to offer various gifts and donations. It was a blessing for me to use my skills for organizing and socializing in a way to bless people I love.

Little did I know that I wouldn't be able to see the job to its fruition, because instead of being the organized helper, I became the frantic one who needed assistance. Once again, our church intervened as others stepped up to become the touch-point people for us. There were many, many people who stepped in to help my family, and much of those behind-the-scenes efforts I will never know. I do know from one of the earliest phone calls that our friends Karla and Sheldon, as well as our pastor, took on that role without us ever realizing how much they were actually doing. Much like my experience a month earlier, I can only imagine love as the motivating force to give so selflessly when they offered a helping hand to what felt like a sinking ship.

I could devote an entire book to the names of all the people who waltzed into our world to help bring peace to the chaos, sense to the senseless. As long as I live, I will never be able to thank them all enough. My gratitude, like an invisible scar, is etched permanently across my heart.

Over the years, I have had many student teachers in my classrooms. All was fine for me as a mentor until the moment I needed to hand the reigns of control over to someone else. As much as I like to help others, I have already confessed how difficult it is for me to allow someone else to help me. Yet in the case of teacher candidates, I signed an agreement saying I would absolutely do so. I remember vividly the first day my student teacher, Nicole, was to have full control of the class. I quietly grabbed some items I needed and walked to the teacher's lounge. I lasted all of about ten minutes before I couldn't take it any longer. No, I didn't go back to my classroom because I knew Nicole had everything under control. Instead, I wandered like a lost puppy to the secondary office and asked if there was anything that needed to be done there. Being idle is just not something I do well. Thankfully, back then, we still had pencil and paper standardized tests, so I was able to assist the school counselor in preparing all the packets for the upcoming testing.

This long illustration simply solidifies my point that having a touch-point person may (under the right circumstances) be extremely helpful. Today there are wonderful online tools where one person can help coordinate meals, odd jobs, and various other tasks to help a family in need. If some minimal coordination can be done with the family, then having someone else manage all the logistics can be a huge relief. The biggest hurdle is helping without making the help burdensome for the recipients, if they are able to let someone else into their storm at all.

When You Have an Uncle Pete

ONE OF THE GREATEST THINGS ABOUT COMING FROM LARGE families (Daniel's parents and my grandmothers come from large clans) is all the extra love that is spread around. There aren't many places in this country I can go where I would not be able to find a cousin or two. That is a huge relief, especially when I find myself stranded on the side of the road. This has happened to us more than once, and family came to the rescue every time. Both of our families have reunions on a regular basis, and they are times of great food, fun, and fellowship.

Over the years, I have discovered that I love all of Daniel's aunts and uncles, but I gravitate to one set in particular. We have kept up a letter writing campaign, and when we can, we sneak in a visit. A few summers ago, I discovered an opportunity to meet one of my favorite authors and take a writers' workshop with her. Since I had just traveled to visit my friend in Kentucky, my travel budget was somewhat depleted. A few quick calls and texts, and I had accommodations staying first with cousins and then my husband's aunt and uncle on the return trip.

I had a blast at the writers' workshop and later a historical tea party based on her books with my sisters-in-law (who also happens to love this writer), but I think I had even more fun just visiting family. Our late-night chats, full of tears and giggles, are what further cemented these relationships in my heart.

My last few days were spent with Uncle Pete and Aunt Susie. We had a blast tending gardens and visiting the Fargo Street Fair. I always say we didn't do anything to write home about, but we sure had fun anyway. We shared meals and swapped stories, and in my mind, that is the best of everything. For my last day, I started to load up my car with suitcases before we were to meet more family in Fargo. On my way out the door, I was handed a huge pile of assorted ink pens with the explanation that "the kids could use these for back to school." I later learned that most of the pens had been gathered at various events like county fairs where vendors hand out pens and other small promotional materials. As I took my stash of pens to the car, I had to smile knowing this was *exactly* something my mother would do (and in fact has done). Uncle Pete's pens have been perfect for replenishing backpack supplies, along with my mom's highlighters from when her workplace changed names.

When I got home with my booty, my husband's perplexed eyebrows told me he had found the bag with all the pens. To some people (including my sweetie), they would see a bunch of office supplies and think, *How in the world did you get all these?* I, on the other hand, see a fantastic deal wrapped up in a whole lot of love. Plus, bonus for me! It means less time spent at the store milling over all the choices of pens.

One day later in the fall, I was busy dealing with some important paperwork when my pen ran dry. I grabbed a notepad and scribbled away, thinking maybe there was a blockage in the ink's flow. Quietly, my husband grabbed the pen out of my hand and tossed it into the garbage. His words of wisdom were ones I wouldn't soon forget. "Life is too short for cheap pens, especially when you have an Uncle Pete." He just thought it was ridiculous to waste time scribbling the life out of a dead pen when there was a whole drawer of pens waiting across the room.

Sometimes, you can never have too many of an item, until you do.

I am always up for a good idea, especially one which will foster my children's imaginations and creativity. Enter the rice table. I had seen something similar in a teaching supply catalog and thought it would be a great thing to have at home for our kids. The table in the catalog featured young children playing politely with huge smiles on their faces while engaged with either sand or water. I love a good idea, but I am no dummy. First of all, I had three children under the age of four at one time, and there was no way I was letting them loose with gallons of water. Second, I have a strained relationship with sand. Most days in the winter in Minnesota, sand sings the siren's call, luring me back to the beaches of my childhood. I daydream about the white sands of my hometown all the time, especially when the thermometer dips below freezing. However, once I do finally find my toes tiptoeing across the grains of sand, I remember how much I hate dealing with it. Trust me: after a day at the beach, you discover crevices you didn't even know existed. I don't even like sandboxes outside, so there was no chance a sand table was going to make its way into my basement.

However, I am not easily daunted when it comes to good ideas. I have been known to ruminate over a great thought for days and weeks until I find a way to bring it to the light of day. Finally it dawned on me. Rice! Rice would be the perfect solution for the not-ever-going-to-be-water-or-sand table. At least I could sweep up rice. The grains are much larger than sand, and rice wouldn't stick to every part of my children.

It was such a great addition to our playtime. We built tunnels and tracks, the construction toys moved the sand over and over, and would-be archaeologists created elaborate dig sites with dinosaur toys. I was a parenting genius, until I wasn't.

About the time we created the rice table, the tattling monster came to live at our house. I could barely get anything done without one of my children interrupting me to tell about some heinous act another sibling had committed. ("He looked in my direction!" Or, heaven forbid, "She breathed in my space!") It was exhausting and just a little bit annoying. When their tattling started to have trickle-down effects while entertaining company, we knew we had to put a stop to it. At this stage in life, we had several close friends whose children were similar in age to ours.

Before one of these impromptu gatherings, we sat our kids down and explained that we would no longer be allowing interruptions involving tattling. They were welcome to sit and watch whatever game the adults were playing (dominoes were our favorite back then), but no tattling was allowed. We provided a clause for catastrophes so that if someone was bleeding or choking, a child could automatically interrupt whatever the adults were doing. The evening's meal was a hit as we tried a new recipe that everyone loved, and the domino game was going quite successfully for most of the evening.

Old habits are hard to break. I knew it was too good to be true, but even mommas need a break some time.

Eventually, Reed came up and stood next to the dining room table with the most pained look on his face. I tried my best to ignore him, thinking some benign slight had occurred in the basement. I went on matching pips to create the best trains for my scoring. All the other grown-ups did the same. As time wore on, Reed's face became more and more contorted. He grew antsy with internal agony as he was trying to decide whether his news met the criteria of the interruption clause. This went on for a good fifteen minutes until, like Popeye, he finally "could stands it no more!"

"The babies are in the rice!" he finally blurted out.

"What do you *mean*, 'the babies are in the rice'?" I asked.

His sad little face said he was disappointed to be breaking the no-tattling policy. He simply pointed to the basement, prompting us to see what heinous act was being committed by Erin and Dylan, who were two years old at the time. Coming down the stairs, nothing seemed to be amiss, and at first I thought we were being hoodwinked by a six-year-old. But at the bottom, we all heard the unmistakable sound of hard pellets hitting the ground followed by uproarious laughter by two pint-sized munchkins. One step into my large laundry room told a tale no momma is ready to unpack. There were the babies with tiny fists full of rice, launching said dietary staple over their heads and howling when it came raining down like pellets of sleet. Every square inch of the flooring was covered in at least two inches of rice. Had there been green plants in there, it would have looked like a rice paddy minus the water. Ten years later, we were still discovering forgotten rice grains in various nooks and crannies.

Having too many pens is not a hardship at all, especially when you are a teacher. A thick coating of rice covering an entire room in your house? Now that's a serious issue (unless of course, you're thinking of taking on micro-scale farming)!

One thing I have learned is that, just like the rice, there can be too much of a good thing when it comes to comfort items. Crafting, just like fashion, has its trends. At the time of the bus crash, the rage in crafting was blankets, especially those made of fleece and tied together. Please don't get me wrong. Soft, warm, and cuddly gifts are comforting and provide an almost daily hug from the giver. However, no family (unless they have forty-three children) needs forty-five of them.

I wish I could say that I'm exaggerating here, but I'm not. I have enough blankets that my great grandchildren are going to have a blanket from "Uncle Reed." They are all wonderful and lovingly made, *and* we appreciate every single one. The problem is we live on what my husband refers to as the "humble end of the street" and we don't have adequate storage for all of our beautiful blankets.

There are times in life when too much is simply too much. I have heard from other grieving families at retreats and gatherings that blankets, stuffed animals, books, and prayer shawls can all fall into the category of excess fairly easily. Each family appreciated the kindness and support, but grief is a heavy burden on its own. Trying to unbury oneself from a mound of good intentions (like piled manna from heaven) is a really daunting task, when there is very little extra energy to go around. If only manna disappeared at dusk, the best result would be the love left in its place.

A Few More Thoughts on Manna

FOR A FEW YEARS IN A ROW, MY GARDEN CREATED A BUMPER crop of herbs (and zucchini, but that's a whole other story). After spending hours tending those herbs and, more importantly, protecting them from the prolific rabbits in my neighborhood, I had a very hard time letting them go to waste. Each year, I would call up my friend Amy and ask to borrow her dehydrator. I would keep the appliance for a few weeks, and day and night it would preserve a bountiful harvest for us to use over the winter in soups, stews, and sauces. The third year I came knocking on the door, Amy met me with on the front step with the box and a declaration. "You've used this more than I have in the last three years. It is yours now. I will call you if I need it." Although it was a rather odd way to acquire a kitchen appliance, I wasn't all that shocked because my friend is a gift-giving guru. What I have always admired about her connection to material goods and gifts was her ability to tell the recipient to love the gift for a season (even if that meant a lifetime). When the gift could be loved by someone else more, her encouragement was to let the item move on to its new home. For years, I have not only heeded her advice but also passed its wisdom along with gifts I have given. Just the other day, another friend thanked me for not guilt giving. I considered this extremely high praise, because I don't think anyone ever wants a gift to be a burden.

When swimming in extra blessings, below are some places where manna is really appreciated.

- women's and children's shelters
- police and fire departments

147

- highway safety patrol and ambulance departments
- missions groups (check with local churches)
- missionary trips or missionaries
- afterschool programs
- nursing homes and memory care units (as gifts for residents to give to family or for the residents themselves)
- children's wings of hospitals
- Ronald McDonald houses
- grief retreats

If you would like to donate in memory of a loved one, all of the above places are great organizations for memorials. The following are also great choices:

- schools and universities
- children's homes and orphanages
- Boy Scouts, Girl Scouts, and 4-H
- animal shelters
- city parks
- parks and recreation departments
- garden clubs
- clubs and teams
- any place that was a passion of the person being remembered

When Greetings Aren't Merry

I HAVE ALREADY SHARED THAT I LOVE A GOOD REASON TO throw a party. I love any reason to get together with friends and family. Sometimes those eleven-minute preparation gatherings are the best ones. I will confess that while I relish planning a really big shindig, I do enjoy impromptu gatherings just as much. The apple doesn't fall far from the tree, because Nannie always loved a good party. She was the life of every one she attended, and I am thankful some of her DNA rubbed off on me.

Over the years, I have been blessed to have like-minded friends who also enjoy celebrating with others. Some of my favorite get-togethers have been ones where a group of us friends planned Easter egg hunts, Halloween arts and crafts, Fourth of July barbecues, and Christmas give-back-to-our-communities gatherings. Several of us organized those Christmas gatherings for a few years, and they were times of great fun. Instead of just a simple affair at one home, we chose to create a progressive party of blessings to spread as much love as possible. We ate separate courses at different homes, and we participated in different charitable acts at each house. One year, I remember writing Christmas cards to veterans at our house and caroling at another home that evening. The friends who organized caroling had access to songbooks, as one of their sisters is a music teacher. We completed a few practice rounds before bundling up and heading out in the neighborhood. Our final destination was the local hospital. We trudged through the snow, going door to door, gleefully sharing a little Christmas cheer.

I can definitely say we carolers forgot about the cold when we saw the looks of surprise and joy intermingled on the faces of neighbors. Well, most of them. Before you think maybe we were horrible singers, I will clarify. I know the Bible says to make a joyful noise (which is exactly what some sweet ladies did in church when I was little), but the truth is we actually made a really decent choir. Okay, maybe we got a little too sure of ourselves and really butchered an attempt at "Mele Kalikimaka," but that is beside the point. Most of us had been in choral groups our whole life and were really enjoying the chance to be out sharing our vocal talents. The evening was a great experience to surprise our friends and neighbors, but apparently we were a little too much surprise for one household.

The couple had seen us coming and going on the street, and we were greeted with quite a shock when we finally assembled on their frozen lawn. Instead of visions of sugarplums dancing through their heads, they saw flashing lights (as in, those of local law enforcement). Our little troupe was told that the homeowners had already called the cops about our merry-making. One among us tried his best to explain that we were not making mischief, just trying instead to spread some cheer. This explanation only infuriated them more, prompting another call to police about trespassers. So, rather deflated, we hastily retreated to our cars to hopefully be of more use to those spending the holidays at the medical center. For the record, our attempt at the Hawaiian greeting was not at that house. In fact, we did not even get beyond a few lines of "The First Noel" before we were made aware of our impending fate as outlaws.

Christmas isn't merry for everyone. In reality, I knew that to be true long before I heard the lyrics to "Blue Christmas." Many people are isolated, lonely, ill, or grieving, and the holidays only perpetuate feelings of sadness for them. It wasn't until our family experienced our darkest day that I realized how incredibly challenging traditions I once adored could become.

Hanging Christmas stockings is one of those traditions. In our family, Aunt Nernie (which is short for Ernestine) and my mom have lovingly cross-stitched stockings for each of us. They are a treasured part of our Advent season. The placing of those socks is an act of hopeful anticipation similar to the way the world waited for a Savior to be born. As a mom of seven, with four of my beautiful children residing in heaven with Jesus, stocking-hanging day paralyzes me with grief. I should be hanging ten stockings (of course, our dog has one), but instead of joy, all I have to offer is tears. I physically have ten stockings (including three for our miscarried babies), yet I always seem to fall apart on tree-decorating day. The last few years I have busied myself in the kitchen because I don't want my children's memories of decorating to be filled with images of a sad momma.

Many other grieving mommas face the same agony when it comes to Christmas cards for an assortment of reasons. One mourning mom friend has never sent holiday cards again after her son's death because she could not bear to not write her son's name on the card. I understood her heart. Instead of not writing Reed's name, for a few years we signed our cards,

> Merry Christmas from Team Stevens
> Daniel, Kandy, Sawyer, Erin, and Cloie.
> And from team members waiting in heaven:
> Noah, Reed, Timothy, and Savannah Kate.

It was just too painful not to write his name, and for years, it was agonizing to not remember our babies. So I marched to the beat of my own little drummer boy, even if that meant making others uncomfortable. That final signature was the only way we were going to send a card. Even though their presence is no longer with us physically, we carry each of them in our hearts and memories. Omitting them from our annual family report (a.k.a. Christmas card) just felt wrong.

How to sign cards is only one facet of the pain of holiday greetings. I never experienced this but have read some deeply personal articles regarding receiving Christmas cards as a grieving mom. One author's point of view was that she did not want to hear about another family's perfect life or see all their smiling faces when her world was falling apart.

Honestly, I have so many friends all over the country, I look forward to catching up on their world by reading their holiday cards and letters. But I do understand her heart, because after losing our first baby, I really struggled to get excited about anyone's pregnancy, baby shower, or birth. It was just too painful to endure because I would never be able to hold my baby, and at that time, the doctors were not positive I ever would.

Over time, my reluctance to embrace anything baby got better, and I really hope that is a transferrable truth for those who are wounded by Christmas cards.

I wrote a blog about this very topic, and a very sweet friend contacted me almost immediately after I posted. My dear friend, Cindy, who was once a part of my church family but now lives far away, wanted to know if I had ever felt slighted by receiving holiday greetings. She had internalized my words, thinking that perhaps she had inadvertently hurt us over the years. This is the blessing and joy of friendship. This sweet woman who was once my children's daycare provider and whose husband started Reed's scholarship fund took to heart the words of a grieving mom and thought they could have unknowingly added more pain to our lives. Quickly, I calmed her fears by saying that was not nor had it ever been my experience. I almost had to giggle at her immediate response of relief and comic genius, which stated that she knew the pain couldn't have been every year because some years she struggled to get any cards mailed out.

This is a perfect example of why I feel as if I have been blessed with the best friends in the entire world, especially the real messy ones, who are a perfect reflection of my own messy heart! She was thousands of miles away, reading an article and thinking of me. When we had an honest discussion on the topic, not only did she warm my heart, but she made me laugh. That is a true friend indeed! As our chat continued, we wondered what we could do differently to help other grieving families in our lives. After much thought, we decided to send our cards and newsletters along with a personal note to anyone who may have lost someone in recent years. Our note would acknowledge the loss and how difficult the holiday season can be, with a promise to pray for them throughout the Christmas season.

It was the best we had to offer to bring comfort at what can be a very difficult time.

All That Glitters Is Not Gold

WATCHING THE OLYMPICS, WINTER AND SUMMER, IS SOMETHING
I have enjoyed since I was a little girl. A dream of mine is to attend
the Olympic Games sometime in my life. I have been known to
rearrange my schedule in order to watch the opening ceremony. My love
for the Olympics is something I have passed on to my children, and the
summer games of 2004 will forever remain my favorite of them all. That
year the games were held in Athens, Greece, and many of the events
were broadcast well after my children's bedtimes. However, Reed's love
of the games was equal to mine, so we stayed up late cuddling in my bed,
cheering for Team USA. We would be on the edge of the bed cheering
and clapping, hoping our athletes would continue to add to the medal
count. Then we would settle back in for the human interest reporting
about each of the athletes and their families.

It was during one of those stories when we quite accidentally
discovered a miracle in our midst. I happened to be almost six months
pregnant at the time, and the baby in my growing belly was just finally
starting to show. She was also getting large enough that I wasn't the
only one who could feel her move. While lying there cheering on the
gymnasts, I realized that Reed could probably feel the tumbling going
on inside my womb. I was right. His face was so precious, a smile slowly
forming as his hands felt his baby sister doing somersaults for hours.
Months before, this same sweet boy had sobbed in my arms when we
told him that we were once again pregnant. His tender little heart didn't
think he could take one more loss, having lost two babies, including this
baby's twin sister, in the previous five months. As he cried, he asked a
question I simply could not answer. "Momma, are we going to lose this

153

baby too? Because I don't think I can take it if we do." That day we prayed and cried.

Here we were, months down the road, and my sweet boy could finally touch the baby he had worried he would never meet. The same scene played out over and over every night of the games. He would cuddle in close and lay one hand on my belly, laughing every time he could feel one of her tiny kicks. And after spilling the beans about the internal gymnastics, my bedroom became the most popular hangout in our house because Sawyer and Erin joined us too.

During those games, both boys developed a real interest in Olympic swimming. So much so that when choosing Halloween costumes, my boys decided on Michael Phelps and Ryan Lochte to go along with their sister's young Laura Ingalls. We bought sweatshirts that resembled the official Team USA uniforms, and I embroidered the USA letters and American flag patches on them. We bought swim caps and made medals with ribbons and cardboard. The silver medals were easy to create because we could cover our cardboard circles with aluminum foil. The gold medals were a little more daunting. We tried several ideas before settling on gold spray paint. If being adorable were an Olympic sport, they were definitely gold contenders. There would be other costumes over the years, but those miniature Olympians were a couple of my favorites.

Like the Olympics, watching the Macy's Thanksgiving Day and Tournament of Roses parades have been traditions for my family as long as I can remember. I wait patiently every year to see the Donate Life float featuring likenesses of the donors chosen for that year. I hope every year Reed will be one of them, but even if he isn't, located next to his bed are two beautiful honors he would have been proud to receive.

I was surprised when one day a beautiful envelope arrived in the mail. I was even more surprised by the invitation inside; Reed was to be honored at the Donate Life ceremony as one of the Donor Medal of Honor recipients by Governor Tim Pawlenty. For a little boy who loved superheroes, it was a fitting honor, and for his momma, one that moved me to tears.

On the day of the ceremony, we were able to meet other recipient families as well as the governor and his wife. I will never forget Mr.

Pawlenty's words to us. When we were introduced to him as the parents of Reed Stevens, he paused and remembered our son as one of the children from the Lakeview School bus crash. Then he asked why no one had told him back then that Reed was a donor. Although it would have been impossible for us to pass on that news because the community service attended by the governor and other officials occurred when Sawyer was still in intensive care, it meant the world to us to know our governor was such a huge supporter of organ donation. When we actually received the medal, I was stunned at its beauty, and I almost dropped it because it was substantially heavier than I expected it to be.

A year later, we received an invitation from the governor of South Dakota requesting our presence at a similar ceremony. Reed had been flown to a trauma center in Sioux Falls, but sadly, rather being able to revive him, that is where he passed away. Because of the strange circumstances of technically being from two states for one day of his life, both states chose to honor him. Sadly, severe flooding in Pierre prevented the ceremony from taking place, and we received Reed's medal in the mail. The honor was not diminished, even without the chance to meet the governor, and today both medals rest atop Reed's dresser next to his bed.

As unexpected as those medals were, the honor bestowed on Reed at the last Reed's Run was one I never saw coming. As the CEM (chief executive momma) of this family, it is very difficult to surprise me. Oh, I love surprises, but when little ears and eyes are always present, a lot of *oopsies* moments happen. Another reason for the lack of surprises in my life is the fact that I am a planner. When looking at details from carpools to holidays and appointments to events, I am usually the wrangler of all that goes on around here.

Reed's Run is the 5K event we held during the years Reed would have been in high school to fund the scholarship created in his name. The ten months of planning it took to pull off Reed's Run each year were fraught with endless lists. Auction lists, T-shirts, website updates, marketing, parade promotions, registration forms, medals, volunteers ... The lists went on and on. All the planning was exhausting but in the end so worth it. Each year on the actual day, I would flit about, being pulled in many different directions. I rarely ate, and I hugged lots of people. I shed a few tears, but none compared to the final year.

Everything was running smoothly, albeit not without a few bumps in the road. Thankfully our amazing committee members shielded me from most of the bumps. As the afternoon shifted into evening, we finally got down to the last parts of the evening: the awards ceremony, the Jesus Painter performance, and an outdoor family movie. I was up on the stage announcing the winners of the various medals and was to introduce the artist for the worship time.

As I concluded the awards, all of a sudden I saw Matthew (my high school best friend) coming toward the stage. I really wished this were videotaped, because I can only imagine what my face actually looked like. My mind was thinking, *This is weird. I haven't seen you in twenty-three years. Have you lost your mind? This is not how this evening is supposed to go.* As he came on stage and took the microphone from me, I am certain I was questioning his judgment and mine.

What happened next, I never saw coming. But as I saw one of Reed's former scout masters in uniform also coming forward, my knees grew weak and the floodgate of tears opened. Matt explained how he was so excited to be here and about our friendship. He then told the tale of how he had made arrangements with Reed's former troop for this special occasion. He shared about his summer long ago at Philmont Scout Ranch in New Mexico and how I was his pen pal while he was gone. They were special memories from a lifetime ago.

Because of some kind of rule on timelines in the BSA, Reed couldn't be awarded the rank of Eagle Scout. Sobbing in front of everyone, I heard one of the sweetest tales ever told. My dear friend decided Reed would indeed be earning his Eagle Scout, just not in the normal way. The gift he gave in honor of our sweet redheaded boy is truly the embodiment of scouting.

We were handed Reed's Eagle Scout award, his Eagle neckerchief, and a Philmont Scout Ranch patch. The Boy Scout Law states all the qualities that define scouts. A scout is trustworthy, loyal, helpful, friendly, courteous, kind, obedient, cheerful, thrifty, brave, clean, and reverent. What it doesn't say is that a scout gives sacrificially, because in one magical moment, that's exactly what happened. The award placed in my trembling hands was Matthew's own Eagle Scout award "reawarded" to Reed. Engraved on the award is the motto "Be Prepared." There was no way my heart would have ever been prepared for the surprise of this truly amazing gift, which rests right next to Reed's medals from the governors.

Those awards are a beautiful and meaningful memorial to the amazing young man Reed was, and they have brought us such joy.

Before my son's passing, I never spent one moment thinking about the word *posthumous*. But after his death, the word snuck up on me in places I never expected. One of those places was the end-of-year awards celebration at our school. A wonderful gentleman in our community started a tradition at our school recognizing top secondary students in each subject, perfect attenders, and exemplary attitudes of students in grades four through twelve. Having formerly been a teacher at our school, I was familiar with the nomination and selection process.

Although he didn't let it eat at him, Reed expressed his disappointment in never earning one of those awards. I struggled with how to comfort him, because I was as baffled as he was. Teachers never said an unkind word about him, and at his services, we were astonished how story after story of his acts of kindness came pouring out of his classmates. Many of the tales were ones we had never heard. At the end of the school year, the year he passed away, we were surprised to be invited to the banquet for these recognitions. Erin had been working for perfect attendance because she had seen the medals of a few friends, and even though her record was spotless up until February 19, she had missed plenty of days at the hospital afterward. We knew after receiving a truancy letter because of being hospitalized for twelve weeks that Sawyer wasn't a candidate for that award either. None of our kids were old enough to be top students in a subject area, so that left only the positive attitude category.

After the very wonderful supper, we filtered into the school's auditorium for the ceremony. When the reason for our attendance that evening was given to Erin in honor of Reed, I wasn't sure what to make of the posthumous award. There is that awful word I never wanted to spend any time on. It was extremely hard to be appreciative of the award when he hadn't been deemed "good enough" in life to earn one. I know my reaction was not in line with the message the nominators intended, but I could never embrace the award with the same enthusiasm as I did the donor or Eagle Scout medals. I sincerely wish I could.

When Back-to-School Backfires

ALTHOUGH BOOKS WERE A BIG PART OF MY CHILDHOOD, I WASN'T always a competent reader. Back in the day before differentiation, kids like me were often seen as a nuisance by some teachers. By "kids like me," I mean those who breezed through their schoolwork and ended up with large amounts of time left to do nothing because everyone else was still working on the assignment. I only had the opportunity to be involved in a gifted program for two years of my K–12 education, but they were the best two years of all my schooling. Other than those years, most teachers either told me to sit quietly (which was incredibly difficult), read a book, or find something to stay out of their hair. One teacher (who probably thought he was being pretty progressive) started a few students, including me, on a new speed-reading program. We finished our other classwork and then were to report to a computer (the first one I had ever seen) to speed-read. Oh, it worked to keep us quiet and out of his hair, because working with the program became a huge motivating tool. We were driven to beat our scores. If any educational researcher would have used us as test subjects, we could have saved many parents and children the heartache of learning how addicting screen time can be. Our rates of reading words, sentences, and paragraphs improved by leaps and bounds. The drawback was that, although we were learning to read fast, we weren't learning to comprehend what we were reading.

The joy of curling up and savoring a book was gone. The point of a book was to devour it, reading the words at a rapid pace. I don't know about the other students, but for me personally, reading became a chore. For years, I would have to read and reread a passage just to make any sense of it, because all my brain was doing was reading the words as if I were in the Olympic speed-reading sprints. This problem continued for a long time until I finally began to discover tools which helped me to read with comprehension. For a long time, gone was the joy I had found in every word written by Beverly Cleary and Laura Ingalls Wilder. Instead of reading for pleasure, I was scared and confused as to why something I once enjoyed had become so much work.

I know my children have experienced very similar feelings. From what we have learned from grief professionals, children grieve in spurts. One moment they can be perfectly fine, playing with friends, and then experiencing the wide range of emotions of grief the next. Just like their grieving parents, grieving kids are required to return to old routines like school, but unlike their parents, they are surrounded by children who rarely know anything about grief. Teachers, sadly, are sometimes the last to know that other students are saying hurtful things to these grieving kids while out of the teachers' sight. The playground, restrooms, and cafeteria can be feeding grounds for those who misinterpret grief and its ugly side effects. I often think that because of the nature of grieving in children, even adults don't recognize the signs of grief because "They look okay today" or "They haven't mentioned anything lately."

As an educator, one practice I value is getting to know my students personally. Sadly, this very activity which is at the heart of effective teaching is one that can stop students in their tracks. Until my family experienced such deep loss, I never once considered how challenging a back-to-school activity can be for some students.

Remember when I mentioned the book I co-wrote with Dr. Seuss? Surviving from my childhood, *All about Me* included blank lines accompanying Seuss's prose and illustrations. To complete the book, the coauthor (the child) fills in the blank spaces to share about her (or his) life. Each of my children has their own copy of this same book, and it will be interesting to see if they, too, fulfill their childhood aspirations. The activity of sharing a little about you is always exciting, until it isn't.

"Getting to know you" activities come in every shape and flavor, and they provide classroom teachers an opportunity to build connections with their scholars. I have used them for years but have now refined my approach after watching my own children struggle with them. Instead of using a predetermined set of questions, I use a list of questions and allow my students to pick which ones they would like to answer. My reason for doing this is watching my bubbly girls come to a crashing halt, tears in their eyes and hands trembling, when they get to the required question, standard on many of these questionnaires: "How many brothers/sisters do you have?" I have sat next to them while they happily write about their favorite food, color, activity, summer memory, and the like, and I have watched as their faces fall as they don't know how to answer the sibling question. Their apprehension is not because they don't know the answer of six. They just don't know how they are going to explain that answer in front of a classroom full of other kids, many of whom don't "get" grieving. If they answer "two," which is the easiest to explain, they feel as if they are betraying the siblings who live in heaven. If they answer "six" but don't have pictures to show, then they feel that they will be considered untruthful. *Who wants that label in the first weeks of school?* No matter what they choose to disclose, the question is one which often brings them anxiety.

Content knowledge, effective pedagogy, classroom management techniques, and technology tools for delivery are all essential for excellence in teaching, and for me personally, being able to build relationships with students is one of my top priorities. I want to be one who believes in each and every student I am blessed to teach. I sincerely hope that is the same for every educator who has ever, is currently, or will in the future teach one of my children. Championing students is hard work, because they all come with diverse backgrounds, personalities, and experiences. Sometimes being a role model requires tweaking what may have worked in the past, but if that staves off unneeded and unintentional hurt to even one grieving student, it is worth it.

PART THREE
Blow Your Socks Off–
Things That Are Most Definitely Helpful

IT WAS ONLY A SANDWICH. SANDWICHES ARE SORT OF A THING MY FAMILY of origin specializes in. I mean, we *know* a good sandwich. Growing up, we cleaned our house every Saturday morning after we had breakfast and snuck in a few Saturday morning cartoons. Oh, how I wish we still had those. Early morning cartoons, which we waited all week to see, were one of the best things about my childhood. The tuna fish sandwiches, our typical lunch fare after our cleaning rituals, were *not* one of the best things about my childhood. Thankfully, my mom would also make egg salad on those days, and that was a sandwich I really did enjoy. But never the tuna fish! I wasn't thankful for it then, but trust me: if you are hungry enough, you will eat anything.

Years later, on a nine-day camping trip with five children under the age of six, it was our friends' turn to make lunch. We were visiting northern Minnesota, taking in all the state parks over the week of the Fourth of July. I don't know how familiar you are with what is referred to as "up north" around here, but I will tell you what I didn't know. *It snows in July!* We were in tents, and it snowed. During the day, it would warm up to a nice sixty or seventy degrees, but at night, it would be cold enough to snow. We were woefully underprepared for the temperature extremes and were forced to buy our children winter jackets at a thrift store to enjoy the trip.

We had gone on plenty of camping trips with these friends and had developed a comfortable routine of traveling with young kids and

163

keeping our sanity. Meal sharing was our saving grace! Each day one family was responsible for breakfast and supper while the other family handled lunch. The next day, the roles reversed. In addition, we tried to keep our supplies light because we were tent camping and we didn't want to haul a bunch of uneaten food home. Looking back now, we never discussed any food preferences: likes or dislikes. We just brought the food for our respective times to serve.

On the next-to-last day of our trip, we prepared for some hiking in the northernmost state park of Minnesota's North Shore, just a stone's throw from Canada. Since we would not be returning to our campsite, we planned to pack our lunch. Our friends had lunch duty that day. We hiked and hiked and by that time thought we were parenting gurus because we had two-year-olds who were becoming excellent day hikers. The falls we explored that day were spectacular, and compared to the prairie where we all live, this seemed like another world—not the same state at all.

By the time we made it back to the trailhead, I was famished and so was everyone else. We quickly grabbed the coolers and tableware and sat down at the picnic table. My friend quickly assessed her supply box and realized she hadn't brought a bowl to mix up the sandwich spread. My sandwich radar should have turned on at this point, but for some reason, it didn't. Perhaps I was too tired for it to kick in. But when she produced a couple cans of tuna and a small jar of mayonnaise, I thought, *I am too young to die of hunger! Of hunger of all things! I love to eat, and seriously I am going to die from starvation right here on this trail!*

I don't know what my friend knew about my dislike—no, let me rephrase that—*loathing* of tuna fish sandwiches, but they were my mother's own particular torture device during those Saturday lunches of yore. Just the smell of them made me want to run for the hills. But instead of curling up in the fetal position, I tried to help my friend come up with an alternative to a mixing bowl. Since we didn't have time to carve one out of a nearby tree (*and* I am pretty sure that would be illegal, seeing as how we were still within the boundaries of state land), we finally settled on kneading the ingredients together in a Ziploc bag. Once mixed, I seriously considered ordering a tuna fish sandwich, hold the tuna fish. The problem with this plan was I had children watching, three of which were mine, and two of those were particularly picky eaters. I mustered every ounce of culinary courage I had to offer and took the proffered sandwich with pretzel sticks on the side.

Since I am still here to write this book, you now have evidence for your children that tuna fish will not kill you, and like I said before, if you are hungry enough, you will eat just about anything. Turns out after all those years of despising tuna fish sandwiches, I actually kind of like them now.

I honestly don't know how or why sandwiches became such a part of my heritage, but I remember having them at my grandmothers' houses. If I had to take a guess, it had something to do with the heat of summer days in the South. Heating up a kitchen for a noon meal just as the hottest part of the day was beginning seemed plain foolish. I still remember all the trips I would make to the deli on old Palafox Road with Nannie to pick up sandwich supplies. Like just everything else, my grandmothers were about as different as night and day. Mama liked solid cuts of meat, while Nannie would exasperate the butcher until the meat was so thinly shaved you could read through it. And let me tell you: I have had some doozies of sandwiches over the years. There were the staples—bologna and cheese, ham and cheese, peanut butter and jelly, peanut butter and banana, potted meat, and the rare BLT ("rare" because it required cooking). I never really wrapped my taste buds around another Southern staple, pimento cheese, but there were plenty of those around too. Maybe I should give those another try someday! But the sandwich that really took the cake was a Nannie specialty: ringed pineapple with mayonnaise on white bread. They were actually pretty good, especially on a hot day!

Sandwiches were a big part of my childhood, and they are still a part of my menu planning, especially in the summer. But there is one sandwich that I will never forget. It was a sandwich that literally came out of nowhere and was exactly what I needed, even though I didn't know it at the time.

I have a dear friend whom I have had the pleasure of knowing for many years. Our friendship starting when I was her son's middle school science teacher. Over the years, our relationship morphed from parent-teacher to the kind of family you create on your own. Her son's was one of the few phone calls that actually made it through to me the night of the bus crash, asking if there was anything he could do to help us.

Much like that final day of camping when we were exhausted and worn out, years later, we stood greeting the people who came to offer condolences the night of Reed's memorial service. After we had been secluded in the pediatric intensive care unit for nine days, people came from all over to tell us how sorry they were. I don't know exactly how many people were there, but the line was endless. And for the most part, I hugged every single one of them.

At some point during that seemingly endless procession, there was a tap on my shoulder. I turned around to see my friend holding a plate with a sandwich and some chips. I looked at her like she was insane. *Don't you see there are a million people here? I don't have time for a sandwich. Thank you for the offer, but no thanks!* After some protesting about not wanting to eat and not being hungry, she made it plain and simple. I *was* going to eat that sandwich. I *was* going to sit down for a few minutes, and that *was* that.

Her sandwich was like manna from heaven, prepared lovingly by human hands. It wasn't until much later that I realized I hadn't eaten much of anything all day and probably would have collapsed from sheer exhaustion if she hadn't been brave and knowledgeable enough to know what I really needed, even if I didn't know it myself. My friend has her own grief story, having lost her first husband a few short days after their wedding in a motorcycle accident, and using her experience she lovingly and persistently forced me to eat a sandwich.

The bread with meat and cheese was only the tip of the iceberg of all the amazing ways people showed up to become the hands and feet of Jesus to us. Their arms wrapped us in love, nourished our bellies, wiped away our tears, and shocked and surprised us in ways that we would have never imagined possible. They were and continue to be the embodiment of love. What follows in this final section are ideas (just thoughts, really) on how to love someone who is grieving, especially if you are at a loss as to what to do. Some may seem obvious, and others are just precious. I could write forever and never run out of stories of the kindnesses shown to us, but in order to give some practical advice, I have highlighted some of the very best.

And yes! As I have shared before, people—friends, church family, and neighbors—fed us for months. That sandwich was one of the first "meals" offered, but it was revolutionary in the tidal wave of relief that flooded my soul. And no, in case you were wondering, it wasn't tuna fish.

When All Else Fails, Prayer Works

WE HAD PLANNED AND SAVED, DREAMED AND BUDGETED FOR our future, but true to our lives since the bus crash, we did have to incorporate plans B and C. For years our kiddos have dreamed of the year they would graduate from high school. That pinnacle moment of launching into the world is one to be revered, but that was only part of our children's dreams. We have made a commitment to each of them that for their high school graduation, we will embark on a trip to a destination of their choosing. Reed's dream was always to go to Africa, and someday I plan to honor those wishes. Up until his actual senior year, Sawyer's trip had been to visit our nation's capital, my original hometown. But after an unplanned first-time-ever get-away with his sister, his plans quickly changed to visiting someplace warm, preferably with a beach. Plan B it was.

We organized a tour of the South, hitting all the favorite places of my childhood and culminating with a beach stay in Pensacola. Then we learned Erin would need major surgery, and once again, we were in hospital and therapy mode. You would think we would be used to it, but every time it happens, I feel like I've been punched in the gut. Suddenly our walking tours and bouncing from city to city all over the Deep South did not make sense, considering our girl would not be weight bearing for six weeks. Good gravy! Plan C—for the love of all zucchini—please be the plan that works! Thankfully it was, and in the end, it was the best vacation of our lives.

We rented a beach house on a southern Florida Gulf Coast island and invited my parents, my sister's family, and Sawyer's girlfriend, Sydney, to join us. Changing plans is tiresome, grueling, and *exhausting* work.

Coordinating travel for six people is tough. Doing the same thing for twelve will wear you out! But Sawyer had been through so much in seven years that I wanted his graduation party and his special trip to be spectacular. I am so grateful God knows the desires of our hearts because he knew how much I wanted this to be amazing for our Boy Wonder, and even though it took plan C to get there, I came away from that vacation refreshed, renewed, rejuvenated, and completely awed by God.

It took Herculean effort to coordinate everyone's schedules, to arrange for our animals, plants, and home to be looked after, and to keep the packing to a minimum for six people for nine days, but the results were worth every minute. When we first arrived in sunny Orlando, we were famished as our flight was over lunchtime and our breakfast at the hotel earlier that morning was rushed. Although my sister was awaiting our arrival, we made the executive decision to take our entourage out to eat before we headed over to her house. Arriving with a pack of wolves might have been the closest equivalent to arriving with three hungry teenagers and one starving middle schooler. I would never do that to any host, not even my sister.

We quickly made our decision for orders, and right then, I had a pinch-me moment. We were here! Plan C worked! If it were not frowned upon, I would have liked to shimmy and shake in a full-out praise dance up and down the aisles of the southern-style barbeque restaurant. The excitement we all shared was palpable. While sipping sweet tea, I suggested we should pray. All six of us bowed our heads, and I led us in prayer.

I don't remember the words exactly, but I do remember thanking God for our safe arrival, for Erin's successful surgery, for the donor and his/her family who gave her the gift of a tissue donation, for Sawyer's and Sydney's successful hard work culminating in their graduation, and for God's faithfulness in the storm for the last seven years. Often, my praise for God's provision pours out my eyes, and that day was no exception. I was humbly moved to see all that God had given us in our darkest days, and on that day, it felt just plain awesome to "taste and see that the Lord is good."

Shortly after our prayer concluded, the platter of succulent smoked meats and slap-your-grandma good sides arrived. We simply ate, laughed, and enjoyed. Looking back, there was a shift in the demeanor of the staff, barely perceptible but definitely noticeable. Since we were eating lunch at two in the afternoon, there were maybe only two other tables with patrons. As things were winding down at our table, I noticed all the employees watching our table. Not in a weird sort of way but with sweet countenances upon their faces.

Eventually our server, who had the best personality, arrived with our bill. Before she laid it on the table, she attempted to explain something to us. The attempt stumbled out, because she was choking back tears. Finally, she composed herself to explain that the family seated adjacent to us had overheard our prayers. Moved by our words of praise, they had quietly asked for our bill and paid it (which to me, at over eighty dollars, was a *large* amount). They explained their reasoning to the wait staff and asked that we be told they were Christians who were touched by our story (which we didn't really share but they had sensed), and they wanted us to know God loved us.

My response while typing this is the same that I had that day. My humbled awe poured out of my eyes. As we left the restaurant, the employees formed a line to wish us all a beautiful vacation.

We floated right out of the restaurant. If we had been excited before that moment, our hearts were soaring at what things God had in store for us the rest of this trip.

Many times I think we forget to "stop and smell the roses." Our lives are so busy that we forget God's creation and his people all around us. I know I have been guilty too many times, *way too many times*, of overscheduling and overcommitting until I'm unable to enjoy the blessings right in front of me. When I do that to myself, I also feel I cannot do one more thing for someone else. *But I couldn't be more wrong.*

I can pray. I can pray while driving to and from events. I can pray while making meals for my family. I can pray while doing laundry. The list is endless. While there were hundreds of people who gave of their time, talents, efforts, and resources to help my family in our darkest days, there were thousands upon thousands all over the world who were praying for our family and every other family involved in that bus crash.

There were days when I could barely get out of bed, but almost like a magnetic force compelling me to move, I was able to do it. There were moments when all the worry, the fear, and the overwhelming sadness were too much, and like a life preserver tossed in a tempest, I would feel a sense of hope. When the odds were against one of my children overcoming another obstacle, the prayers of God's people would literally be our lifeline to make it through the next breath, moment, minute, hour, or day.

The Bible calls us to pray fervently. I believe those prayers, above anything else, are what kept us going—especially when we weren't sure we would be able to do it.

Our CaringBridge sites were places to share our progresses and our stumbles, but mostly they were an outlet to reach those who were praying and were asking for specific prayer guidance. The journaling I did there chronicled the highlights of what I could share and stressed where our most immediate needs were at the time. One time I deviated from the norm and used the site almost in desperation. When we returned from Sawyer attending his last Camp-We-No-Wheeze, we were met by some neighborhood kids who told us they had witnessed one of our dogs getting hit by a truck when they were playing street hockey. We panicked, thinking that one had been killed. When we saw Lucy limping along, we were sure it was her that had gotten too close to a truck tire. The neighborhood kids told us it hadn't been her but Huckleberry—Reed's dog—the same sweet dog who lay next to his boy's casket at his service and never made a peep. No matter how much we tried to explain it, every time we would return in a car, Huck would jump in and scour every inch looking for Reed. Despite having an electronic fence line, our gentle giant of a golden retriever had started running all over town in what we could only describe as a desperate attempt to find his boy. The boy he last saw at that service was not the full-of-life young man who worked with him to earn ribbon after ribbon at the county and state fair.

At first glance, Huck looked okay and we were certain the boys had been wrong. But after unpacking and spending a night at home, it became apparent we were the ones misguided. Crying out in agonizing pain, Huck let us know that he had made a brave and valiant attempt to cover up his injuries. Before I loaded him into the van to go to the veterinarian's office, I did something I still cannot believe I did.

This was Reed's dog. Next to Jesus, I don't think Reed loved anything more than him. They had spent countless hours together on adventures, including the time the two of them overtook the entire tent, leaving the other five of us pressed against the outer edges. This was the dog who honorably paid his last respects by lying next to his boy. *I could not lose him too. Not now. I wasn't ready.* Having Huck was like holding on to a small vestige to the boy who helped raise him.

While the other kids did their best to comfort him, I got on the computer and begged people to pray. I explained this was unconventional, but I was desperate. I poured out my heart and explained that we were not ready to say good-bye. After hitting post, I rushed Huckleberry to the vet's office.

When we walked in, their faces were grave. "Big dogs and truck wheels do not have happy endings" was written all over their faces. We were given a private room to await the doctor's arrival. I just kept whispering assurances to Huck akin to the inspirational messages given to Rocky Balboa when he was taking a beating.

When the doctor arrived, she did a manual examination, vowing she was 100 percent certain his hip was broken. I lost it. I cried like a baby. I asked her what his chances were. I explained I would do whatever it took to save his life if it could be done. To her credit, she cried too. Before any further decisions could be made, Huck needed to have an X-ray to see the extent of the damage. A tech came and helped the veterinarian carry our sweet boy to the diagnostic room. I simply sat and cried, thinking this might be the last time I would get to see the best dog in the world.

The doctor came back without our golden-haired guy, shaking her head. I misread her incredulous as devastated. She plopped down in the extra chair and said, "I have never seen anything like this in my entire career." Although my heart was breaking, I hung on her every word. "I know when I examined him that right hip was broken. I could feel the broken bones. But when we got him on the table and took the X-ray, there isn't one single bone broken. Huck will be back in a minute. He is just getting some extra special love in the back from our techs."

I was flabbergasted.

A sheepish smile broke across my face as I wiped away the tears of joy mingled with those of my earlier grief. "I think I know," I quietly said.

"Before I came here, I asked everyone on CaringBridge to pray. I'm pretty sure they did." It was the only answer that made sense.

When all else fails, prayer never does.

God might not answer in the way we expect or hope, but he hears every word. He loves us without fail. Even when we don't feel that love or his presence, he is tenderly cradling us with the rhythmic message of "You are loved, you are loved, you are *loved*."

Sometimes that love manifests itself in the most magnificent ways—ways that prior to February 2008, I never dreamed possible. Grief and loss have a profound way of changing you. I have already confessed to becoming a gentler, kinder version of myself, but the acts of kindness documented here have and will never leave me. They have become my equivalent of the Bat belt—tools I can rely on to help someone else in need.

One of the most heartfelt things anyone did for us was done by a complete stranger. Seeing our distress signal in the sky prompted this amazing, incredible, and loving woman to recall her very own deep, dark valley. She too had experienced unfathomable losses. Yes, losses. Several in her family passed in one tragic accident. She recollected how through the power of prayer she was able to go on all these years later. When she learned of the bus crash, she wrote a simple message in a card to us, documenting how she was forming a deeply personal type of prayer contract with us. She vowed a covenant of two years of praying for our family. When the first card arrived, we were blown away. We could barely make it through an hour without some overwhelming flood of grief or another medical emergency needing our attention. Yet here she was just a little over an hour away, believing in us. How did we know that? She didn't just say she was praying for us. No! She made a "contract" with us to pray every day for two years. We couldn't see through the immediate, and she was looking to a future—one where we would feel joy again, one where our children would be physically healed, and one where not every moment would be spent thinking about how much we had loss. In the onslaught of cards and letters, there are a few that still linger in my memories. Hers is one of them.

Periodically she would pen a quick little card to tell us that she was keeping up her end of the bargain and encouraging us to keep clinging to God. Her message was clear: there is always light up ahead. I embraced her message, and it became my own personal battle cry in the chaos. We are going to make it! We were deep in the valley of the shadow of death, a dark and isolating and wearisome place. Grief and our responses to grief forced us to spend some time in that cold, dank pit, but God never intended for us to stay there and put up curtains or, as Mama would say, "set up house." Her aptly timed cards of encouragement and commitment of praying for us just plain oozed hope, something we so desperately needed.

The messages would arrive every few months or so, and each one would move me to tears. Grief could be an absolute nightmare of a companion, creating the worst possible day, but her penmanship would tilt everything in a different direction. We would reverently thank God for her presence and her prayers in our lives, almost rubbing the life out of each note, so precious was her uplifting covenant.

Her devoted prayers were just a few among many. We couldn't go anywhere, from church to the grocery store to a sporting event, without someone personally expressing their prayers. We didn't go a day for a very long time that someone didn't post on social media or send us an e-mail telling us they were, had been, and would continue to be praying for us. The deep love expressed by praying continually for someone is revolutionary.

It changes everything.

I have run a few 5K races and one triathlon. Running is still one of my least favorite things to do, and I still abide by my early mantra: "I don't run, even if it's a good sale." But even a reluctant runner (the thought never crossed my mind that I could simply write a check for a good cause and not run) can become infatuated with the cheers and well wishes from bystanders. Each person's shouts of encouragement or clapping gives the runner that last little turbo boost to finish strong. It's hard to hang your head and drag across the final line with so many cheerleaders present. When we felt we had nothing left to give or were at our breaking point, the prayers of others gave us one more nudge to keep going. I began adding a line to our CaringBridge journals on occasion, which explained that we could hear all the people cheering us on at the top of the hill and slowly, and steadily we would climb—crawl if we had to—out of the mire and muck of sadness to rejoin them and begin truly living again. The prayers of this sweet woman and countless others were truly the spirit of peace and the gift of hope.

When all else fails, prayer never does.

I wish that the worst day of our lives could be the last worst day any parent would have to experience. I know that isn't going to be the case, as our own community has lost many beloved children since the passing of Reed, Hunter, Emilee, and Jesse. There have been countless devastations and unspeakable horrors around the world since that day as well. At times, I feel utterly helpless because I would love to pack myself up and go to those families, scoop them up in a heartfelt hug, and give whatever I could to help lessen their pain. I know that isn't feasible much of the time. Remembering all the prayers shared for me and my family, I can do one simple thing. Those prayers changed my life, and when I feel that I have nothing more to give to anyone else, I couldn't be more incorrect. *I can pray.* Many times, that is all God wants me to do. It was the one and only suggestion I could give to several who desperately wanted to do something for the families in the aftermath of the Connecticut school shooting. Everyone wanted to do something, but most felt their hands were tied by indecision. The feeling of wanting to help but not knowing what to do is devastating. My idea of praying was practical, but it was the one thing most of my revolutionary-hearted friends had missed.

When all else fails, prayer never does.

Prayers can give someone the ounce of hope they need to take the next step.

Trust me: I am living proof.

Pink Is the New Red

I RECENTLY HAD THE OPPORTUNITY TO BE THE KEYNOTE SPEAKER at an event sponsored by our local newspaper. This event honoring exceptional women in our region of the state is what I like to refer to as a "pretty big deal." I would be lying if I said I wasn't telling my voice not to sound "too excited" and telling my heartbeat to slow down when I got the call asking if I would be the speaker. I was giddy with enthusiasm, honored and delighted to be asked. What I didn't realize in the agreement was that my face would be plastered on the newspaper (think a quarter of the page) and on flyers all over the county. I still think of myself as the quintessential girl next door, so to have that type of media coverage was humbling, especially since many days I did not look like the stunning woman looking back at me from that page. I was often out in no makeup, hair in a ponytail, and sweat clothes (that I actually use at the YMCA and don't just wear because they are comfy). The girl in the photo got lucky with a beautiful (albeit freezing) day with a slight breeze giving her flowing diva hair for the photo shoot.

In the days leading up to the event, I worked on my speech and prayed *a lot*. I asked God for the right message to share with this group of amazing women, and that my words and stories would be inspirational because they all deserved the very best. When the evening came, I was thrilled to look out in the audience and see friends, neighbors, former coworkers, and families of former students in attendance. These were my people, and the ones that didn't know me personally were about to become my people. At the end of the evening, as typically happens following one of my speaking engagements, there was a line of those who simply wanted to hug me. Good thing I am on my way to earning a

PhD in hug-ology. One of the attendees was a dear friend and colleague. She is the real deal, a writer and literature professor. I admire her for all the ways she has loved our family in the last few years, but even more so for the talents she possesses. After our warm embrace, she said what I consider to be one of the best compliments I have ever received. "Kandy, you are the embodiment of Southern storytelling!" *Did you hear that, Papa Noles? I have made it! All those years of listening at your feet to you and Jerry Clower and around the tables of every relative I have, I made it to the big leagues.*

Those words carried me home as I walked that beautiful spring evening. Well, honestly, I felt like I was more floating than walking. Storytelling is something that isn't just a part of my cultural heritage. I feel like it is an integral part of my DNA. Most of my friends, especially those who are fellow speakers, often chuckle because I have a story about *everything.* Some people collect knickknacks; I collect friends and their stories. I consider those words and memories my greatest earthly treasure because I plan on taking a whole bunch of people to heaven with me.

Those memories recalled over and over again have been the way that we keep Reed's memory alive for Cloie. She was simply so little when he died that she doesn't remember the details. We tell the stories again and again to help her keep a piece of Reed alive in her heart. For us, telling stories and speaking about him is as natural as breathing. It may be off-putting to others, but to those who find it weird or uncomfortable, I simply don't care. It isn't that I don't care about them or their feelings (because I really do), but Reed is a member of our clan, our tribe, our family, and speaking about him helps us heal. In addition to collecting stories, I am also a big fan of quotes. Words move my soul. I saw this quote once and it stuck with me, although I don't know who is the original author. "When you find people who not only tolerate your quirks but celebrate them with glad cries of 'me too!' be sure to cherish them. Because those weirdos are your tribe."

This is why speaking about Reed is just second nature to us. He was one of our weirdos, the same bunch that loves how their momma sometimes serves ice cream for breakfast and calls us it healthy because she wraps it up with bananas and crepes. He was also the weirdo who loved to get ice cream in the form of a Dairy Queen blizzard for supper. He loved superheroes and animals and the Minnesota Twins and traveling and laughing as much as all of the rest of us weirdos around here. It simply would be foreign to us *not* to talk about him. We do it to bring ourselves comfort and have learned along the way that our open sharing brings comfort to others, which we believe is exactly God's call for our lives. Not talking about him would definitely be a sad, sad day for us.

A few weeks before one of the Reed's Runs (our main fundraising tool for the Reed Stevens Memorial Scholarship), a former student, now dear friend, sent me this poem. Tears streamed down my face for the love she shared and for the aptness of the sentiment. She knew my feelings on what I would consider the second worst day of my life, the day no one speaks Reed's name, and she thought these words would speak to my heart.

His Name Sings my Soul

The mention of my child's name
May bring tears to my eyes,
But it never fails to bring
Music to my ears.
If you are really my friend,
Let me hear the beautiful music of his name.
It soothes my broken heart
And sings to my soul.
—*Author unknown*

She was right! Every word of that is true for me. I know in the beginning people were afraid to tell us stories, but as I became more open about sharing our story, it was as if a treasure chest of stories was opened. My soul was sung the lullaby of his name. One of the greatest gifts I could ever receive now is someone sharing a story about Reed that I don't yet know. I don't even mind if they have become embellished a little over time. Hearing about his story is an incredible gift, just like the one that ended up on my dining room table one cold, wintry day.

Our town is pretty small. For years and years, it was safe enough to not lock our doors. Sadly, a rash of burglaries a little too close to home stopped that practice, but not before the unexpected pink and red baby roses accompanied by a little teddy bear clad in a pink Green Bay Packers sweatshirt showed up. No note was attached. No card was found, and no one in our family had any idea of who in the cat hair (you can thank my college physics professor for that saying) would have left this gift. Days, weeks, and months went by before I received a call from the mother of one of Reed's classmates. She asked if I had ever found some flowers and a little teddy bear at our house. Incredulous, I asked if she was the gift bearer. She stated that indeed she was and wanted to share the story of her gift. She remembered our boys' love of football and of the Green Bay Packers. On a recent trip there, she saw the little bear with the pink sweatshirt, and she was transported back in time to a mother's coffee group.

For a few years, a group of us mommas got together to have coffee (or in my case, sweet tea) and a Bible study, to pray, eat, craft, or have a book club. It was an eclectic mix of moms, but we always had a marvelous time. Sometimes, we would share parenting struggles, and because our children ranged in age from college to toddlers, there was always someone who could offer some advice. It was also a safe place to share funny parenting stories. (Of course I would be hooked. We were sharing *stories*.) Although our boys had been classmates for five years, we were mere acquaintances until this group formed. During this time, I learned that she is a hugger extraordinaire. My kind of gal! She too is a collector of stories, and her timing in the retelling of one of mine could not have been more impeccable.

Once upon a time, I had a captive audience in the selection of my children's clothing. I was not only the washing, drying, sorting, and storing person, but I was also the person who purchased most of their wardrobe. Of course, my run with this glorious job came to a crashing halt one day in the Macy's Department Store in Fargo, North Dakota. If you have to go out, you might as well go out on top, I say. For years, I would purchase matching or coordinating ensembles for my precious children to wear for special occasions and holidays. For this particular year, Reed must have been in fifth grade. I had purchased these beautiful pink and spring-green argyle dresses for the girls, and I wanted to purchase the boys pink oxford cloth shirts. We were walking through the young men's section when Sawyer, who was always the more dapper of the two boys, spied a gorgeous seersucker suit that would have been darling. (This, of course, should be pronounced *dah-ling* for dramatic effect in this story.) Reed was having none of it. No way was he wearing that suit to match his brother. We found the shirts I really wanted to buy. Sawyer tried the shirt on *with the suit,* and he was right: it would coordinate with the girls' outfits perfectly. Reed, on the other hand, came out of the dressing room wearing exactly the same clothes he wore to the store. He handed me the pink shirt and simply said he was *not* doing it. No way, no how. He was not wearing a pink shirt. Sawyer, who really wanted the whole outfit, tried his very best to convince his big brother to relent, but Reed's mind was made up. I don't think I will ever forget what happened next. It was the equivalent of the whopper of childhood persuasion, just like the triple dog dare. The little brother in his best plea said, "Aww! C'mon, Reed. Don't you know pink is the new red?" I thought I was going to die from laughter right there in front of my four children in the Macy's children's department.

My friend had relished this story. She explained as soon as she saw that little bear at Lambeau Field she knew she had to get it. She had carried one of my stories in her heart for years and wanted to do something to say she and her family had not forgotten Reed. As I listened to her share her laughter over this moment, tears pooled in my eyes that she not only remembered but had taken the time to travel down memory lane with me. My friend knew that stories matter and sometimes, just sometimes, they only get better in the retelling. In this case, the music of her heart mixed with my memories. I could clearly picture my girls in their dresses and my boys in green (not pink!) shirts.

Hugs and Kisses

GROWING UP, MY PARENTS MOSTLY SHIELDED US FROM THE chaotic aspects of hurricane season. In the event that we were called to evacuate (which did happen a few times), as kids we knew nothing other than adventure. Usually we packed up a bag of stuff, swung by to pick up Nannie and Granddaddy, and headed on up the road to Mama and Papa's house. I remember one time in high school when we were told to evacuate, we all piled into my grandparents' RV and headed up to Opelika. Rather than natural disaster refugees, we looked like tailgaters ready for an Auburn football game.

About midway to our destination, we phoned my aunt and uncle, who had decided to ride out the storm, and soon we were heading back to Pensacola after hearing a change in the expected landfall location. They confirmed that the new forecast was for the storm to come onto land somewhere in Mississippi or Louisiana. Since we were only halfway to my other grandparents' home, we turned the traveling party (oh yeah, we were playing cards with Nannie and having a good ol' time) around and got back into Pensacola just in time for the hurricane to switch courses once again and head right at us. We waited out the storm at Nannie and Granddaddy's, and it was not the party atmosphere we had in the RV earlier. It was not the worst hurricane in Pensacola history, but it did leave a huge impact in my memory. What other people were doing while I watched lawn furniture go whipping through the neighborhood is something I never thought about.

My children know nothing of the perils of hurricanes, other than my stories and news media. They do, however, understand the craziness known as "a blizzard is coming." As gardeners, outdoorsmen, and

181

4-H'ers, our freezers are usually full, so we don't go to the store when the weatherman predicts another big blizzard. Inevitably, we end up there to pick up one small item and are met with wide-eyed shoppers, baskets overflowing with food, and supplies for storm preparation. I am not saying they are wrong in their thinking, as we have gone as many as thirteen days in frigid cold without power. But I am just not a "sky is falling" kind of girl. We pick up a few supplies, knowing we can whip up something from our freezer. We aren't going to starve, but we might have to get creative for a few days. A little bit can go a long way.

One snowy winter day, Daniel and I were waiting to see if school was going to be closed early. We had a dozen eggs that needed to be used soon, so we boiled them up to make egg salad. I was distracted by then-toddler Cloie and asked Daniel to add the finishing touches to the salad. He chopped the eggs and added the good dollop of mayonnaise, but things went very wrong when he went to season the dish. Something slipped from the saltshaker and instead of maybe a teaspoon of salt, we ended up with more like two tablespoons of salt in the mix. We didn't think the potato trick for a little too much salt in soup would work in egg salad, and frankly, with the wind getting worse by the minute, we didn't want to brave the crazy at the store for more eggs. We just put on our adventuring spirit and tried to bravely go forward. After a couple of bites, we decided that perhaps the Gulf of Mexico would have been less salty! Toast it was, rather than trying to deal with all the people going crazy for the last loaf of bread or gallon of milk in the store.

Just like salt in egg salad, when it comes to tokens of condolences, a little bit can go a long way. Some very dear friends wanted to come and see us following the crash. They were traveling from the town where both Daniel and I went to college. I had the privilege of once being the family's nanny, and the mom and twin girls (now college graduates themselves) were coming to hug us and tell us how much they loved us. Over the years, they had remained part of our adopted family, which included the tables turning and those little girls, now grown, watching my kids on more than one occasion. Their presence was an incredible gift, even if the time they could stay with us was brief.

Many from the town were unable to travel all those miles but sent their offers of sympathy with our friends. One sweet lady sent a lovely note about how much she wished she could come all those miles just to hug us. She was unable to do so, but she put a lot of love and thought into her second choice. She had filled a small metal bucket with Hershey's Hugs and Kisses. It was a small gesture, but this friend is one of the most personable, kind, and sweet people you could ever meet. It was a small gesture but felt like invisible hugs from a bunch of people who were part of my story a long time ago. And that little bit of love went a really long way!

Just Sit Next to Me, Mom

For few years following the bus crash, we would go camping with a pretty large group of friends. We were making steady deposits in the bank of family memories. One of the other mommas and I really hit it off and grew close. While sitting around the campsite one afternoon, we decided we would make great companions for a girlfriends' getaway. Despite the fact that we both love to visit, we mutually respect some quiet time to cuddle up with a good book. Our dream trip (which we still have yet to take) would involve just the two of us heading off somewhere warm with nothing but a bag full of books. We discovered we could be content simply sitting next to each other.

The year Reed was entering sixth grade, our family moved away briefly. Because our move was a few hours away, I gave up my teaching position at the school where our children attended. When we returned three months later, it was almost a breath of fresh air to be a momma— nothing more, nothing less. Instead of a frenetically busy and chaotic momma with lessons to plan and papers to grade, I was a momma much more available to be with my kids. Our nights became much more enjoyable as we had more time to spend together. One evening, Reed was working on homework while I was knitting in the other room.

"Mom, can you sit by me? I don't need your help with my homework, but it would be really nice if you could just sit with me."

Wow! Can I? You bet. I would love to sit with you. And sit I did. Almost every night, when it was time to do homework, there we would be just sitting together, simply soaking in each other's company. When homework was done, some nights we would watch television. We continued this routine every night for both sixth and seventh grades.

Back then, we had basic cable, and during this time the television writers' strike took place, so for the channels we had there wasn't much to watch. One evening after homework, we were cuddled up on the couch together when some reruns of *The Carol Burnett Show* came on. Talk about a blast from the past. I shared with Reed how much I loved watching that show when I was younger. He soaked it all in, being a true fan of physical comedy and a good laugh. When the episode came on where Carol played Scarlett O'Hara and had a curtain rod through the shoulders of her drapery dress, Reed's belly laughter was contagious.

Watching my son laugh out loud to something I had laughed at years ago was priceless. Looking back now, I had no idea how much I would come to treasure those times, because I didn't know how little time we had left together. Sitting side by side with my son, who as a preteen wanted me to be there, is a timeless treasure. I am so thankful that for a brief period I walked away from teaching, because if I hadn't, I would have never had these moments of sharing the same space with him.

I have learned comforting others can often come with no words. Sitting together quietly can be almost as healing as a hug. The physical presence of someone else is both an acknowledgment of your pain and an understanding that there is probably very little they could do to take it away. My dad always told his basketball players they could earn at least a B in a college course just by showing up. His logic was that showing up was the biggest obstacle many college students have. The same can be said about being a friend. Showing up to simply sit with someone is a remarkable gift.

There were many people who did this for Sawyer in the early days, when it was especially difficult for him to get around. One young man would often stop by and just sit with our Boy Wonder. The heavy doses of medications would often have Sawyer wide-awake one minute and knocked out cold for the next hour. Daytime was bad, but the nighttime hours were epically worse. This true friend would sit by Sawyer's side for hours. He was not fazed by Sawyer's moments of sleepiness. He simply wanted to comfort his friend. One night, this sweet young boy captured my heart. He wanted so desperately to sleep over, but we wanted to shield him from the night terrors that plagued us. When we explained that nights were plain horrible, he still wasn't daunted. He looked me straight in the eye and said, "It's okay, Mrs. Stevens. I'll just lay on the floor next to Sawyer, and if he has a really bad moment, he can squeeze my hand."

Stole. My. Heart.

In a completely different way, a dear friend from church came to hold my hand one afternoon when once again the world made absolutely no sense. Following the bus crash, our youth pastor, Andy, whom our children adored, asked if he could start spending regular time with Sawyer. He told Sawyer that he could never be Reed, but he would love to be like a big brother to him. Weekly, he would come and hang out with Sawyer or take him out on one adventure or another. They were a perfect match. Andy had recently bought "Rock Band" for Wii, and the two of them were valiantly trying to improve their score. Right before Sawyer left for his last year at asthma camp, they did, moving from "sucks" to "stinks." They did guy stuff that only guys enjoy, and for a little boy missing his big brother, it was the perfect remedy.

No matter where I am, if an ambulance or air ambulance crosses my path, I stop whatever I am doing and pray for the paramedics, doctors, nurses, the injured or suffering, and all their families. For as long as I have breath, I will say those prayers, because I remember watching all those first responding units go flying by, not knowing that it was for my kids and their friends.

As we drove back into town from asthma camp, the typical calm and quiet of the prairie was replaced by the mournful wail of sirens. My prayer instinct kicked into overdrive. What I didn't know was that I was praying for people I dearly loved, who had been involved a crash eerily similar to ours. When the news reached our house, we were devastated. Several were injured, and Andy—the same Andy who our kids loved watching as a college basketball player, the same Andy who was the best youth pastor ever, the same Andy who had those weekly "man dates" with Sawyer—was gone.

Knowing we would be overwrought with grief, this friend did the only thing she knew to do. She drove down the street and came to sit with me. She was as shocked as we were, and through her pain, she came to comfort us. Sawyer and Andy's relationship was well-known, and I believe she understood that now he would be grieving the loss of two brothers. Her presence was a divine one, bringing comfort just by being there to cry and hold my hand.

Two other friends, one who had known Reed since he was tiny and one who moved into our neighborhood two years following the bus crash, have been constant companions. They both make a concerted effort to just come and console me when needed. So steady is their love, they show up without being asked. And sometimes they arrive within moments of a call for help. We have walked around the park, driven around town, cried in parking lots, and sat on the deck watching the birds in Reed's garden. A love like theirs reminds of me of one of my favorite parts of A. A. Milne's *Winnie the Pooh* book.

> Piglet sidled up to Pooh from behind. "Pooh?" he whispered.
> "Yes, Piglet?"
> "Nothing," said Piglet, taking Pooh's hand.
> "I just wanted to be sure of you."

Just like Reed wanted to be sure of me when he was doing his homework, I don't have to reach very far to be sure of these friends. A better gift would be hard to imagine.

The Crazy Way Traditions Start:
Battling Blue-Hairs in the Dairy Aisle

IT ALL STARTED INNOCENTLY ENOUGH. WELL, IF YOU DON'T count the weather. Our school had been dismissed early due to a blizzard. The white-knuckled drive home was one I will never forget. The seventeen miles between school and home seemed to be much longer as the blustery conditions made visibility near impossible. Thankfully, my children and I were traveling in a caravan of others who, like us, lived and worked in different towns. It wouldn't be the last time I drove in whiteout conditions. This is Minnesota after all. In all honesty, there were times much more harrowing than this one. The memorable factor came from a conversation I had with my "copilot" that day as we slowly trekked back to our home. It was on this day I learned how much little traditions truly define a family.

The conversation started innocently enough. Reed wondered if we were going to embark on our snow day tradition when we finally and safely made it home. I can thank the weather that I needed to have my eyeballs glued to the road, because my perplexed thoughts would have been written all over my face. *Um. Reed. I'm a little distracted here. Can you remind me what our snow day tradition is?*

In only the way he could, he laughed without a care in the world. "Mom, you know the tradition where anytime school gets out for a snow day you make us your famous hot chocolate and homemade chocolate chip cookies." Now I am going to be utterly and completely honest here. Up until that moment, I didn't even know we had such a tradition, but I wasn't going to tell Reed that.

Every family has their traditions—big and small—that truly define who they are. If chocolate chip cookies were going to be ours, a trip to the grocery store (which would be a madhouse reminiscent of World War II rationing) was needed, and I was willing to take my chances with those who thought the world was coming to an end because of a snowstorm. Friends and family from the South, blizzards create the same chaos at stores that hurricanes do. I love people, but I hate crowds. If I was going to join in celebrating this *well-known* family tradition, if nothing else than to acknowledge its very real existence to my redheaded wunderkind, then I was going to have to succumb to dealing with those who want to buy every last gallon of milk and every loaf of bread in the store. The momentary flicker of discomfort was not enough to deter me from stopping by the grocery store, where I quickly grabbed all the necessary ingredients for cookies and Irish hot cocoa. Visions of sugarplums swirling through our heads, the final mile home was the most peaceful. Of course, the plowed roads might have helped quite a bit too.

We quickly got ourselves and the groceries inside. My kiddos could barely contain their excitement as they started to gather all their winter attire to head back out into what most people were rushing home to escape. While they chased down the elusive mitten or snow boot, word of a celebration at the Stevens home must have spread like wildfire on the prairie. Hustling and bustling in the kitchen, thankful to be home and not taken out by the bad roads or little blue-haired ladies in the dairy aisle, I was momentarily distracted from my praise time by a noise outside the patio door. Wiping my hands on my apron, I walked over to see what was causing the commotion on the other side the door, in a world full of frigid temperatures, swirling snow, and howling wind. I somewhat expected the wind to be the cause of the clanging noise. Right now, I am incredibly thankful I looked first before opening the sliding door, because standing there looking at me (I am not making this up) was a possum. Like the chocolate chip cookie tradition, I didn't even know these marsupials lived in Minnesota. Standing on its back legs and lifting the lid to our grill, this super possum turned and looked at me as if I had interrupted his winter wonderland barbeque. I cannot be certain which one of us was more shocked. Just as I called my kids to come see, the possum looked at me with an air of righteous indignation as if to say, "Show's over, lady! I'm outta here!" His hasty exit was punctuated by what I think was a little over-the-top flair, pointy nose held high and pink, scaly tail slithering westward in search of more accommodating environs. Never in my life had I seen a possum that large or uppity.

Meanwhile, back at the coat closet, my kids were still searching for their lost items and never made it in time to corroborate my story. My absolutely 100 percent true story!

Even though the lost snow gear was eventually found, I made my sweet cherubs wait for the cookies and cocoa because I wasn't exactly sure where our gray-furred visitor had ended up. My last up close and personal encounter with a possum was when one stumbled into Nannie and Granddaddy's backyard when I was in the sixth grade. Momma possum, replete with tiny, clinging baby possums, hissed and spit at all us grandkids. I don't remember which one of the boys ran for help, but the rest of us cousins just stood there wide-eyed, wondering why in the world a possum would end up in this neighborhood. Remembering the fight that tiny momma put up when animal control arrived was etched deeply in my memory, and there was no way I was releasing my babes out into the potential harm's way of the snooty super possum, especially one big enough to open a closed grill.

This being Minnesota and all, the third part of the day I never saw coming was when mid dunk (some of the kids like to dunk their cookies in their cocoa), in walked our backyard superhero. Rarely do businesses in Minnesota release employees during bad weather, which more than once has resulted in snowbound refugees camping out for the evening at the local National Guard armory. But on this day full of twists and turns, my husband's workplace decided to let everyone leave early. With him home to protect us, we could enjoy the backyard.

With the whole family home, it didn't take long to polish off a few mugs of cocoa and way more cookies than any of us needed. Family snow day! Sweet freedom! Snow days are infinitely better than the one extra hour of sleep every year when Daylight Savings Time ends. The freedom to have nowhere to be and nothing required to be done elicits feelings of time travel to the carefree days of childhood. This particularly day was no different. The whole family bundled up to play in the snow and enjoy every second of our freedom.

The wet, heavy snow that had bogged down our drive home had become a snow paradise in the backyard. Not all Minnesota blizzards produce snow that is ideal for snowman building. This day of memories, it did! We set forth to recreate Steve—our family's snowman and (before you think I had too many things going on to remember them all) our tradition. I think Steve's first appearance on the scene—the white and blinding scene—came after our boys went through a fascination with all things *Blue's Clues*, but given my whack-a-doodle bunch, the name *Steve Stevens* and the ensuing giggles might have been the origin. Whatever his humble beginnings, Steve comes back each year in various forms. On this particular day, we used up all the snow in the backyard to make two snow creatures. This too is true, because while Steve looked dapper as ever, white and gleaming, Jabba the Snow Hut appeared even more menacing with the traces of forgotten fall leaves sticking out of his large and looming form.

After more mugs of cocoa and later steaming bowls of homemade soup, we all fell into bed wishing we had more days like this one, where battling little old ladies for chocolate chip cookie ingredients seemed to be our biggest concern. Magical ordinary days and unique family traditions will be the legacy we leave for our children. God blesses magical memory-making days.

He also blesses the people who embrace those traditions even when they are not their own. Two of my most often read and reread blogs stem from a tradition from my childhood. The blogs feature my annual letter to the leprechauns, whom my children try each and every year to entice with a very cunningly crafted welcome (a.k.a. trap). You would think for a momma whose recent answer to "What would you consider a peaceful and restful day?" was "A picked up house," that my fascination with the little green men who annually wreak havoc on my normally quaint and quiet existence would be long over. Yet the magic they bring our family is worth much more than their pot of gold waiting at the end of the rainbow.

The St. Patrick's Day tradition is one which dates all the way back to my kindergarten classroom. My tiny classmates and I had never seen our teacher so distraught. As true little Southerners and united in our mission, we were ready to unleash a pound of hurt on whoever had dishonored our teacher when just the moment before we were arguing over who got to enter the classroom first. Our teacher quickly deescalated the situation before one of the boys offered to duel the culprit while several others humbly offered to be the first brave soul's second. Even in kindergarten, honor meant something, and nobody (I say, *nobody*) messes with our teacher. Soon we began to notice the cause of our sweet teacher's alarm.

Our classroom looked like a hurricane had swept through it, even though we were months away from that season. One tiny clue stood out in the disarray of classroom staples. Footprints! Tiny green footprints were everywhere. Our very astute and now pulled-together teacher was very wise, finally deducing the cause of our disaster to be leprechauns. Our pint-sized bodies belied the alacrity we possessed, as we banded together like a tiny brigade of Merry Maids to restore truth, justice, and order to room 1B.

Now all these years later, those same menacing—yet somehow charmingly magical—tiny green men visit my family. Only, the year of the bus crash, all our energy was zapped. Caring for an extremely wounded child, while numbly crawling through the fog of our own grief, stole every ounce of energy we could muster.

While our view of our lives was somewhat myopic, our friends sensed, saw, and felt every ounce of our exhaustion, always offering to step in when we didn't have energy to do one more thing or, oftentimes, a single thing. Our friends came to the rescue as often as we would let them. As March 17 rolled around, other than to go to the doctor's office, we had barely left our home, making any celebration difficult. We were just going to be kind and gentle to ourselves and hope the leprechauns decided to take a cruise to Barbados that year.

But our tiny green friends apparently hadn't earned enough airline miles or didn't realize there were blackout dates for their favorite holiday, because despite the heaviness of their grief, our children announced they were highly anticipating the arrival of their Irish friends. That is children's grief for you. One moment they are distraught, crying their little hearts and eyes out, and the next, they are envisioning how they are going to spend their gold. Thankfully some of our dearest friends—yes, those of Irish heritage—knew exactly what to do. Our kiddos desperately needed to be children who believed in the magic of traditions, again. Fortunately, our friends must have caught a leprechaun or two in their day, because they knew exactly where to find the gold of my children's dreams.

Not all of our friends are fortunate enough to be of Irish descent, but we love them anyway. Despite our melting pot of cultural heritages, one mission which bound us all together was a common love for our children and keeping the traditions they enjoyed alive. Our friends watched as the story of our lives unfolded before them, always looking for a way to help us live up to our once voicemail greeting.

> Thanks for calling. I'm sorry we can't come to the phone right now. We're busy making memories. If you leave us a message, we'll get back to you as soon as we can.

Those same friends remembered a line from one of my St. Patrick's Day blogs.

> Today's childhood is something to be savored.

Much of our belief in that statement stems from the wonderful traditions of our own childhoods. The traditions we hold dear are exactly the ones that make families unique. Oh, and our friends didn't just chase little green men. They boiled dozens of eggs to dye for Easter, they bought pumpkins to carve in the fall, and they took our children Christmas shopping. They showed up with vim and vigor when we were exhausted, and they preserved a slice of childhood for our sweet kiddos. I cannot imagine a better memory than that.

Grandpas-R-Us

Every childhood should be filled with memories of loving people. Mine certainly was. I have so many stories of times spent with friends and family and all the love found in those moments. True to being raised in the South, most of those stories have something to do with food, but not all of them. When we were little, my parents did ordinary things with my brother and me, but they made them feel extraordinary. Nothing beat flying kites in the park on Sunday afternoon or lying on a blanket and looking at the stars. Playing farm in the backyard while my dad grilled supper is still one of my most special childhood memories, and going to the library and swimming pool with our mom is a tradition I passed on to my kiddos.

A smile creeps across my face whenever I think of those times from years ago. There are three moments from my childhood so uniquely special I will treasure them forever. Each moment involved a very important woman in my life who took the time to make me feel as if I were the most loved and important child in the universe.

For as long as I can remember, we spent a week or two with our grandparents in the summer. My parents would drive us down to Pensacola and drop us off at Nannie and Granddaddy's house. They owned a commercial wholesale nursery and summer days began before the sun was up; otherwise, they would roast in the greenhouses. We were usually up about the time they would take a coffee break in the morning. My brother used to love to drink coffee loaded with milk right along with them, but I never developed a liking for coffee. Since my grandparents were in the floral business, their Floridian yard teemed with beautiful flowers. Their front yard had grass, but the backyard was as sandy as the beach. It was ideal for creating elaborate places to play. We would take sticks and draw out rooms for houses, businesses, and exotic places to travel far away. Our cousins would often come over and join in on the fun, as did the little girl who lived across the street who was a year older than me.

Most of the time, we played some version of house. The summer I was eight years old, I was enamored with earrings. Every woman in my family on both sides, except my mother, had pierced ears. My mom's mantra was "If God wanted holes in my ears, he would have put them there." There was zero chance I was ever getting my ears pierced.

Every morning we had a clean slate to start our day of playing, and every day I would have to get properly "dressed" to assume my role as the mom. My getting ready consisted of going to find a blossom from one of Nannie's camellia plants, which I would break off and place above my ear to be my "earrings." Every day. Blossoms for earrings.

One day Aunt Nernie saw my beautiful adornments and asked if I really wanted my ears pierced. I replied with a completely impassioned and enthusiastic "Yes!" Her response was "Well, let's do it!"

To me, it was as if choirs of angels circled the room and flooding light from heaven descended upon us. *Do you mean it? What will my mom say? Can you actually do this? Oh, this can't be happening!*

Aunt Nernie is my mom's baby sister, and from what I understand of family history, she has always been the more daring of the two. She is also the mother of sons, and for many years, I was the only little girl in this family. Almost sensing the internal conversation I was having, I am pretty sure her thoughts were along the lines of "What your momma doesn't know won't kill her."

The next thing I knew, we loaded up in her old VW bug and were off to University Mall a few miles down the road. Into Bojangles we walked. (Well, I kind of floated in with a mixture of anticipation and nervousness because I was pretty sure my momma was going to kill both of us, but I figured if I died in a couple of weeks, at least I would have stylish gold studs to be buried in.) Back in those days, I wasn't much for pain, and getting my ears pierced hurt like nuts. But out into the hot Floridian sun I sashayed, head held up at my first real act of rebellion, tiny flashes of gold sparkling for all to see under my Dorothy Hamill haircut.

Aunt Nernie and I would go on to have many more adventures, but that one act of defiance bonded us for life.

Another aunt on that side of the family made a huge imprint on my heart a few years down the road during my teen years. My mom has one older brother, Uncle Buddy, and Aunt Nernie is her younger sister. My uncle lives over in Louisiana, and even though the physical distance isn't that far, we didn't see him often because of his work in the oil fields. I loved Uncle Buddy, and any time we did see him was always great. Most of our visits were around holidays, especially Christmas, but one year he and his wife at that time, Aunt Linda, came early for Thanksgiving. My late November birthday was always close to Thanksgiving, and Aunt Linda called and asked if I would like to go shopping with her. *Would I?* That was like asking if I wanted to breathe air that day!

We made plans to head to another big mall in Pensacola, Cordova, which at the time was just down the road from our family's home. Aunt Linda was a tiny lady from humble beginnings who had a larger-than-life personality. We spent the afternoon walking around the mall, looking in one store after another. We finally landed in one of my favorite stores, and Aunt Linda did something she had never done before. She told me to go and try on some outfits. At that time, my family's finances were pretty tight as my dad was working as a public school teacher and coach. Florida is a beautiful place to live, but it can also be a very expensive place. So trying on outfits was about as far as I could normally go.

Aunt Linda and I had fun traipsing through the store, picking out one outfit after another to try on. There was one outfit that day I absolutely loved and just plain made me feel radiant. My time in the dressing room came to an end, and I was heading out the front of the store so we could meet up with everyone else for supper. Aunt Linda stopped me and asked which outfit I was taking home. My perplexed eyebrows told her I had no idea what she was talking about.

"Your Uncle Buddy said for me to take you out and to let you buy whatever you wanted."

He did what? When? Is this really happening? Are you sure? I can't ask you to buy this outfit. It's too much!

Aunt Linda wasn't stupid, then or now, and she knew exactly which outfit I wanted. She just marched back to the dressing room attendant, grabbed it from the return-to-the-floor rack, and headed to the checkout counter. I still remember the goose bumps I had that day. I wore that outfit until it was threadbare. Getting the new outfit was special, but having my aunt and uncle go out of their way to invest not only money but time in me was a blessing I never forgot.

Growing up as a child with siblings, I will tell you that having individual time with an adult family member is one of the rarest things ever. Those moments are ones to be savored, wrapped up, and collected.

The third special memory of someone doing that for me actually occurred chronologically in between the great earring moment of my childhood and the great shopping excursion of my teen years.

It happened when my family briefly moved to North Dakota in my junior high years. My dad had accepted a teaching position at a university there and eventually became the head basketball coach. One of his players had a grandmother who lived in town who loved to watch basketball. The only downside to that love of the game was the driving to all the away games. Enter my mom. She volunteered to transport Grandma to and from the games that we would be attending as a family (which meant the ones not too far on a school night). On our very first road trip, my mom was explaining to her that despite all the differences (and trust me: there were a lot) between living in the South and the Midwest, we were all growing accustomed to it. Her only regret was that we were so very far away from family, especially her kids' grandparents. Without batting an eyelash, Grandma said, "We'll just solve that problem. I will be the grandma!" It was a promise she kept until her dying day. That kind of love is revolutionary, and it is truly the kind of love our whole family needed at that moment. Thankfully, Grandma's family understood and they, too, welcomed us into the fold.

Grandma Leone was an amazing woman, with a love for Norwegian heritage and a good Scrabble game. (Do not ever challenge a word she put on the board, because she would be 100 percent correct). Several times she volunteered to watch my brother and me so our parents could get away. On one such occasion, she took us to a pizza place which allowed you to choose three toppings. Having been a former schoolteacher, she handled this decision in the most democratic way. We each got a vote! This on the surface seemed like a good plan, until we had a

Canadian bacon (my choice), pineapple (my brother), and sauerkraut pizza. While her taste buds might have been questionable, she was an amazing Christian lady who loved the Lord and serving others.

One day, I received a call from Grandma Leone asking if I could solve a problem for her. I was puzzled before I had even heard her dilemma. She had an event at her church, and since her other granddaughter about my age lived so far away, she was wondering if I would be interested in being her guest at a "Mother-Daughter Tea" at her church. I happily agreed because even though I wasn't fond of her pizza topping selection, I loved just being with her. She always made us feel included and loved. She came and picked me up in her big red car, complete with a stuffed white cat in the rear window, making it impossible for her to pick the wrong car in the parking lot. As we drove into town, we chattered about what was new in our lives. At some point, she asked if I could grab something from the backseat for her. The only thing I saw was a medium-sized white box with an elaborate bow. I grabbed the box and tried to hand it to her.

"I must be mistaken, dear. I think that is for you." Unsure what to do or say, I held the box in my lap as we headed toward the church. "I would love for you to open it," she encouraged me. I carefully untied the bow and lifted the lid to reveal a beautiful teacup and saucer, ornately decorated. Other than ones with imaginary supplies, this was my first tea party, and I had no idea what to expect. Having my own cup and saucer was an amazing gift. It made the day that much more memorable for me. I still have that teacup and saucer all these years later.

I share all these stories not because they are truly about earrings, outfits, and teacups. Rather, they are about the love I felt when someone invested in me. I can only hope that my own children remember the people who did the same things for them in the weeks and months following the bus crash.

There were gifts ranging from handmade sweaters to custom NFL jerseys and from teddy bears to gift cards. They are too numerous to mention. Others gave love in the form of service. There were those who came to just sit with Sawyer because he wasn't able to do much more than that. Others planned special lunches at school with Erin, because early on, she was somewhat lost in the shuffle. Another offered to watch Cloie when Sawyer was rehospitalized and the stay was much longer than we thought it would be. Every single person who invested time in our grieving kids was a part of their healing. They were the living embodiment of God's love to some very broken-hearted little people and their parents.

Sadly, all the things we had done with our children prior to the crash were put on the back burners while we were focused on just surviving. Thankfully, friends saw this and stepped in as they could. One of the times that stand out most poignantly for me was during one of my driving times. Due to the fact that Sawyer was being treated by two hospital systems in two different states, there were days that I would get up and load him, medications, wheelchair, and some fun stuff in the van and drive the ninety miles to see the orthopedic surgeon in Sioux Falls, drive home, replenish supplies, and drive the four hours to the Mayo Clinic in Rochester to see the rehabilitative doctors. It was a lot of miles, but I was willing to do whatever it took to help Sawyer heal. With all the time spent at therapies and hospitals, a special day at our school snuck up on us.

Annually, our school hosts a day inviting grandparents to visit the school for a special lunch and usually a preview of the evening music concert. On this particular day, Erin didn't have any of her grandparents or "adopted" grandparents available. I knew that we would be traveling to the hospital on that day, but I didn't want her to feel neglected. In desperation, I called our church secretary and told her the situation, asking if there would be anyone in the church who could step in to help us out that day. She said she would certainly try but wondered if I had any ideas on who to ask first. I gave the name of the one man who in recent months our children had gotten to know and who is the quintessential teddy bear of a man. He was involved in leading worship at our church and was a huge Chicago Bears fan who, stereotypically, reminded me of the characters in the 1980s "Da Bears" skits on Saturday Night Live. I left it at that and kept on driving down the road to Rochester.

I think it was ten minutes later when my cell phone rang. After answering, I heard a booming voice on the other end. "Well, hello. This is Grandpa Dave from Grandpas-R-Us. I was just calling to learn more about this wonderful experience I am going to have with Erin." Right there, he melted my heart. He could have just asked when and where to be, but instead he projected so much love, enthusiasm, and care into two sentences. I choked back the tears as I explained all the details. True to form, when the day arrived, Grandpa Dave didn't miss a thing. He brought a camera, documenting all they did that day from lunch to tour of the school to playing on the playground, and of course the musical selections the third graders had prepared. Erin felt loved and honored and special all wrapped up in a bear hug!

Thankfully, this wasn't just a "Rent a Grandpa" situation. He has stayed in contact with all three of our kids over the years, even after moving away. His steadfast love and support has meant the world to them and to us. Someday, I hope their "earring" story starts with "I got one of my grandpas at 'Grandpas-R-Us.'"

Where Is That List?

FORGETFULNESS IS SOMETHING I COME BY NATURALLY. Unfortunately, grief has a way of compounding this particular problem by clouding thoughts even more. I lose my glasses (seriously, I don't know how I do this because I need them to be able to see), my keys, my favorite lip gloss, important papers, my purse, and about a dozen other things. Most recently, I left my cell phone on the airport shuttle bus, which cost me a pretty penny to have shipped to me on vacation. My sweet husband should have realized what he was in for during the drive to Yellowstone National Park from North Dakota on our first vacation. After a wonderful evening spent in a cabin at a KOA campground in Cody, Wyoming, we were ready to experience the wonders of the park. We drove the hour-long, winding but breathtaking route to the east entrance. All was well until we reached the park's gates and couldn't find my regular glasses. Because my eyes are extremely sun sensitive (a trait I passed on to Reed), I require prescription glasses and sunglasses. I never embraced transition lenses, so I am forced to carry a case with one pair or the other at all times. We scoured every inch of our car and were forced to retrace our steps (or miles in this case) back to Cody. My husband was nothing but patient, understanding that I really could not go about the lodges in sunglasses at night. Well, I could, but it would look rather strange. We retraced our steps to all of the locations we had visited that morning, which were thankfully few. Nothing. Nada. No trace. No one had seen them.

This was long before the advent of cell phones, so we drove around looking for a pay phone to call our optometrist back home, praying that we would find a one-hour eyeglass location in cowboy country. The odds were not in our favor. We eventually found a pay phone in a grocery store parking lot, and while I was punching in numbers from a phone card (oh good gravy, remember those things?), my sweetie did one last car check out of nothing but sheer desperation.

When I turned to face out of the phone booth (another one of those things our kids will likely never encounter), I saw my husband of one year hold up my glasses case. It had been hiding between the passenger seat and the center console the entire time. I am so thankful I married a patient man, because that was only the first of many things that I would lose or leave behind.

A friend recently posted on her Facebook page a meme that frankly sums up most of my shopping excursions.

> I like to make lists. I also like to leave them laying on the kitchen counter, then guess what's on the list while at the store. Fun game.   —SnarkEcards

My response to her post was "All. The. Time." She is a dear friend, who has also walked in the shoes of a grieving parent, but more than that, God has shown us that we are really cut from the same cloth on many things. When I post quirky items, she really understands where I am coming from.

As challenging as the "What's on my list?" game can be, going to the store following a tragic loss is almost impossible. Mix together grief brain, muddied thoughts, a penchant for distractedly leaving your list at home, and the uncomfortable feeling of just going back out and living, and you are left without much of anything, particularly a successful trip to the store. In our case, Sawyer's care was round the clock for a very long time, and doing anything beyond meeting everyone's basic needs was exhausting. List making we could handle, but getting out the door for anything other than medical appointments and school or church would wipe us out.

I have been blessed with amazing friends who see things long before I realize they are even an issue. On a regular basis, we would get a call stating, "Hey! I was just coming into town (from the farm or from a neighboring town without a grocery store). I was wondering if there was anything on a list that I could pick up for you at the store."

I have been and shall remain a fairly independent person, but with very little extra energy to go around, I accepted the help I never thought I would need. Thankfully, a few years back, I had a conversation with a very good friend from our church who helped me realize how much we all need each other.

My friend, who led a Bible group at my church, was using an example in one of our group discussions. This friend has an incredibly witty sense of humor. She was sharing once about how she was trying to reach her husband at work (again, long before cell phones). It had been an exasperating day and she just needed his assistance. Rather than realizing her guy was going to be her knight in shining armor, she was getting more and more annoyed by her inability to reach him. Her annoyance turned to frustration after several unsuccessful phone calls. Eventually, the company's receptionist placed her on hold. While listening to the music, a message broke through explaining that if you are unable to reach your party, press 0 for assistance. As she was pressing 0, she blurted something about her husband being a zero in this story. Suddenly, she felt convicted by God to remember all the ways her husband had helped her through multiple life challenges and health crises. The conviction didn't end there. God also opened her eyes to how many times she had shrugged off an offer for help from a friend, family member, or member of our church. She was highly successful, upwardly mobile, and had the world by the tail. She believed she had it all under control and felt she would be a nuisance asking for or accepting help. Then she was reminded that God calls us to a body of believers. If she turned down help, then she wasn't allowing someone else to be God's blessing that day.

It was a powerful lesson that has never left me.

What I learned from her is that all the times I have been able to help someone else were less about me and more about the humble acceptance of a friend or stranger. My opportunities to be a blessing had been plenty, and thankfully the recipients allowed me to live out God's will for me that day. Now it was my turn to humble myself and receive the blessings from others.

It never seemed to fail that just as we really needed something from the store, the phone or doorbell would ring. It became second nature to gratefully and humbly accept the help, although most days it would have been much easier to do if I could have remembered where I put that list.

I Always Dreamed of Having a Rosie

WHEN WE WERE LITTLE, MY BROTHER AND I WATCHED A LOT OF cartoons, particularly on Saturday mornings before cleaning house and eating tuna fish sandwiches. One of our favorites was *The Jetsons*. My love of science and engineering was really piqued thinking about what the world would be like in the future. Our love of the show carried into our later lives. My brother's first dog was named Cogswell, and the moment we broke down and bought a Roomba iRobot vacuum, I christened her Rosie. All those Saturday mornings of my childhood were spent daydreaming about how awesome it would be to someday have a maid just like the one the Jetsons had. After each child we brought home and the exponential volume of laundry accompanying each one, I continued to wish technology would catch up to my imagination. Sadly, many of my friends now refer to laundry at my home as if it has earned a spot on a "cartographer's best" map. While I do appreciate this is a First World problem, I often do battle with Mt. St. Laundry. Taking a page from another animated favorite, *Superfriends*, MSL is the archenemy to my Supermom!

The offers for help often felt otherworldly as the never-ending to-do list became my Kryptonite keeping me from ever accomplishing much at all, other than surviving on most days. There were times when friends stepped in to do tasks that would have never been accomplished without assistance. One friend took on the task of sorting through all the medical bills and prioritizing who needed to be paid. My prayer group helped with addressing and mailing the countless number of thank-you cards. Another friend still comes to visit and ends up tackling one or more jobs that just never seems to get accomplished.

She would probably take the comparison to Rosie as a badge of honor, but her help in a really sad time was astronomically helpful. My cousin—well, actually it is our husbands who are cousins—has cheered my family on every step of the way. Auntie Ellen, as my kids call her, is a teacher just like me. When Sawyer and I were living at St. Mary's hospital, we would regularly receive cards and letters from her students at Midway School. While we are part of the same family, we really didn't know each other that well until a phone call came one beautiful summer day.

Ellen called and said she just *had* to come and help. She didn't care what we asked her to do, but she was coming and we were to begin making lists of where we needed help. Her thinking correct, there was plenty to do around here, but I didn't even know where to begin. The insistence in her voice caused my eyes to pour out what my heart was feeling. She had two little ones at home, but she had made arrangements because nothing was stopping her.

Looking over the calendar, we both decided the week right before the county fair would be the most helpful time all summer. I'm not too proud to admit it, but many of our children's final touches on 4-H projects are done in the last minutes leading up to judging days. That summer was no different. All the loose ends were never going to be tied together without help. Auntie Ellen arrived with extra energy (that this momma did not have) and jumped in, helping put the finishing touches on every single project. She came to love and to serve, and she did both beautifully. She put photos in frames, glued, painted, shellacked until every inch of her was covered in what looked like a Pinterest eruption. The bigger the mess, the more she relished cleaning it up.

Once judging day rolled around, she painstakingly loaded every project into the van and stood in line holding the ones that wouldn't balance on a wheelchair. The heat of a metal show barn didn't deter her enthusiasm for keeping her promise to just come and love us.

In *The Jetsons*, Rosie would often help Elroy and Judy with various projects. Auntie Ellen isn't exactly Rosie. She was much better, especially as she held my hand as we submitted the one project that had been completed the previous fall when the garden harvest was ripe and bountiful. Tearfully, she held me close as we handed over one jar of

Reed's "Sweet and Spicy" salsa, which he had proudly made and which eventually walked away with a Grand Champion Ribbon.

Another time things were starting to get pretty rough around the house, it was advertised through our church that there would be a garden work day in our backyard. Our youth group wanted to be a part of remembering Reed and helping us with some pretty labor-intensive work. It was only supposed to be youth group leaders and members, so I was surprised when a knock came at the door and there were a few ladies from our church standing there, gloves and cleaning supplies in hand.

One lady explained they would not be much help hauling and placing garden bricks, so they had come to clean my house. I was so embarrassed because it was a disaster. They didn't care. They simply saw how much we were trying to help the kids heal while all of us were grieving. They showed up and took charge. They swept and dusted and washed and shined. Our home sparkled when they were done. The sacrifice of their time and the love they invested was more than we could have ever dreamed possible.

Again, not Rosie, but the love shared was more than a robot could give any day!

My Husband Thinks I Am Preparing for an Ark

I HAVE ALWAYS LOVED ANIMALS. ALL ANIMALS. OKAY, MAYBE not fire ants. My Nannie and Granddaddy once had a weekend place we called the Fish Camp down in Caryville, Florida. The trip there always seemed to take forever, but once we arrived, we were in another world full of alligators, electric eels, snapping turtles, beavers, snakes, bugs of all sorts, and baby frogs. Almost all my stories of growing up at the Fish Camp, which was really a canal system with trailers built up on stilts because the gators were thick in those parts, involve one animal encounter or another.

The best part about going to the Fish Camp was seeing my cousins, Joey and Jimmy, who were often there too. Along with my brother and me, all of us cousins spent most of our days adventuring around those backwoods. One time our investigations took us a piece down the road. We had explored every inch of the meadow closest to the camp and had grown bone weary from it. Joey and I spotted an old log sitting in a clearing. In our elderly wisdom, or bossiness, we decided our little brothers were not fit to sit upon that log. While they camped on the sandy ground, we enjoyed being the royalty on the log, until we noticed our skin was crawling, literally. Every inch of us, scalp to toe, was covered in ants—fire ants. We hooted and hollered all the way back to the camp. Our howling preceded us, and our parents and grandparents came running to our rescue. We spent the next few days nursing our wounds, mostly soaking in oatmeal baths while our little brothers were free to enjoy the outdoors and play with Nannie's collection of Weebles. After that experience, I was never a fan of the fire ant again. Of course, all these years later our little brothers still bring it up. Sometimes, it doesn't pay to be the queen.

211

Although there were many adventures with animals at the Fish Camp, not all of them ended with excruciatingly painful acidic bites covering my body. One of my favorites was a time when only my parents and grandparents were there. This was back in the days when we played hard outside all week and made sure to take a really good bath on Saturday evening before church on Sunday. This particular time, we happened to be at the Fish Camp with our Mom while the rest of the adults were fishing on the Big River. She decided that we should get our baths early because it was her job to drive down and pick up most of the adults before we all headed into town for supper. Being a good momma, she thought she had this bathe-the-kids plan all wrapped up. Sparkling clean and dressed in some of our best going-to-town-clothes, we arrived at the Big River just as a major run of fish was coming through. None of the adults were ready to leave because they were catching 'em as fast as they could reel 'em in. Such is the life on the river; plans change. My brother and I were left to do what we normally did: explore.

Now before you think that my parents were crazy to let two little kids wander around without adult supervision in a place crawling with gators and snakes, just know that we lived in a different time, when parents let kids be kids. We knew it was time to come home when the city whistle blew or the streetlights came on. We were never far away, we hardly ever played inside, and we had the general sense to stay away from things that harmed us.

On that particular hot and steamy afternoon, our adventures led us to a moss-covered trail that wound its way to a small creek which fed into the river. Cooled by the mist of the creek and the tall shade trees, we made the best discovery of the trip: tiny baby frogs (my favorite animals) everywhere. There were hundreds of them. We watched and caught them then put them back. We played back there for a long time before sharing with the adults what we had found. I would have loved to keep one or two, but I knew our parents would never let us.

By the time we made our way back to the fishermen and women (Nannie *loved* to fish), we were getting hot, and they had no intention of quitting anytime soon. (Meal times were not centered on us kids back then either. A lot has changed in a few generations.) A little more exploring and just down the hill from where the fish were biting was the boat launch. I heeded the warning to not get us or our clothes dirty (because our momma meant what she said), but my brother could not resist the lure of that cool, muddy water. His pleading finally wore our mother down. She acquiesced as long as we didn't go in past our knees. The first step was so cool and refreshing with the water lapping just over our toes. The second step went just past our ankles. I decided that was probably about as far as we should go. My little brother had very different plans because his next step was just far enough to be where the boats would drop safely into that river. The next step for that tiny little guy came up to his eyeballs standing up. He just stood in the water and cried. He knew he was in trouble for exceeding his limit, but thankfully the same momma who meant what she said also has a good sense of humor. She, like everyone else, just laughed, and my brother knew he was safe. Looking back, maybe we should have just kept on frogging.

My love of exploring nature and loving animals has never really died down. When we were first dating, Daniel and I went to visit a miniature bunny farm with his sister and niece. While we were there, we decided to purchase our first pet together. This should have been his first clue as to my love of animals, but I don't think he saw what his future held until many years down the road. My parents were less than enthused when I came home with a bunny, but Daniel took the time to build Annabelle her first home away from the farm. All was going well until the pair of bunnies his niece had picked out, Fred and Wilma, were done in by the family dog. We were so heartbroken for her we offered Annabelle as a replacement, complete with his master builder rabbit hutch (read: definitely dog proof).

Over the years, I have drug home one stray animal after another, and sometimes our animals have done the same for us. Our first dog loved to find baby animals. After a few encounters with baby skunks, we thought Bubba, a German shorthaired pointer, had learned his lesson. We could not have been more wrong. One spring, he found several rabbit holes on the farm where we were living and brought his treasures home. He was an excellent hunting dog with a really soft mouth. I was pregnant with Reed and was astounded to open the door to find four nearly hairless, crying baby bunnies on my front step. Bubba, with the face of an angel, seemed to say, "Look, Mom! Look what I found! Aren't they great?"

Despite being a gigantic hunting dog, he always had a soft side. He couldn't stand to hear those baby rabbits cry any more than I could, so he laid down next to his little buddies. Several had already passed away, but two were still hanging in there. I had no idea where they came from, and even though I needed to get to work, I couldn't just leave them to die. I wrapped them up in an old towel and drove into town to the vet's office. The vet just shook his head and said to try to feed them with a dropper but that nature was probably just going to do her job in this case.

Sadly, they didn't live for more than a couple weeks, and my husband was not impressed that we were paying to take care of garden pests. Shortly after their passing, we learned Daniel's beloved Aunt Lou had lost her courageous battle with lung cancer. On our drive to North Dakota for her services, an otter ran out in front of me. I cried because despite doing everything I could to avoid hitting it, I still did. My husband asked, not all that nicely, if I wanted to go back and try to rescue it too. If I'd thought it would do any good, I certainly would have tried. In his defense, between the science experiments in the kitchen and the animals I've loved, he has had to bear it all.

What can I say? I simply love animals and the joy they bring to the world. Our family pets over the years have been as beloved as children. Each has had their own personality, and the love they have given back has been a big part of our family's story. In the immediate aftermath of the bus crash, the scene at the school was chaotic at best. If you know nothing about small towns and small town truisms, this one is 100 percent positively true: *word travels fast*. In fact, word traveled so fast that day that others knew our children were hurt before we did. All telephone lines and cell phone circuits were completely busy. The grapevine was hard at work that day.

Despite having known his children for many years, that was the first day I met one of the daddies from the bus. I will never forget that I was frantically trying to reach my husband and I could not get a call out. This sweet man walked over and handed me his cell phone, telling me he had a connection, and I was finally able to get a call to my husband's work. I don't think it was more than a few minutes later when a former student who is like one of my children (our families are that close) somehow got a call in to my phone. His request was simple. "I know your kids are involved. What can I do to help you?"

Even though Josh was in college, he was someone I trusted explicitly with my home, my children, and my animals. I explained that the situation wasn't looking good and that most likely we were heading to a hospital somewhere. The first thing he offered was the thing I didn't even think we needed. "Can I take care of your pets?"

A quick yes was all he needed. For all the days we were gone to the hospital, I knew I didn't have to worry that our animals were starving for food or attention. He had it under control.

It became very apparent following our brief stay at home that our cats and their natural curiosity were going to be too much for a boy writhing with unending nerve pain. The two feline friends were so used to jumping from chair to couch to seek attention from one of us that the mere sight of them hurling through the air simply was too much for Sawyer. Anything or anyone touching his left leg or foot was unbearable, and how do you explain that to a cat? After his doctors confirmed he would most likely live with that pain for years, we knew we needed to find a place for our cats, Shadow and Rescue, to live for a while. A wonderful, selfless couple from our church offered to take them in. (These were the same sweet people who once when both Daniel and I had terrible stomach flu came and took care of our three children under the age of four one night, and the parting gift they received was the stomach flu.) The girls lived with them until it became abundantly clear that the prediction of years of recovery for Sawyer was going to be accurate. Heartbreakingly, we made the decision to find both our rescued girls (one from the golf course and the other from the engine of a truck driven into town) a new home. We all cried when we said good-bye, but it was the best decision we could make for everyone involved.

Every time since those immediate days, whenever a surgery or procedure has arisen that takes us away from home, someone in our beloved circle of friends has stepped up to take care of our pets. It may not seem like much to others, but to us, having the animals we love very much being well taken care of has relieved some of the stress and burden we faced. At times, our pets saw what no one else did. They saw the anguished cries, the desperate prayers, the late nights spent on the couch because of the *I can't sleep because this can't really be my life* moments. They see the tears of sadness, joy, and laughter and have been ever-faithful companions and friends.

Having someone love them, even if only for a moment, has been a true gift!

You've Got to Get Out of Town

FOR MANY YEARS, OUR FAMILY DIDN'T HAVE CABLE TELEVISION. For the bargain price of around nine dollars a month, we had access to basic local channels and a few superstations. That was it. During most of that time, our children were allowed to watch public broadcasting cartoons and preselected videos. There were a couple of old TV shows they loved to watch: *The Andy Griffith Show* and *The Little Rascals*. I almost died from laughter the night that my husband graduated with his master's degree and we spent the evening celebrating with his sister's family. That evening's entertainment was taking six kids swimming at the YMCA. We live life in the fast lane.

As we were waiting a few minutes for the car to warm up that freezing December night, I remember hearing a conversation all four big boys were having. From oldest to youngest, the span was thirty-three months of age difference, the oldest two in third grade and the younger two in first. They were talking about what movie they wanted to watch for their "late-night snack fest." They were all debating which would be the best choice when Reed blurted out, "Hey, guys, we have to watch *Andy Griffith*, because Don Knotts is the best comedic actor ever!" That was Reed, an old soul in a tiny body! I don't even remember if that was the movie they watched, but I do remember his impassioned plea.

Mama Cloie had given my boys about 102 *Andy Griffith* videotapes, and I think Nannie Katie had given them a few as well, adding *The Little Rascals* into the mix. One of their favorite episodes from the latter was one we gave them for Valentine's Day. Because the restaurants in our little town are packed on that February day and I detest crowds, we have always opted to stay home and have a family celebration with a date night on another day. The year we gave them the video, we chose to have a picnic supper with candles on the family room floor and watch the show together.

In the episode, the gang learns that their beloved teacher is going away for Christmas break, and when they return, a Mrs. Somebody will be coming back. The rascals misunderstand that their teacher "Miss" is getting married and will be coming back as a married woman with a new name. The kids hatch a plan: go to the engagement party and break up their beloved teacher and her beau. But of course, this plan has its own hijinks because they decide to create another boyfriend who comes to steal Miss Teacher away. To accomplish this, they get a large overcoat and have a mustachioed and fedora-wearing Spanky stand on the shoulders of two others, pretending to be the other love interest. Eventually, the rascals have their chance, and they corner the betrothed groom, telling him, "You stole my girl! Now you gotta get out of town!" Fits of laughter erupted from the basement that night. Our kids just howled at that scene, which of course, caused Daniel and me to burst into giggles. Laughter is always good medicine.

Apparently so are respites and vacations. It really is true, because God gave us clear instructions to follow his lead and observe a Sabbath rest. So much in the world is about hurrying up and accomplishing more, which for many years summed up our life. This harried, frenetic pace of life was even more exaggerated during the early months of grief, especially with all the doctoring we needed to do for the other kids. We were bone tired and weary, often going through the motions without even realizing how worn out we really were.

We may not have seen it, but others around us certainly did. Although it wasn't Spanky on Alfalfa's shoulders, the message was about same. "You've done too much! Now you've got to get out of town!"

Our sweet pastor, who embodies the spunk of the gang, was the one to tell us of a plan hatched by our church family. Unbeknownst to us, several had pooled their money and made us reservations for a few days at a hotel in Sioux Falls, arranged for one family among them to keep our kids, and gave us a bit of pocket money to spend on a nice supper for our anniversary. They implored us to go and not call every two minutes, but most importantly, to spend time together and make it memorable.

I'm not certain what happened that weekend was exactly what they all had in mind. After doing a little sightseeing, we decided to jump onto the interstate to return to our hotel before heading out to eat. There was a huge motorcycle rally going on and the traffic was at a standstill on the freeway. The next thing we knew, law enforcement cars were screaming alongside our vehicle, surrounding us and the vehicle in front of us. Guns drawn, they dealt with whatever police business was involved while we were stuck behind them, front row seats to the action as if we were a film crew.

We had planned to go out to dinner and then to one of our all-time summer favorites: a minor league baseball game. Due to that delay, we decided instead of being late to the game, we would just merge dinner and the baseball game into one. After a quick rest and time to get ready, we headed off to the ball diamond. I am definitely certain our friends were not envisioning hot dogs when they bid us adieu for the weekend, but somehow that dinner was just perfect for us. Well, sort of perfect. Even though we didn't go out for a lovely dinner, we were still a tad bit late arriving at the Bird Cage, home of our favorite minor league team: the Sioux Falls Canaries. We found our lower level seats about the time one of our boys hit a home run, at which point my sweetie forgot he was holding a full ballpark beverage. A flicker of whooping it up left his wife of fifteen years (on that day) wearing a very drenched outfit the rest of the game.

Well, the least I can say is it was definitely memorable!

The gift was so much more than just the monetary value we could place upon it. Our church family took care of all the logistics: reservations, childcare, and the funds to do it all. Sometimes, since the bus crash, I have had days when I feel like I am doing all the heavy lifting. There are days when the minutia of life has a chokehold on my existence. It was a gift immeasurable to have someone else tackle the details, giving me and my husband a rest. Priceless and memorable, even if it involved eating hot dogs!

Just a Little Note

I'VE SHARED THIS STORY DOZENS OF TIMES WHILE SPEAKING AT women's conferences, but it was a profound moment for me, even if it occurred in the most unlikely of places. One evening while I was teaching a night class at the university, my sweet tea had finally caught up with me. During the evening break, I practically raced to the closest restroom, which happened to be one of the large private wheelchair-accessible sorts. To this day, I don't know how I missed the bright pink Post-it note stuck prominently on the bathroom window. Well, okay, that is only half true; my vision was singularly focused on one task, clouding my vision of the neon note waiting for me. When I was washing my hands, I began to read the beautiful words penned upon it.

The message was concise, but it changed my life forever. Thank God for sweet tea! Written in simple penmanship was

> I may never have the chance to meet you, but today I want you to know that you are absolutely beautiful.

Truth be told, after running like a maniacal circus act to the bathroom, I was looking and feeling anything but beautiful. As a grieving momma with three busy kids, I often just looked tired but saved exhausted for my evening apparel. I am not too proud to admit that I stood in the bathroom with tears running down my cheeks. Thank goodness I had used waterproof mascara that afternoon, because I am sure mascara-stained tear streaks would have only added to my beauty at that moment.

I still don't know who left the note, but I did learn a little more from a website scrawled in tiny letters across the bottom of the note. The founder of this note-leaving movement did so in hopes of stopping women from sending themselves negative body messages, which is something our media-saturated culture is already quite adept at doing to young girls and women of all ages. If what I felt after wiping away my tears is any indication, her movement worked, because I left that corner bathroom on the second floor with a spring in my step and a smile on my face.

Something so little (seriously, it was just ink on a three-inch square of paper with some glue) was transformational. And although they weren't messages about my beauty, random notes would arrive in our mailbox that often lessened the sting of grief. It inspired me to want to do the same for others.

There were countless cards and notes that told us the sender was thinking of us. Some were signed, others anonymously sent. Many arrived around milestones like Reed's birthday or the anniversary of the bus crash, but others were simply short messages of encouragement that told us the giver was thinking of us, remembered a story about Reed, or were touched by something in my blog or on one of our CaringBridge sites.

In the aftermath of the crash, the community did their best to provide comfort for the families waiting to learn what was happening or had happened to their children. Pastors were called in. One such gentleman, a local pastor and father of two of my children's classmates, came and sat with me for a while that awful day. I remember very little about what he said that night, but I do remember the notes with heartfelt encouragement he sent for years to follow.

His words and those sent by so many others were a continual reminder of God's faithfulness in the storm.

A little paper, a little ink, a little time, and maybe even a stamp can make a huge impact on the life of someone else, especially when they are grieving.

The Red Bed

Taking one of the biggest risks of my life, I only applied to one graduate school during my senior year of college. Having grandparents who lived in the neighboring town, "War Eagle" was more than just a saying at Saturday ball games. Being an Auburn fan ran deep in my veins. I took that gamble, hoping my dream would come true. As a chemistry major who worked her tail off to earn good marks, my leap of faith paid with rich dividends when I was not only accepted but offered the prestigious Patricia Roberts Harris fellowship (read: full ride). Title IX and being a girl in an underrepresented science field also paid off. Yep, I got paid to go to graduate school. When my brother and I arrived at our grandparents' house in my first vehicle, a little Ford Ranger pickup truck with a used topper on it, I basically had some kitchen items, clothes, books, and a few household decorations.

Mama and Papa had spoken with Nannie and Granddaddy, and between them, they were putting together a bed and mattress for me. We would pick up the mattress in Pensacola, and Papa and I would go exploring in the barn for an old metal bed frame which he had picked up when the neighbors, the Baileys, had passed away and their kids didn't want any of their old furniture. As a little girl, I remember visiting the elderly couple when I was out helping in the garden.

It didn't take us long to find the rusted iron bed frame in the rafters of the barn. We loaded it up and rode on down to Tuskegee to visit Papa's body shop guy, who was located back in the woods. Papa and I had a nice conversation on the way to get the bed sandblasted and painted. He told me I could pick any color I wanted, which, of course, was *not* true. Oh, I could pick any color, but expect the wrath of Southern gentility

223

if it didn't meet with his expectations. We walked into the old barn turned body shop, and the proprietor told me to go pick a color from the various paint chips he had hanging on the wall. I walked back with a beautiful, shiny, metallic red that I later learned was Porsche red. I thought Papa was going to faint. He tried all of his persuasive techniques to get me to change my mind, but I wouldn't budge. Red was and still is my favorite color. I knew it was going to look great, but my selection seriously offended his decorating senses. I loved Papa, but he lived life on the bland side. The entire drive home, I heard one lecture after another about how I was ruining a piece of history. It was a *long* drive back to the supper Mama had waiting for us.

The lecture continued even after we got out of his old green truck. He walked into the house announcing how I was going to be the death of him and how he would need to bring a stack of blankets when we went to pick it up so that he would not die from the shame the neighbors would surely inflict upon him. Woe was he! I did my best to avoid the topic with him, but secretly, Mama told me she thought red would be a nice color.

The day arrived to go pick up the bed, and true to his word, the back of the truck was piled with blankets and quilts of all sorts. Mama came along for the ride. I'm not sure if she came for my protection or her own entertainment, but either way, it was the three of us bouncing down back roads for the big reveal. When we arrived, the owner had the bed all set up, polished and sparkling. Papa took one look and realized she was as pretty as a hot rod coming fresh off a Detroit assembly line. He was smitten. He loved every red square inch of her. Suddenly the blankets became cushioning pads rather than coverings. He asked the boys at the shop to set the bed up in the flatbed of his truck so all could see her grandeur as we rode back home. Strutting like a peacock, he walked a little taller as we took one detour and pit stop after another to parade that truck all over central Alabama. My disgraceful choice morphed into his best idea, and who was I to argue with his logic?

A similar situation happened when it came to Reed's final resting place. As much as we love our community, we have never felt that it would be our final home. Someday, we hope (maybe after we retire) to move closer to one of our families. When Reed died, we had a multitude of decisions to make. Cremate or bury? And if we buried him, where should we do it? Sawyer was still in intensive care when we began our planning via conference call. Our pastor helped coordinate the call with hospital staff as we spoke with the funeral director back in our hometown. We left with some very rudimentary plans and everything else up in the air because Sawyer's release date was still tentative. Our heads were swirling with what to do, and we decided, as much as we loved Reed, so too did his siblings. We asked for a time of privacy, and we left the choices to them. We explained our thoughts and feelings not to persuade them but to at least give them some foundations. In the end, Sawyer and Erin (Cloie was just too little to understand) chose that Reed would be buried in North Dakota next to Daniel's dad. Reed loved North Dakota, and the cemetery is in a beautiful field, with waving grain surrounding it and wildlife of all sorts visiting throughout the year.

Normally, due to the amount of snow cover (which that particular winter was substantial), burials are held off until the spring in the northern climates. Our North Dakota family pulled some miracles off to allow us to bury Reed at the end of February. Waiting until the spring would have been simply too painful.

We buried our child and went back home the next day because Sawyer had to get back for therapy. In the days following the crash, our mailbox was flooded with cards and letters of sympathy and support. One family from Iowa mailed us a letter telling about a biblically based grief recovery program they had attended that really helped them following the death of their daughter on her graduation day. The couple explained they had heard stories of our faith and of Reed's faith, and they felt compelled to tell us about GriefShare. They were right about the healing nature of that program, and a few years later, we became hosts of a local group. I have no idea whatever possessed them to do this, but they closed the letter with some pictures. I am guessing their own experience with losing a child led them to know that one thing grieving people strongly desire is authenticity—in relationships and in comfort. One picture was of their sweet girl's senior photos, another was of her on her motorcycle, and the third was of her headstone with a colorized bronze marker featuring pictures of their daughter. As soon as I saw it, I knew that is what I wanted for Reed.

Yet no one locally had ever heard of it. Some even went so far as to tell me it couldn't be done. Others tried to talk me into settling for something less than what my heart desired. If Papa were alive, he could have told them I wasn't going to budge. I would wait forever if I had to, but I was not going to choose something to mark my son's life that didn't adequately tell the world his story.

Our North Dakota family, who all live in and around the town where Reed is buried, spends a lot of time tending to Grandpa Earl's and Reed's graves, and my insistence of no headstone until I got what we wanted (because Daniel loved it too) was driving his sister Lori crazy. One day during one of our regular chats, she broke down and asked me when we were ever going to place a headstone for Reed. I was firm in my conviction that I was not going to do it until I could get a colorized bronze marker, telling her the story of the letter and the pictures.

"Do you still have that letter?" she asked.

"Yes, I think so. I know it is around here somewhere," I replied. "Actually, I just gave a copy of the letter to our pastor because we wanted to learn more about that grief program."

"Can you get me a copy of that letter?"

I had no idea what good it would do, but within thirty minutes of e-mailing her a copy of the letter, she called me with a name and phone number. She had researched the young lady on the Internet, found the funeral home her family had worked with, located the manufacturer of the bronze markers of our dreams, told them our story, and had an agent ready to work with us.

Not one single time had it crossed my mind to do what she did! Oh, I have the skills necessary to do that, but it just never occurred to me with everything else on our plates to go straight to the source. One phone call later, and the ball was rolling toward creating a marker that shared not only our sweet boy's face, but also a little more about his story.

Sometimes monuments and red beds aren't all that different. I am guessing Papa would have thought I was being completely ridiculous on that marker until the final product was done, but if he were with us, he would have driven it all over town too!

What Have You Done to Your Kids?

THE MOMMY WARS DRIVE ME INSANE! I BELIEVE WE ARE ALL doing the best we can to parent the children God has given us. In my thinking, there is no room to say what you would do different if you were another child's momma. I am not a perfect mom, but I am exactly the momma God chose for these beautiful, flawed (yes, I said it: my kids are not perfect either) people. Often, I say to my friends when they are disappointed in their parenting skills, energy, creativity, whatever, "Remember to be gentle and kind to yourself." Just a few days ago, I was having one of those sad momma moments, lamenting how I should have caught something going on with one of my kids. One of those sweet friends repeated my own words back to me, reinforced with a "You're a great mom!" message.

After the bus crash, our school did provide some counseling to all the children on the bus both on and off school grounds, and I believe that was extremely beneficial. There was also a camp organized by area grief specialists and held at the school, made available to anyone with a connection to the crash. Unlike most of the other counseling, this was also made available to Cloie, which was a blessing. Camp Faith was paid for by donations and staffed with amazing volunteers.

Our family chose to participate in a few other opportunities that were amazing investments in our healing, individually and as a family.

When Sawyer was still in intensive care, we were given a packet of information in relation to Reed. The nurses in the Avera McKennan Children's Wing were truly genuine and handled our family with the sweetest of care. In the packet was a brochure about Faith's Lodge (a grief retreat for families who had lost children). The pictures were amazing, and we showed it to our pastor, who stayed with us for five days before returning home to shepherd his flock. One of the requirements for attendance was a letter from your clergy. We all agreed when Sawyer was able, spending time together at a place where others understand the unique pain of losing a child would benefit us all. Faith's Lodge was the absolute best investment we made as a family in our healing. Each of us met people—moms, dads, and kids—with whom we have bonded for life. We attended all three years we were allowed to go, even coordinating to go back with friends we had met previous years. There are activities planned, but participation isn't required. The grounds are breathtaking, as is the lodge itself. The Lacek family, who built the retreat after losing their little daughter, Faith, put every ounce of amazing into each detail, from architecture to programming. While a retreat-like setting isn't for everyone, we highly recommend the opportunity whenever we get the chance.

Our first year at the lodge, we attended during the week dedicated to traumatic grief. All of the families in attendance had losses with powerful backstories. It is hard to explain, but traumatic grief is a beast unto itself. The whole world changes in the blink of an eye with absolutely no warning. Being surrounded by others who understood what we were going through was such an incredible gift. If we achieved nothing but being validated, our time in the Wisconsin woods would have been worth it. There were so many other benefits, but I want anyone who goes there to be able to have their own experiences. In my opinion, Faith's Lodge is time well spent for grieving families.

During that first year, the director of the then Camp Amanda (a grief camp for children) came to do a program with all the kids, grieving siblings, and later a parent program on raising grieving kids. For those of us from neighboring Minnesota, she shared about her camp and the benefits of children attending a camp where they could grieve out of the eyesight of their parents. I was really shocked by this assertion. But when I stopped to think about it, Erin, at age eight, had yet to cry for Reed. Coral, the director, explained that many children don't grieve right away because they don't want to hurt their parents any more than they were already hurting. They do everything possible to protect their parents, delaying their own grief.

Returning home, we shared this information with two of Reed's best buddies' families, who decided it would be wise for both boys along with Sawyer and Erin to attend Camp Amanda together. The three of us moms drove them up together, and we planned to spend the weekend together while our kids were at camp, wishing their reason for being there was something so much different from reality.

Other than our family being separated when Sawyer was hospitalized, this was the first time our kids were away from one parent or the other for any significant amount of time since our lives had changed forever. The counselors were in-the-trenches folks who had all experienced losses of their own. Each of them volunteered to give back to hurting children. They were energetic and enthusiastic, but also comforting and available. The staff also understood the difficulty most parents, guardians, or caretakers were having when leaving their children, even for just a couple days.

The closing day of the weekend camp included a family program, sharing some memories, singing, and a beautiful balloon release. My merry trio of moms pulled up to the camp's location, and one of my children's counselors met me on the sidewalk. When I had left my son in her care, she was the most bubbly, energetic, understanding, and accommodating (Sawyer was still using a wheelchair) person ever. She was still that same person standing outside in the softly drizzling rain. What she said, though, made my knees shake.

"What have you done to your kids?" she asked me.

Those are not the words any momma wants to hear. I panicked, thinking that the nightmare we were living had finally become too much for my sweet kids. My eyes flooded with tears, and she quickly realized that she needed to rephrase her question.

"No, no, no! I'm so sorry! What I was wondering was how in the world did you get your kids to be such hearty vegetable eaters? We have a camp full of kids here, and your kids are the only ones who went back for seconds, and sometimes thirds, of veggies."

A relieved laugh came bubbling out before I explained that I let my kids grow their own gardens, with one caveat. They can pick any vegetables (seeds or plants) in the spring they would like to try, but if we put all that time and effort into watering and weeding and tending those plants, they had to eat them. I don't think I have any magical formula, but that method sure worked for my adventuresome kids.

This counselor was so sweet that several times before we left, she reassured me I had wonderful children who were very resilient. I remember thinking she was pretty incredible herself to annually give up a weekend or two to invest in building up someone else's children. I must have been correct in my assessment of the influence she and the other camp staff had, because on our drive home, both of my kids expressed interest in being counselors when they were old enough.

More than just kid tested and mom approved, these wonderful people earned my children's seal of approval. I cannot think of any better praise than that.

SPECIAL NOTE: MANY OF THESE CAMPS AND RETREATS ARE FUNDED BY donations. Donations in memory or in honor of someone are the best ways to keep these opportunities available for every child and every family.

I Pledge My Hands

I LOVE OUR LITTLE CHURCH. WE WORSHIP AND FELLOWSHIP together. We are not better or worse than any other church, but we sure do an amazing job of taking care of each other. Our church family members are plain real people who are doing their very best to love Jesus. They are so real, in fact, that a few years back our pastor asked us to raise our hands if we had ever been involved in 4-H. Many in the congregation raised their hands.

The most transparently real among us, our pastor shares many stories about his childhood. Not one to mince words, he communicates the good, like his grandfather's airplane, the bad, like the milk money brought home, and the poopy (well, you get the idea) about his days as a farm boy in Iowa. All of his stories have some connection to the sermon material that day. Thus, none of us found it out of the ordinary to get asked about participation in 4-H. This is, after all, Midwestern farm country. For those of us with our hand in the air, he asked us to recite the 4-H pledge, stating he knew after all those recitations earlier in life that we probably all remembered it. He helped get it started, and sure enough, about half of those present joined right in. I was amazed by how many recalled those words from years ago.

His sermon that day talked about how the pledge from one of the world's largest youth development organizations asks us to commit our hands to larger service, just as the Bible calls us to be of service to others.

Although not members of our church family, a family from our school took that 4-H pledge very seriously. I only heard about it after the fact, but when the story was relayed to me, I was moved to tears by this kind of revolutionary love.

From what I was told, this family had been on the fence about whether to join our local 4-H club. While we were still in the hospital, I had shared that we were going to need a ramp built so Sawyer could come home with his wheelchair. At that point, we were barely functioning, so building a ramp into our home was about as possible as Daniel and me building one of the pyramids. Our only option would be to lift Sawyer in and out of our house unless that ramp was built.

Serving others became more than just words in a pledge for our Swan Lake Skippers 4-H club. The leader organized the help of a dear teacher friend and her husband, Barb and Larry, who had become like family to us. They had expertise in building ramps, as it had been a necessity for one of their children. The blessing of their experience would provide not only a ramp, but a ramp built safely, securely, and to code. When word traveled that the club would be building the ramp, this family, who had been on the fence about joining, signed up for 4-H to be a part of loving our family.

I cannot explain how overwhelmed with emotion I was upon hearing this story. *Who does that?* Apparently, the answer is there are the sweet people in our community who wanted to help and who had the skills needed to really find a way to serve our family. I am pretty sure both Jesus and 4-H can be proud of that.

Well, That Is Deceiving!

I WAS HONORED TO BE ONE OF THREE PEOPLE ASKED TO SPEAK AT Nannie's services when she passed away. I joined Uncle Buddy and Nannie's pastor at the podium, sharing memories and saying good-bye. My uncle shared about his and his sisters' (Mom and Aunt Nernie) growing-up years and how Nannie sewed all their clothes. I shared stories about us grandkids pretending we were eating in Paris at every holiday meal, even though we were just at the kids' table in the carport-turned-dining room. I shared about Nannie lighting the neighbor's roof on fire with Christmas Eve fireworks and about how she did something magical with boxed macaroni-n-cheese because no one made it like her. I explained how she spoiled us rotten, like the time when all I wanted for Christmas was a Darcy Doll. When she went to purchase them, they were sold out and she convinced the department manager at the old TG&Y store to sell her the display model. When every other little girl got a fashion doll in a box, I got three of them in the store display, which was about as big as me. Mark my words: Nannie did not do average.

Saying good-bye to your mom and grandmother is never easy, but I think both Uncle Buddy and I did a great job of sharing who Nannie was to us and to our generations. But as well as we did, her pastor hit it out of the park. He had one great Miss Katie story after another, and it was evident she had an amazing relationship with him. Their jovial camaraderie was present in every encounter. A true Southern storyteller, he shared about their unusual greeting. One time, he waltzed into a gathering of the grannies' Sunday school class. When he saw Nannie (whom he called Miss Katie), he let out a whopping "Hey, girlfriend!"

233

Without batting an eyelash, her response was "Hey, boyfriend!" If you have never witnessed Southern people greeting one another, the four-word exchange was dripping with about every ounce of sass and drawl one could muster. Even though the pastor was a happily married man, that greeting, although unconventional, just sort of stuck.

The family Nannie created at her sweet little Baptist church was a big part of her life. She loved her church body, and I was always thrilled when we were able to worship with her. To my mom and daddy's credit, they would often forego attending their own church so all three generations could worship together. One particular Sunday, along with my parents and girls, I drove over the bridge to go to church with her. Daniel and Sawyer were away on an excursion, otherwise known as fishing in God's creation that day. Nannie cried and patted my hand or Erin's the entire service. She was just so happy that we could be there with her, the joy leaked right out of her eyes.

After the service, Nannie had a little business to tend to. As the rest of us waited in the foyer, a perfectly coiffed Southern grandma came up to greet us. White hair cut and combed into a bob, nails done, and wearing a pink suit with matching shoes and handbag, she looked as if she'd stepped right out a scene from my favorite movie of all time: *Steel Magnolias*. She walked up to my daddy and asked if we were Miss Katie's people. He assured her we were, explaining that he was the son-in-law, I was the granddaughter, and my girls were the great granddaughters. He introduced us all by name. She stood about four feet, ten inches, if she was an inch. Trying to make small talk, she marched over to Sister, who at the time stood almost five feet, eight inches.

"Erin, are you having a good time in Florida?"

"Yes, ma'am, I am."

"Well, Shug. We have some great youth group activities going on. How old are you?"

Sister's prompt reply was not the one this sweet little lover of Jesus was expecting.

"I'm twelve."

Sister Pink Shoes put her hand on her hip, did a once-over from Erin's toes to her head, and then in true dramatic stage whisper fashion blurted out, "Well, *that* is deceiving!" I thought my daddy and I were going to die from laughter, but we held our composure long enough to state that we grow tall, proud kids up in Minnesota. I still get the giggles thinking about it.

In her defense, she was tiny and probably came from tiny people and made tiny people. She didn't mean any harm or offense, but she just expected our Sister to be much older. It was something that happened to Erin many times after that.

We rarely acknowledge that our perception of situations based on our own observations can be deceiving. We see people living their lives and assume (often incorrectly) that they have it all together. In the case of grieving people, I have been guilty of wanting them to return to living, that I have taken their small steps back into regular life as an assessment that they are doing okay. In our experience, it took many years before we felt even a tiny bit of normalcy return to our lives. There is no timetable on grief, and no one should ever feel rushed to move on.

For as many helpers and prayer partners who rushed to our aid in the early days, the one who caught me off guard is the one who wasn't fooled by the "they look to be doing just fine" mentality. She saw my version of the Bat signal (posting on social media) that I was looking for a place for Cloie to take some Irish dance lessons. My friend, who at that time was more like an acquaintance, responded with super speed about an idea she had put together. She and her family are world travelers, and she is a planner extraordinaire.

She planned a day away for four, including herself, her daughter, Sally Gal, and me. We spent an entire day having fun in Sioux Falls, which included Irish dance lessons with a former principal dancer in *Riverdance*.

On the drive there and back, the little girls watched a movie in the back while we moms got to know each other better. We learned that we had many similar interests, including our faith. While we were just having small talk, she told me that I wouldn't be paying for today's lessons. *That wasn't the plan. What in the mayonnaise is going on here?* She explained that she and her family had been praying for us for five years, asking God to show them when they could step in and be of assistance. Five years of waiting on God!

"Today is going to be our treat. We knew that early on there were many coming to help you, and we wanted to wait until things slowed down. When I saw your question, I knew now was the time!"

It is a good thing she was driving, because I couldn't contain the tears that fell down my cheeks. They were humble tears of astonishment at a love that would wait five years to bless our family.

Almost Heaven

JOHN DENVER IS OUR COUSIN. OR AT LEAST, YOU MIGHT THINK so, if you joined us at a Nowatzki family reunion. With all our talented guitar players and singers, we sit around the campfire for hours singing John's greatest hits. Of course, Johnny Cash and many other artists could be our cousins too. Those old songs are perennial favorites as we gather, often cuddled up in blankets, next to each other, soaking up every moment of the precious few hours we can all (well, mostly all) be together. In the days leading up to every reunion, someone will post on social media that they've dusted off John Denver's greatest hits in preparation for our biennial family jubilee.

One of the second-generation pickers has begun to take charge of the musicians, and he leads us all beautifully (I am not at all biased) as our voices meld together to sing the songs that capture the hearts of four generations. In fact, at Reed's celebration, our sweet pastor asked this same cousin, Chris, whom we had asked to do the special music, if he could squeeze in an extra song at the last minute. He shared about Reed's last family reunion the previous summer, when Grandma Sheran and Granpa Junior had given him an MP3 player for his birthday. At the campfire, the first where we allowed him to stay up half the night, a rite of passage for all Nowatzki children, Reed kept requesting his favorite songs ("Blow up the TV/Spanish Pipedream," "Almost Heaven," and "Homegrown Tomatoes") to record on his new technology. Chris shared that he was about on his last nerve with our redheaded boy shoving the mic in his face that night. As annoying as it was for the musicians, his impromptu recording is one of our favorite memories, perfectly preserved on his tiny white device.

At the service, the unusual request was met with some quick thinking. *Why not honor Reed with one campfire favorite?* Chris shared our family's tradition and asked if for one moment "we could all be Nowatzkis," asking all present to sing along. Reed, who loved people, would have loved the moment when, completely unscripted, all present sang their hearts out to "Back Home Again." I don't know if they've met in heaven, but I think John Denver and Reed would have reveled in that moment. Looking back, the memory still brings tears to my eyes, not in sadness but that in true celebration of a little boy, a whole gymnasium full of people who love us would have a campfire moment in his memory. Several later shared they either dusted off their greatest hits CD or purchased one, just to savor the moment.

Reed was definitely my child. He loved a good adventure and inherited the rambling gene passed down from my parents to me and from me to him. From the earliest days of our marriage, I shared with my husband that I would rather travel than own a great big house. We have lived our lives that way ever since. Trips, vacations, and adventures mark the days, especially summer days, of our family's story. A few years after the bus crash, a dear, dear man approached me and said he wanted to see those adventures continue again. He was well acquainted with the details of the hours we had spent traveling, not for fun but for doctor visits and surgeries. His solution to this dilemma was to generously give us a week's vacation. We simply had to choose the location, and he would cover the expense of the lodging.

The gift was too extravagant, in our opinions. So too was a similar gift from church friends who gave us a very large check within a month of the crash. They tied one condition to the money—it was not to be used for bills. We were to use the money to do something together as a family, something that would bring us joy. Joy was so far off our radar, we thought we would never use the money, most likely gifting it to someone else. We tucked the money away and forgot about it, until this friend offered to send us away. I felt unworthy. At first, we brushed off his offer as too large a gift; God helped us wash away that nonsense. It wasn't that we were any more worthy than the next family, but it was the way this friend chose to bless us. God used the generosity of two families to show us how deep His love truly is. This man loves our family, especially our children, Reed included, and he wanted to see us live again, rather than numbly enduring our days. If only for a week, they wanted to see us have something fun to remember. It took a little coordination of schedules to finally pick a week and a location, but we settled on Vail, Colorado. Our friend covered the resort lodging, and our other friends' generous gift paid for everything else.

We drove out to the mountains, full of anticipation of a week of relative respite. We were wiped out after our long drive and spent the first evening enjoying the heated pool, shadowed by amazing mountain vistas. While we were enjoying our peaceful surroundings, we overheard that the next day, the largest farmers' market in Colorado would be right there in Vail. In our minds, attending a huge farmers' market equals time well spent. We will pick homegrown veggies, artisan foods, and freshly cut flowers over store-bought items any day of the week. We were not disappointed. The open-air market, over a mile long, had family activities ranging from puppet shows to mechanical bulls, artisanal cheeses, pastas, and breads, and every kind of fruit and veggie imaginable. There were also about a thousand pairs of Keen shoes, which made us feel right at home, since that rugged footwear is our standard summer wear.

For hours, we walked and slathered ourselves in sunscreen, being that much closer in altitude to the sun. Taste-testing and purchasing enough groceries to feed us for the week, we shared a blissful time, reminding us of the ones we had previously shared at our hometown market with Reed. Sawyer was still using a wheelchair some of the time, and we were all reaching veggie-lover overload when we decided to make our way back to the parking structure. Just as we turned around, the band playing changed songs. I stopped in the middle of the busy sidewalk with tears in my eyes as the familiar chords were played. It was our first vacation, real vacation—not grief retreat—without Reed. In just a few notes, a warm rush, like one of Reed's sneaky behind-the-back hugs, filled my senses as I felt God hugging me while the band played John Denver's "Annie's Song."

Gonna Need Some No. 2s

THE MOST GRUELING QUESTION I WILL EVER FACE IS "How many kids do you have?"

"Seven! I have seven! I am a mom of seven!" is what every fiber of my being wants to answer, but I often don't. The answer of seven requires a really long explanation, and sometimes I simply don't have the energy to give all the details. Well, that and the looks of pity and sympathy and sheer uncomfortableness most people give after I answer with seven and its accompanying explanation make my heart hurt.

My kiddos once loved the cartoon *Seven Little Monsters*, and that was one momma with whom I could totally identify. She could say seven, and all she would get were looks of astonishment. Of course, considering the head of one of her little monsters was detachable and would often get lost, she probably received a few disparaging looks as well. There were times in the show when her heart would be sad because one of her kiddos was hurting.

I understood exactly how she felt, because since the bus crash, I have, at times, been the embodiment of the proverb "A mother is only as happy as her saddest child." While my voice doesn't often speak "I am a momma of seven," there is not a single day my heart forgets. The anguish of my heart cries silently until it crescendos to a deafening roar on two days out of the year. Both days bring me heartache, and if I could erase them from my existence, I would.

On these two days, the ache of not holding seven within my grasp is too much to bear. Thus far, time has not lessened that wound, but thankfully there are 363 other days in a year. "Back to School Eve" and "Christmas Stocking Day" are those two days. Anniversary dates pale in comparison for me. I should be helping pack seven backpacks or college laundry baskets and helping hang seven stockings. The three children I have are amazing and wonderful and the joys of my life—period. There are no buts here. There are simply holes where their four siblings should be, and no matter how hard I try, I feel it acutely on those two days.

Ironically, these same two days were the favorites of my childhood. I believe not being able to share those same moments with all my children is the source of my angst. Aunt Nernie made our Christmas stockings, which are cross-stitched and quilted. Every year pulling them out, I remember the year we received them. My own momma continued the tradition, making one for my sweetie and each of our children. And I have always, *always* loved school. I enjoyed my summers, but I anticipated school like some do Christmas morning. I still remember our back-to-school shopping excursions buying supplies and a few new outfits, like the peach gauchos from the downtown Sears store that were legendary. Tough to top that fashion sense in the fifth grade!

Of all the supplies I have needed over the years, the ones that brought me the most joy were pencils. The pencil, good ol' No. 2, holds so much promise. There is nothing like the potential of what those golden jewels will produce. The best answer to a question, the perfect solution to a challenging math problem, or the perfectly crafted sentence is just waiting inside. I have never been a fan of pens, preferring a perfectly crafted and sharpened pencil any day. Apparently, so too did my college physics professor.

The first day of my sophomore year of university studies was a scorcher on the North Dakota prairie. Not equipped with air conditioning, the physics laboratory and classroom was sweltering by three in the afternoon. As we sat listening to the syllabus and introduction to the class, I could tell that Mr. Wymore was going to be one of a kind, a gem of a man and a teacher. I was not disappointed in any class I took from him. On this first day, however, he and I made a huge impression on each other. He was explaining the rigors of his course and his expectations for all of us, which culminated in what I refer to as his "evils of pen" lecture.

For this science course, we were required to have a hardcover graphing notebook for all of our lab work. Unlike many of his contemporaries, he did not—I mean don't even think about it—want us to use pen in there.

My heart jumping for joy because I adore pencils, I found his adamancy odd because many professors expected the use of pen to prevent cheating in lab results. While my heartbeat was doing little pitter-patters, Mr. Wymore was still extolling the evils of pens, of which he had many examples.

Eventually the oppressive heat got to him as much as it had to us and he removed his sport coat, laying it over his ubiquitous overhead projector. When he turned back around, his white dress shirt had a large black ink stain on the chest pocket. Anyone who knows me knows exactly what my reaction was. Yep! I let out the largest, heartiest chuckle ever. Apparently, I was the only one in the room who found it funny, and I was beginning to question the character of the science scholars who failed to see the irony in the "evils of pen" lecture and his ink-stained shirt. Thankfully, Mr. Wymore forgave me, his daughter became one of my best friends and a bridesmaid in our wedding, and we girls spent hours studying in his basement.

Long before the bus crash, while I was still teaching at our children's school, I was blessed to work alongside some amazing women: teachers, staff, and administration. One of these women was a paraprofessional in my classroom. She is personable and engaging, and both students and teachers (me included) were enamored with her. One time I shared with her my sadness over the weekend with Christmas stockings, at the time having four to hang and longing to place three more. True to her larger-than-life personality, she embraced me in the biggest hug and cried with me.

Friends like this are truly a treasure.

Fast-forward to the summer after the bus crash. A phone call out of the blue was one that saved me from a heartache I was trying desperately to avoid. Miss Linda, as my children have always referred to her, asked if my kiddos were busy in the upcoming days. Considering our lives revolved around doctor appointments and therapy visits, "busy" wasn't exactly what came to mind. After confirming they were not, she stated they had a date with her. She would be taking them "back to school" shopping so their momma would not have to face that ordeal this year.

When I got off the phone, I crumpled to the floor and sobbed. Not only had she remembered our moment a few years previous, she put words into action, especially when I would have been a sobbing mess in the school supply aisle.

As a teacher, I have always waited with great anticipation to the upcoming year full of possibilities, but still this is one day I struggle to endure. What should be buzzing with excitement isn't for me, and my friend became the hands, feet, and heart of Jesus by making the excursion a shopping adventure for my children. Imagine their glee when they returned home and recounted that Miss Linda had allowed them a few splurges (like character folders) that their momma would have never allowed. Through my tears, I rejoiced at every gift they had been given, and there in the midst of the beautiful back-to-school bounty were the staples, and this momma's favorites: the old faithful No. 2s.

Grace of Strangers

As a third-generation teacher, graduation is a big deal. A really big deal! So the thought of Reed's high school commencement was looming *large* and *foreboding* well before the actual date arrived. I was quite shocked when we received a call from a school administrator stating he would be asking other area administrators what protocols were followed at their schools when a student had died, specifically mentioning suicide. It was disheartening to hear that he felt a mimicked commemoration would be appropriate when, unlike other area students, Reed and Jessie died during a part of their school day. I want to extend grace, and I believe this is a challenging situation for all involved, but the uncomfortable comparison broke my heart.

Long before the call, the mailman crushed our spirits and didn't even know it. One incredibly cold, snowy Friday, in the mail arrived an innocuous-looking postcard, advertising how much fun Reed was going to have at some private school next fall. As proud state college graduates, my husband and I were surprised that an area elite school would be soliciting our child. Our pride runs deep for small, public schools.

There I stood in the snow next the mailbox with tears dropping on the fluffy accumulation around my boots. My immediate shock turned to disgust, dismayed at how this had happened at all. He died in the seventh grade. *How in the mayonnaise did his name get on this list when he never took the ACT or the SAT?* Thankfully, it was a Friday, giving me a few days to cool off before phoning the admissions department of said school and asking to have Reed's name removed.

That one little mass mailer sparked an avalanche of information I never knew existed. After Daniel and I shed a few tears over the dream

245

that would never come to be, I composed myself enough to call the college the next week. The admissions person was apologetic but was really an innocent bystander in the unsolicited mail heartbreak. He gave me the name of the service whereby their potential student lists are generated. After a brief pause, he was kind enough to locate the number to the College Bound Selection Service.

New information in hand, I wasted no time in reaching out to save ourselves from more college and university marketing mail. The sweet receptionist I spoke with was grace filled and delicate as I shared my story. Miss R was sweet enough to explain how they got the names in the first place. Believing scholastic achievement testing corporations probably made the bulk of their business, I was deeply saddened to learn I was only partially correct. Schools, across the nation, are the main suppliers of potential future student lists. Miss R took all of Reed's information and assured me that she would have his name removed from all their databases. Throughout our conversation, she apologized several times and assured me that while she had never walked in my shoes, she could only imagine how heartbreaking this experience was.

The grace of a stranger saved my day. She was so kind and gentle. We said our good-byes, and I felt God place on my heart this message: "When you have good service at a store or restaurant, you make your family wait so you can tell the manager how exceptional the service provided was. Why not call and tell Miss R's manager?" So I did.

Miss R was shocked to hear my voice again, and was in tears when I explained why I was calling back. Her manager was as kindhearted as his employee. He was also moved to tears when I explained the whole story. His parting words were "I am a father. Your story makes me want to go home and hug my children." I assured him that would be the best decision he made all day.

I was able to finish my conversation and compose myself before I needed to be at the university to teach my afternoon class. Despite the sadness of the reason for the call, their kindnesses really buoyed my spirits. Mistakenly, I believed this was the end of the story.

About a week later, I received a note from Miss R on company stationery, reminding me of our conversation and thanking me for sharing such kind thoughts about her to her boss. She then explained she had learned of some new information that would probably solve this issue once and for all, because they are not the only company to provide this type of service. As soon as the IT guy told her about the Deceased Do Not Contact Registration, a tool used by a large group of direct marketers, she knew she needed to write me immediately to tell me how to contact them.

Her final bit of information must have done the trick, because after registering, we never received another heartbreaking postcard again. But more importantly, I saw how miraculously God works through the grace of strangers to help heal broken hearts.

Note: Please see "Really Good Stuff" for more details on the Deceased Do Not Contact Registration.

Welcome, Teenager!

WE HAVE A TRADITION IN MY FAMILY FOR BIRTHDAYS. MY parents call and sing "Happy Birthday" to us. Before cell phones, they would each pick up a house phone and sing. With the advent of speakerphone, they gathered around one phone to use that function. I am not sure where the tradition began, but I do know that even if they have to wait until late in the evening to catch a busy teenager, they will do it.

Nannie loved a good party. I have always had a love for Miss Frizzle from *The Magic School Bus* stories, and as much as I think Miss Frizzle has an outfit for every scientific concept, Nannie had an outfit for every celebration known to mankind. We have enjoyed a hearty chuckle over some of them, but Katie Campbell was nothing if not her own woman. She wouldn't have given two hoots (let alone one hoot) what anybody else thought. She was one of a kind, and I miss her terribly.

Nannie loved all her grandkids and great grandkids, but Sister held a special place in her heart. Arriving with my parents just the day before, Nannie was present at the hospital when Erin was born. She paced the halls trying to figure out what was taking so long. We should have gone by Nannie time because she knew there were troubles long before the doctors and nurses figured it out. After Erin was released from respiratory intensive care, Nannie was there to welcome her home. One of my all-time favorite photos is of her kneeling down soaking in the wonder of her first great granddaughter with our two boys on either side of her.

She loved us all, but Erin was special to her. For Erin's thirteenth birthday, Nannie called and left a message on Sister's cell phone because she was unable to catch her directly. Her birthday message is still on

Sister's phone. When I was traveling to Florida for Nannie's funeral services, Erin did the one thing she could do to try to cheer me up. She forwarded that message to me, which to this day is stored on my phone as well.

While sitting in my sleeper car on the *Spirit of New Orleans* train, I laughed through my tears because that message was full of everything that made Nannie special. The words written here will never do it justice, but every bit of the message showed how much she loved Erin and how she was about as Southern as turnip greens.

> Happy birthday to you!
> Happy birthday to you!
> Happy birthday, dear Erin!
> Happy birthday to you!
> (dramatic pause)
> And welcome, teenager! (pronounced like teenag-ah)
> Love you, darlin'.
> And miss you so bad.
> Come on back and stay with Nannie this summer.

We had been down to Florida to visit a short while before Erin's birthday, and Nannie would have loved nothing more than to have Erin come and stay with her.

Several of our friends have expressed the same wistful sentiment in relation to visiting Reed's gravesite. I never in my wildest imagination could have dreamed how many just want to go there. Do not misunderstand me! Their desire makes this momma's heart so happy and brings us both tears of joy and of wonder for the depth of the visitor's love and friendship. There have been more than a few dozen who have made the long venture between southwestern Minnesota to north-central North Dakota, a trek of over four hundred miles, to go "see" our son.

Once at a 4-H gathering, I saw my husband speaking with the dad from a fellow 4-H family. The Swan Lake Skippers is a fairly large club, but friendships run deep in our roots. These two guys chatting was nothing new, but when my husband came over shaking his head, I knew something was definitely amiss. His demeanor immediately told me he was blown away with some new knowledge. I have loved that man for many years, and he has a way of just letting unexpected information slowly settle upon him. I would liken it to an old percolator slowly dripping one ounce of goodness at a time.

"I just got done talking over there, and do you know what he did when he was up in North Dakota on business? He realized he wasn't that far from Leeds, and he decided to go visit Reed. He was telling me all about how peaceful of a place we chose. I can't believe it. I just can't believe it."

His percolating is only rivaled by my tears. *He did what?* I simply had no words.

Some have made hunting and fishing trips to the area. Others have rerouted their family vacation to get there. Business has brought quite a few to the edge of that tiny little town. No matter what the reason, we are humbled by their love and their willingness to go such a great distance.

Speaking of the beauty of God's creation and of the grandeur of the headstone, each and every friend who has made that journey has shared with us how much their visit touched them. Their words are like a beautiful song of comfort to our souls. The lyrics tell us how much Reed's life impacted theirs and how, like us, they miss him too. And our hearts sing back. We are truly blessed to have friends like you.

Watch Out, Mary Poppins

You will never win! Trust me! Admit defeat now before you take on my mother at baby showers or home parties. Home parties, where women gather together to shop for things, are what my husband refers to as "one of those 'parties' (imagine him doing air quotations) where Kandy and her friends get together and guilt each other into buying stuff they don't need." Prior to my priorities shifting, as grief has a way of doing, I would always scoff at his description. But now, I am content with collecting memories rather than anything I will ever have to dust. Of course, this rule doesn't seem to apply to party or crafting supplies. But I digress.

I am *serious*, though. If you are locked in a challenge with my mom in the parlor game known as "who has this item in their purse," she will annihilate you. Even Mary Poppins's bottomless carpetbag is no match for Sheran. You need a Band-Aid? She's got you covered. Maybe a wet nap? She knows no KFC that doesn't offer one just the right size for her purse. Exactly four crayons? Oh yeah, she's got them! Just a little snack? She didn't need that in-flight biscuit. A nail file? Way too easy! Supplies for a science experiment? Give her a minute, and she will find them.

If there was an award for the person most likely to be able to create a MacGyver contraption from her purse, she would be a perennial recipient. I don't know a Boy Scout who would even come close to challenging her. My mom is prepared for every scenario. Taking a page from Teddy Roosevelt's life quotes, her motto is "Speak however you want (she is still a mom, after all) and carry a big purse."

Whenever I think of her ever-faithful accessory, I am always reminded of the jokes about how if there had been three wise women, they would have brought much more practical gifts than gold, frankincense, and myrrh. They would have brought a casserole, a giant package of diapers, and a gift card for a cleaning service. Oy, the barn dust! Wives, women, and mommas who know the things that once helped them are often the first to pass that wisdom on to the next person who could use it.

I was completely surprised one day when a friend who had experienced several losses showed up with a minivan that looked like it had been involved in a successful warehouse supply store robbery. Instead of another blanket or casserole, she brought something that was completely practical and extremely helpful. We had no energy left to accomplish much of anything in the early days of grief, and her gift helped alleviate the need to do so.

I truly believe in protecting the environment, and I know that God gave Adam and Eve the charge to care for creation, thus giving all humanity the charge to do the same. Yet I will tell you washing dishes was close to the last thing I was interested in doing for a long time, especially when there were more people than usual staying in our home just to help us out.

Apparently, she wasn't the only one who knew about practical gifts, because a few others brought or sent similarly practical things. Buying gifts for my husband is about the most torturous experience on earth. I usually buy him something thinking it will have real meaning to him, only to have it sit in the box unused. If I ask him for suggestions, his reply is always the same. "I don't want anything. I have everything I need." *Helpful. Really helpful.* Like our friend who came bearing paper products, we had a few other like-minded folks who gave from their heart in ways that I would have never thought to do and who gave thinking we might have just about everything else covered.

My husband had an idyllic childhood, living in the same town his whole life until college. He has had friends from childhood that are still his friends today. Coming from nomadic Southern Baptists, I didn't have that luxury. Had we lived closer, I am sure his classmates would have plugged in their crockpots or baked a casserole or two. But it is hard to keep food warm and drive it over four hundred miles to be delivered. As I have already shared, without the care of others, my family would have survived on junk food or pocket lint. His childhood friends wanted to help feed us in the way that all good Midwesterners have a knack for doing. Instead of long-distance deliveries, they did the next best thing. They researched what restaurants were available in our town and pooled their resources to purchase hundreds of dollars in gift cards for us. When someone locally wasn't feeding our family and we were sick of cold cut sandwiches (okay, I wasn't sick of sandwiches, but everyone else was), we could place an order to go, pick it up, and—*voila!*—instant meal.

There were several groups that brought cases of pop (or, as some in the South call it, "Coke"). Again, we would not normally subsist on sugary beverages in our diet, but it was helpful to have a variety of sodas to offer guests when they came to pray or offer condolences to our family. Hospitality is a part of my DNA, and whether the friends who provided those cases of drinks knew it or not, their gift was one that helped me honor a small piece of my Southern upbringing. Although no one visiting would have expected it, I felt better having the ability to, at the very least, offer our guests something cold to drink. In the craziness of our daily life, it was the lifeline that let me live as close to my authentic self as possible.

Another gift came from my sister-in-law when she overheard my overwhelmed comments at the outpouring of love from people near and far and all over the world. Barely perceptible, I uttered, "How are we ever going to thank all these people?" Thank-you notes are just another one of those Southern staples. Frankly, I would feel horrible if I didn't thank everyone. Hugging necks, penning thank-you notes, and offering hospitality are simply parts of who I am. The morning of Reed's services, in she walked with a stack of embossed notes and a pile of stamps. In that same fashion, a local printing company donated our programs for the services and personalized thank-you postcards for our family.

All were things we could and *did* use. All were things that gave us a tiny bit of the life we had lived prior to the crash or that were helpful in the midst of our struggles, beautiful and well thought out and much-appreciated gifts. These are ideas to help those who want to help but perhaps don't know what to bring or who want to bring something a grieving family would find really useful. For each item on the list, I cannot guarantee you will find them in my mom's purse, but I wouldn't bet against her!

- paper plates
- napkins
- plastic/paper cups
- boxes of tissues
- plastic cutlery
- toilet paper
- paper towels
- baby wipes
- disinfectant wipes
- dish soap
- laundry soap
- thank-you cards
- pens
- markers
- stamps
- gift cards (grocery store, restaurants)

With the Comforter You've Been Given

THERE ARE A NUMBER OF THINGS I REMEMBER VIVIDLY ABOUT our wedding day—some wonderful, others comical, and some I would just as soon forget. One of my favorite memories, other than the actual "I got to marry the boy of my dreams" part, was during the receiving line at our reception. We were married in a standing-room-only, packed-to-the-gills church. Despite a dusting of snow that morning, the temperatures rose to a cozy warmth by afternoon, meaning we had a church full of hot people. We chose to receive our guests at the reception hall rather than making friends and family sit squished together a minute longer. Guests came from all four corners of the United States from both of our families, and there were many introductions made.

As one of our bridesmaids and her husband came through the line, we exchanged hugs and well wishes, thanking them for the heirloom gift they had given to us the day before. During our brief moment of small talk, my college best friend's husband blurted out, "I made love in your quilt." My eyebrows shot up to the roof about the time that my friend smacked him and emphatically corrected his grammar. "Noooo! *Put* love in the quilt! Put love in the quilt."

Now about thirty shades of embarrassed, my fellow scientist and favorite zucchini deliverer explained her family has a rule when they make a quilt for a gift. Each person must sew at least one stitch in order to get their name on the card for the quilt recipients. Since one stitch is all some ever do, there was at times an occasional needle-pricked finger which deposited a drop of blood on the quilt. Rather than stew over such a moment, the women of the family have a saying. "You put love in that quilt."

Every time I wrap myself in that comforter, I smile, thinking of that hilarious, albeit somewhat awkward, moment. Thankfully, it wasn't *that* loved when we received it.

Little did I know that crazy story would someday become a symbol of fellowship and working together to love and support others. The women of the quilt family have been my friends and at times mentors. Their spirit of fellowship of gathering around a quilt frame at the lake cabin to work side by side to create a treasure of lasting beauty and comfort is something I've always carried with me. Through hours of hard work, and at times tedium, theirs was a true model of loving others.

Along with many others in my "growing up days," I developed a true appreciation for what it means to serve others. One of the greatest benefits of growing up in my family and within a church was the opportunity to serve others. Over the years, my role has morphed from helping with children in my teen years to helping their mommas in my recent years. I certainly don't have all the answers, but I am more than willing to listen and to offer words of encouragement. I can also pray, and of course, offer those hugs my husband say "should come with a warning sign." One such spring evening will forever be marked in my heart. The weather outside was beautiful, the perfect Minnesota day, as a sweet momma poured her heart out to me, sharing the troubles in her life, while her preschool-aged daughter played with our Sally's toys. We spent hours talking, crying, and praying. At some point, her precocious little girl began asking me a litany of questions. Very observant for her age, she noticed that we were doing some construction in our home. She asked if we had fixed just about everything she could see and name—walls, floors, ceilings, and windows. I told her that we had indeed replaced almost all those things but shared that we would have to wait on replacing our windows because we didn't have enough money.

In one of those moments that literally take your breath away, my tiny friend jumped up next to me, cradled her chubby little hands around her momma's face, and asked perhaps the sweetest thing I have ever heard. This dear family has been in turmoil for many, many years, which is part of what brought them to my doorstep that day. Many in the community and in our church specifically have helped bring their ends closer together. I am certain with heartfelt prayers, each time they thanked the Lord, in front of the tiny dynamo wedged between us on my faded living room couch. "Let's give her our money. She can't fix her windows, and she needs it."

Not having two mites to rub together, this sweet momma assured her daughter they would help "fix" our windows, while I wiped my eyes, which were now overcome with emotion.

Lord, help me to have this child's giving spirit. Let me not hold on too tightly when one of your beloved is in need.

All of my days I want to remember the moment a very tiny one taught the teacher a very big lesson.

My little friend was not the only one who showed our family what true comfort giving looks like. In the immediate aftermath of the crash, I was only able to squeeze in a few calls, the circuitry backlogged from all the people calling—some to check on loved ones, others to share the news. One of those calls was to one of my best friends, who along with her husband eventually helped locate our children as we desperately tried to navigate the red tape of chaos. When it became apparent that we would need to travel to a bigger hospital, this same friend swung into action, alerting her family and our church family. One among her family had walked in our shoes years before. He remembered the kindnesses poured out to him during his time of need. He called my friend and told her to arrange for our family to have a place to stay for as long as we needed it while Sawyer was hospitalized. There was an inn closely connected with the hospital, so it was a welcome respite from the all-eyes-on-us environment of the hospital. Although the pediatric intensive care allowed us to room in with our child, the recliner that folded out into a bed wasn't nearly large enough for two parents and two children. The privacy of our room was a much-needed retreat.

During our initial stay at the hospital, another dear friend sent well wishes for one son and condolences for another. This friend and his wife had walked alongside us for as long as we had lived in Minnesota, celebrating the births of children together and mourning the losses of babies together as well. I still have the card, penned in the husband's handwriting, when he learned of our second miscarriage. *We grieve the hands we do not hold.* It was one sentence, but it was the one sentence my heart yearned to hear, its message reminding me our friends knew our pain intimately. Ours is a comfortable friendship, reminding me of a summer pair of sandals when you first take them out after a long winter. You remember how amazing they fit and how happy you are to have them around. Our families don't see each other as often as we would like, but we seem to pick up right where we left off when we do get together. They weren't able to join us at the hospital, or perhaps it was because they wanted to give us a time of private mourning. Whatever the reason, they once again sent their thoughts via a simple handwritten note.

The brief message said that others had helped them in times of need, and they wanted to do the same for us. *Comfort others with the comfort you've been given* was his motivation. Tucked in with the note was a large amount of cash. The currency of the world could have been salt for all we knew at that moment, and given the enormity of the medical bills we were facing we would be living a fairly salt-free diet for a long time. Our friend recognized we were going to need some financial help and gave generously. Enough to hold our heads above water while we tried to sort through the difficult days and decisions which lay in front of us.

Both men hold very special places in our hearts, and always will. They gave generously without any expectations because once upon a time someone had done the same for them. Like our ladies at the lake working over the quilt frame, they have become the models for us to give generously, particularly to those who are in need of the comfort we are equipped to give.

On Easter Rabbits and Turtles

MUCH LIKE OUR AVERSION TO CABLE TELEVISION WHEN OUR children were younger, I had very strong (vehement, actually) feelings regarding video games. Their pleas for one gaming system or another fell on deaf ears, knowing I was never going to give in to their requests. Eventually, they stopped asking, resigned to enjoying a game or two when visiting friends' homes. My unbending system worked well until one summer at Crazy Days. Each year our local newspaper, the *Marshall Independent*, has a few contests or drawings down at their end of Main Street. This particular summer was no different. Imagine my shock when I received a call from one of the writers alerting me to the great news. I am certain my reaction was not the one he was expecting after telling me Reed had won an Xbox system. Without hesitation, I asked if they could award the prize to someone else. Much to my chagrin, the surprised caller responded equally as swiftly with, "Um, no. We already printed his name in the next edition of the paper." And with the click of typeset, my house built upon the sand crumbled.

As annoyed as I was, Reed was elated. In his mind, Christmas really came in July that year. He and Sawyer were thrilled to try their skills on the newly acquired treasure. As parents, we scrutinized every game they purchased and rented. I may have lost the battle, but not the war. Turns out, it was a great bonding activity for Daniel and the boys. Many hours of giggles were heard from the basement, and even though I wished for a different activity, they were all having fun. On more than one occasion, they tried mightily to persuade me to join in. Even though I came from the age of ATARI, I was never much of a gamer, so it was pretty easy for me to say no.

Eventually they finally wore me down. The boys had rented a copy of a Teenage Mutant Ninja Turtle game (which was about as far as this mom would relent on games involving fighting). Those boys needled me with the stories I had told about how we would search high and low for TMNT items for their oldest cousin. I agreed reluctantly to play as one member of a four-person game on one condition—I got to play as my favorite turtle, Raphael. They agreed, and my brief foray into video gaming began. I was startled when the controller vibrated in reaction to my movements. When it came to game technology, we weren't in Kansas anymore.

Even if I hate to admit it, I was having a good time as the four of us took on some bad guys. We were taking names and kicking the tar out of those dudes. Or at least I thought so, until Reed rudely asked if I was ever going to help out. Shocked at his insinuation that I wasn't pulling my own weight, I told him, "Reed, what are you talking about? I am over here kicking some bad guy booty." I will never forget his deadpan, yet honest, reply.

"Mom, no you're not. You're the Ninja Turtle walking into the wall."

And just like that, my gamer lifestyle was over as quickly as it had begun. For my kiddos, the game system provided hours of entertainment, and for me, the laugh of a lifetime. Who knew one little box could offer so much?

Just as one little drawing on a hot summer's day brought the Xbox I never wanted, one little basket brought a friendship I never knew I needed.

Easter Sunday 2008 was filled with many twists and turns, including making the first meal for my family since the bus crash. A traditional meal of Easter ham, twice-baked potatoes, deviled eggs, and homemade rolls was served to our family and a couple friends. It was a short-lived return to normalcy because that very afternoon we loaded up the entire family, including a wheelchair, boxes of medications, and medical devices of every sort, to travel four hours to Rochester, Minnesota. *The Beverly Hillbillies* had nothing on our vehicle, except the granny on top. Even though Sawyer would be returning for a long-term hospital stay a few weeks later, his needs were not the reason for this trip.

Originally, a few days after the bus crash, our littlest had been scheduled for surgery to remove her tonsils and adenoids and to repair her eardrums (because she had what is known in layman's terms as mechanical deafness). This was to be her third and final surgery, and time was of the essence. We were still so overwhelmed with everything going on at home I am shocked we had enough sense to cancel the original surgery. Eventually, we received a call from the Mayo Clinic explaining we really couldn't wait much longer, which is how we ended up celebrating a favorite Easter tradition in the lobby of a hotel across the street from St. Mary's hospital. While packing, we threw in a few extra items that most holiday travelers might forget—like one uncle and two family friends to help take care of Sister and Sawyer and keep us company during the procedure.

While we were trying to keep our minds off the idea of another hospital stay, we decided to host an egg hunt in the breakfast area of the hotel. Brightly colored eggs were hidden in every possible nook and cranny. My kiddos were just getting ready to hunt when the most adorable little girl I had ever met started gathering the eggs, despite the protestations of her sweet Grandma.

My heart melted at her innocence. Little did I know this tiny girl was a BIG part of God's amazing plan. After explaining our family's story to our new friends, Grandma Bonnie hugged me with an intensity that left both of us in tears. As our family lingered in the lobby a bit longer to regroup emotionally and physically, we heard the familiar ding announcing the elevator's arrival on our floor. Out came the tiny-bodied but big-hearted Miss Kennedy with her Easter basket, which she gave to my children because she "wanted to make them happy."

More tears and more hugs.

Over the course of our next few days while our little Sally recuperated, our friendship grew with Grandma Bonnie, Granddaddy Warren, and their precious granddaughter. We learned they were living in the hotel because of an extended work contract, and little K was there visiting. When it was time to head home, we exchanged contact information because, well, I have a habit of collecting new friends.

Eventually we headed back home, where things took an interesting turn. We weren't getting answers on Sawyer's care, and after some strings pulled by another bus family, we were referred to the Mayo Clinic for him as well. Once again, we loaded up the family and headed to the southeastern corner of the state, packing along our friend, whom my children call Miss Amy, once again.

Our appointment was somewhat delayed because the Mayo Clinic was hosting a distinguished guest and many, including our doctor, had signed up to hear his discussion. This time our visit produced answers—only not the answers Sawyer wanted to hear. We were told the best way for him to begin real healing would require time spent in a rehabilitative hospital. In our attempts to comfort Sawyer, we weren't paying close attention as we drove out of the parking garage. The next thing we knew, we were smack dab in the middle of the motorcade for the Dalai Lama. And right there in the long line of black Town Cars was a maroon minivan that had once been owned by family friend and adopted Grandpa Warren. Never in my life have I been in the middle of such a ruckus. There were protesters on both sides of the road. Shouts of "Free Tibet!" were matched with equally charged ones of "Tibet has always been free!" It was a sight to behold, and for a small moment we were able to laugh and not think about the decisions we needed to make which would rip our family apart again.

Looking back, it was the best decision we could have ever made for Sawyer, but it was an incredibly painful one for Sister. She felt neglected, misunderstood, and forgotten, but knew that her big brother needed this more than anything. Adults were kind to her, but some of her classmates were not, which only compounded the struggles she was facing. Sawyer was facing other kinds of nightmares as well as emotional and physical pain, as thoughts of returning to a hospital plagued him. To complicate matters, Cloie, who was only three years old, needed a daycare to attend. Trying to coordinate all those details was almost too much, but again, friends, neighbors, and church family came to the rescue.

Convincing Sawyer this new adventure was going to be great and would hopefully allow him to walk again was entirely another hurdle. In desperation I called Grandma Bonnie, who was still residing in the Rochester area. Her words were encouraging and comforting. She asked me to relay to Sawyer that for every third day he worked hard in therapy (which would be every day of the week for six to eight hours), she would buy him a new Webkinz. Her proposal worked, and he began dreaming about which stuffed animal he would earn first, determined to work hard.

Since he was a juvenile patient in an adult ward, I was allowed to room in with him. Originally we were told he would be there a week to ten days, but after an exploratory surgery to determine the extent of damage to his nerves, we learned our stay would not have a finite ending. Grandma Bonnie sat with me every minute of that surgery, which lasted many hours past the original 45 minutes we were told to expect. After hearing the outcome, she and Granddaddy Warren became more than just some nice people who we had met in a hotel.

They became my lifeline to the outside world. They brought me meals and the daily newspaper. They provided company in the quiet moments and a shoulder to cry upon in the dark ones. On the weekends when Daniel and the girls joined us, they provided a room to stay and offered to watch the girls if we needed a break. Grandma Bonnie and Granddaddy Warren were the embodiment of love and a "home away from home."

That Mother's Day weekend, I received a call from Bonnie and Warren's daughter, telling me she was praising God for me that day. I was completely baffled because I had been the recipient, not the giver, of any number of blessings from them. Her kind explanation moved me to tears. Because of my family, her mom had found a purpose far from her home, while temporarily assigned to the region for Granddaddy's work. She was able to use the gifts of hospitality and loving others God had given her to help me and my family, something she hadn't had the opportunity to do prior to the oddest Easter egg hunt ever contrived.

Their kindnesses were the embodiment of the same things being done for us by countless others, but it was the words of their daughter (who happened to be the momma of the sweet little basket giver) who reminded me that many times God places people in our paths to create opportunities for us to love them.

Pizza from California

Sometimes classes and teachers really leave a mark on my way of looking at the world. Since taking a graduate class on educational ethics, I have dreamed of seeing one of the studies we read become a reality in our neck of the woods. The study proposed solving two problems society faces: hungry senior citizens and children without loving support systems. The plan was simple enough in design, if not in application, and involved bringing senior citizens into the schools every day to have lunch with the school children. If implemented properly, the program would provide substitute or adopted grandparents to have safe and loving relationships with kids. If every lunch table isn't realistic, then having adopted grandparents in neighborhoods is something that every child should experience. Thankfully, my children have had that opportunity.

Our relationship with Grandma Beulah began innocently enough. During one of our neighborhood events (a baby shower), she mistakenly called and asked if I would be attending and if I could walk with her to the shower. I was happy to oblige, but the shower was being held at my house. I simply walked across the street and escorted her over. She was a tad embarrassed at the oversight, but was truly touched by my willingness to drop everything and run. That tiny act began a long relationship filled with banana bread, trips to the store and doctor, birthday parties, family meals, Christmas gifts, a grandma for school events, and garden produce crossing the street between us. For many years Grandma lived alone, and I believe the hustle and bustle at our house helped alleviate some of her loneliness. For us, her presence became a special part of our lives.

We love to tease her about the time we were working like crazy to paint our bedroom. Our tiny house was crowded because all our furniture had to be moved out to paint the room. While we were sweating away in that August's sweltering heat, we heard a rap at the door. Here was Grandma Beulah dressed in her Sunday finest (even though it was not the Lord's day), and she had brought some oatmeal cookies she had made. Rather than dropping the cookies and returning home, she stayed and supervised, even pointing out a few spots we missed. My husband loves to tease her about how she purposefully wore church clothes so she couldn't be forced to work. Other times her unexpected visits were a divine interruption, especially when I was dealing with postpartum struggles. She came and read to me one day while I ironed clothes. Having once been a Minnesota farm wife and mother to a large family, I think she just knew that I was the lonesome one now and that all I needed was a little company.

Over the years she has slowed down, and family members have moved into her home to help her continue living there. Before roommates became a necessity, she began having to give up a few things that she truly loved. One of those things was gardening and yard work, and she had mentioned her love of flowers to the right young man, Reed. The next thing she knew, we had rented a sod remover to create a garden space in her backyard. Another neighbor helped with vegetable gardening, but planting flowers was Reed's responsibility. He planted, weeded, watered, and loved that garden, just to see her smile. In return, she would send a few cut flowers for our family to enjoy every now and then.

When we first brought Huckleberry home, Reed and his canine friend spent every waking hour outside. Reed's imagination was so incredible that hundreds of adventures took place right in our backyard. If I didn't see them in our backyard, then I knew to check Grandma's because those two houses were the most likely places to find Reed. Huck must have sensed the sacredness of the ground they trod, because while Reed was not at home, he would walk the perimeter of our property with his stuffed cow in tow. Eventually, we called Huck "the sheriff" and his faithful bovine sidekick "the deputy." The redheaded wonder, the sheriff, and the deputy not only kept our neighborhood safe from all varieties of imaginary bad guys but also grew a fine garden or two.

When Reed passed away, we decided we wanted to create a garden in the area where he had played for so long. The school also has a beautiful garden in memory of Jesse, Hunter, Emilee, and Reed and in honor of the other children on Bus 5 that day. But we wanted something right in our backyard that would allow us to look out the back windows and smile, remembering the adventures he once had there, but the amount of work it would take to go from green grass to memory garden was gargantuan and impossible for us to accomplish alone.

Four months out from the accident, we were still barely making it through the days, let alone the nights. We had so many people asking how they could help, and doing something big just felt right. It gave us something positive to focus on. We did something we never thought we would do but that would have made Reed proud. We alerted the Bat Signal. Okay, we really just put our idea out on CaringBridge. Offers for help and supplies started pouring in.

For our first workday, I think more than twenty people showed up. A friend who has experience planning gardens took charge, and another friend great at organizing people worked her magic. One friend who raised worms brought mineral rich worm-cast soil to enhance the health of the ground. Others brought rakes, hoes, positive attitudes, and a spirit to help. Because the area is extremely shady, we put out a request for hostas and other shade-loving plants. Hostas started arriving one after another. One friend from New York State arranged for five miniature varieties of hostas to be delivered straight to our house. The outpouring of love was incredible.

As the evening wore on, we knew we needed to feed all these people. We were beginning to talk about how to do that when a pizza delivery guy walked into our backyard. *Well, that was rather unconventional!* Since our home is often confused with another home in our neighborhood (Thank you, city planners! Whoever thought it was a good idea to put 206 St and 206 Ct across from each other was not thinking!), we assured the pizza guy that he had the wrong house. He checked his bill a few times and assured us the big stack of pizzas was for this house. We argued that we hadn't ordered the pizzas, until finally he showed us the receipt. Five large pizzas had been ordered and paid for by a friend in California (the same friend who started Reed's scholarship), because he really wanted to be there to help but couldn't.

Everyone shared a very good laugh because none of us knew it was possible to order pizza from thousands of miles away. The fellowship was wonderful, but I can tell you, pizza never tasted as good as it did that night. This wasn't just any pizza; it was a heartfelt message of love. Just like that garden. For one brief moment, one small redheaded wonder united an entire nation from New York to California, all coming together in a humble Minnesota backyard. That is a moment to be proud of, and we certainly are.

The garden became a magnet for groups wanting to see it all come to fruition. Youth groups worked on landscaping and hardscaping, placing bricks as edgers and around the fire pit. One youth group came all the way from Iowa to work in Reed's garden. Missionaries home on furlough came and dug in plants, Boy Scouts spent hours back there, and one local school still comes every year to rake the leaves in the fall.

Today the garden is thriving, with bird couples raising families there. Vegetables flourish. Trees blow in the wind. Flowers bloom throughout the growing season. All of it possible because many hearts and hands worked together in honor of a young man who loved a good adventure and a good growing season!

And if you listen carefully, you will hear the redbird sing his song of hope.

Chewbacca Seriously Needs a Pedicure

Now, before I get nasty messages from die-hard *Star Wars* fans over that title, read on. *Star Wars* has been a big part of my life. My love affair with the franchise began in the backseat of a 1976 Chevy Vega at the drive-in movie. Before any tawdry ideas cross anyone's mind, I was eight years old, my brother and I clad in our jammies, taking in a double feature with our parents. We were hooked from that moment forward. As we both grew up and had families of our own, my brother and I passed the love of all things *Star Wars* on to our children. This fact was known far and wide (okay, really just amongst our friends, family, and Reed's poor classmates who had to sit through an hour-long presentation on the lesser-known details of the franchise in computer class).

There is just something about forces banding together to fight evil powers. It gets me every time.

Our sons were hooked too. Action figures, light sabers, Christmas ornaments, and T-shirts are staples in our world. We've even had a motion sensor R2-D2 fish tank. "Luke, I am your father," is more than a movie line around here, serving as a reminder that while we all have earthly dads, our heavenly father is FAR more than we could ever imagine.

When we planned Reed's services, I refused to call it a funeral because that denotes an ending. I explained to the funeral director and Pastor Don that I would need a whole lot of grace, because at the end of the Celebration I had one desire: for Reed and Jesus to look down from heaven and smile. While both men agreed to extend a latitude of grace, I don't think they could have ever foreseen what my heart would envision.

We planned an upbeat remembrance, complete with worship band, campfire songs from the Nowatzki clan, and Reed's faithful companion and furry best friend as a pallbearer. I wanted the world to know what it had lost, an amazing young man—full of faith, love, and "The Force." There was no way we were ending on a somber note, but how would we leave the service saying, "So long for now," for a twelve-year-old boy?

We chose to have a processional for the entrance including family, friends who were like family, best friends, classmates, teachers, and Boy Scouts. The entourage was so large the worship team sang, "How Great is our God" at least eight times before we all were seated inside the school's gymnasium. If that was some kind of entrance, the recessional was electrifying. After a beautiful telling of Reed's incredible faith and how if the audience members knew Jesus like Reed did, they would all see him again, story after story was shared of his love for others and how he truly made a difference in those twelve short years. Eventually the time came. The service was over. The Boy Scouts rose, filling in both sides of the aisle, fingers at the ready. The funeral director came to roll our boy's American flag draped casket out of the gym, which was the cue to our sound technician to give it all he had. We had arranged through one of our local stores to purchase light sabers, and as the funeral director prepared, the scouts stood, and classmates rose sabers at the ready. Unbeknownst to us, the three pastors had brought their own light sabers and created a lighted final blessing. Subtle at first, the melodic notes of the *Star Wars* theme began to play, almost drowned out by laughter, creating exactly the "ending" Reed would have wanted.

Sitting in the audience that day was one of Daniel's cousins who shares our love of a galaxy far, far away. She knows what it is like to love a redheaded wonder, and while she knew both her son and ours were June bugs (Mama Cloie's way of referencing someone born in the month of June), she didn't know they actually shared a birthday. Sometime later, she heard an announcement that the Science Museum of Minnesota would be opening a *Star Wars* exhibit on what would have been Reed's thirteenth birthday. She somehow knew in her heart (without ever uttering a word to us) that if Reed had known about the exhibit, he would have asked his parents to be there on opening day. She was one hundred percent correct because when he saw the sign while visiting the museum's Pompeii exhibit a month before his passing, he begged us to make sure he and his buddy, Quinn, could be there the minute it opened.

Those birthday plans fell by the wayside as we spent long days and even longer nights in hospitals with Sawyer's recovery. In fact, we weren't even sure how to plan to spend the day celebrating Reed's birth without him (which is still a struggle each year). We phoned a grief mentor and friend, asking how they celebrate their son's birthday. She shared what they do but in the same breath said we would know when we found the right thing. To make matters worse, that particular year Father's Day fell on Reed's birthday. We lamented for quite a while because nothing felt right. Then in God's divine providence came an e-mail from Cousin Anne. She took her hunch straight to the Science Museum and told them the story of a little redheaded boy. They were so moved by her story of Reed's love of *Star Wars*, they gave her tickets for our entire family to be their guests on opening day. We were blown away as our answer to the unanswerable question fell right into our laps.

Knowing the day would be painful, especially for Daniel, we embraced the bittersweet irony of celebrating by doing exactly what Reed had chosen to do. We had honored Daniel and my dad and remembered Granddaddy earlier for breakfast with my parents and Nannie, and then quite by surprise, folks in the elevator gave us an extra pair of tickets to the exhibit. A quick call to my brother and his wife, and we had a real party going on. Sawyer, still using a wheelchair for mobility, scooted around from one costumed character to another on the plaza while we waited for the extra guests to arrive. When we all entered the exhibit, it was a surreal moment.

Remembering how we had lost track of Reed at the Pompeii exhibit because he was absorbed in learning everything he could, it was an easy leap to imagine his excitement over even the tiniest details in every piece of *Star Wars* memorabilia. I flitted about with Clo, who was still too little to understand all the hoopla and mega-fans who showed up for opening day.

While Erin was trying a hover racer with Daniel, and Sawyer was building with Uncle Davy, our little one and I were admiring all the details of the costume of one of my favorite characters: Chewbacca. We were taking in every inch of the gigantic frame when she let out an "Ewww!" with a turned-up little nose. On her tiny frame, her line of vision for the pedestalled figure was Chewbacca's feet. True to my sense of humor, I blurted out with every bit of sass you can imagine, "You are right, Clo! Chewbacca was seriously in need of a pedicure!"

Apparently, more die-hard fans than me do not take it well when someone disses the nail fungus of one of their beloved characters. I didn't have the time nor energy to explain the hardship of the day to their contempt-filled faces. In fact, I know for certain my comment would have earned an "Only you would think of that, Mom," followed by a chuckle from my redheaded boy! Even though I was almost escorted out of the exhibit faster than Han and Chewie in the Millennium Falcon, my broken heart had to laugh over a joke that only my boy, the boy I missed with every fiber of my being, would have understood that day.

A Comforter's Guide to the Grief Galaxy

THIS GUIDE IS MEANT TO SERVE AS THE "CLIFFSNOTES" VERSION of the final section of this book. As a quick reference guide, I created smaller takeaways from each chapter. Use this guide to spark your own creativity as to how you might use your gifts and talents to help someone who is grieving. These "blow your socks off" kindnesses are some of the ways our family has been and continues to be blessed by others. We are forever grateful for their love.

When All Else Fails, Prayer Works: Prayer is a literal lifeline, connecting us to the author of peace and the model of comfort. When someone is hurting, praying for them is something that can be done anywhere, at any hour of the day. When you aren't sure if there is anything that you can tangibly do to help, prayer is a fail-safe solution.

Pink Is the New Red: When a loved one is lost, those who remain quickly realize that new stories involving their loved one are no longer able to be created. Old memories and stories become treasures. If you know a story about the deceased, sharing that memory may bring a tear to someone's eyes but will also often bring incredible joy to their hearts.

Hugs and Kisses: Like the widow's mite, many times it is the little things that can bring big smiles to someone's life. So many times we cling to the false belief that bigger is better, but, comforters, rest assured that a small treat or practical act of service can go a long way.

Just Sit Next to Me, Mom: I've been there. Instead of saying something comforting, I have said something harmful rather than helpful to the ones I was trying to comfort. Grief can be extremely isolating. A great gift to a grieving person is giving of your time to be physically present, just sitting with them and listening. Showing up is a powerful treasure.

The Crazy Way Traditions Start: Battling Blue-Hairs in the Dairy Aisle: Grieving parents are exhausted parents. One of the biggest desires of grieving families is to return to normalcy (acknowledging that it will be a "new normal"). One way to help grieving families is to offer to help maintain traditions for them. Some may want something simple, while others may desire to embrace larger longstanding traditions.

Grandpas-R-Us: Grief takes an enormous toll (physically, emotionally, mentally, and spiritually) on a person. Any way you can help grieving parents by being involved in the lives of their children will help them. More importantly, grieving children will work tirelessly to protect their parents from more pain. Having another trusted adult spend time with them provides a safe place for children to grieve.

Where is That List?: Trips to the store are often overwhelming. Not being ready to return to everyday life can also be a deterrent to completing such chores. Friends' willingness to do such mundane tasks, like calling to ask for our current shopping list and to pick up those items, was a huge blessing.

I Always Dreamed of Having a Rosie: In our early period of grief, we were numbly enduring our days, just barely making it through. Having enough energy to do more than exist was rare. Several friends came with cleaning supplies in hand and cleaned our house, spic and span. I have been the giver of this gift before, and somehow cleaning someone else's house seems like a lot less work than it does cleaning my own.

My Husband Thinks I am Preparing for an Ark: Family members come in a variety of sizes, shapes, and number of legs. Our pets were lovingly cared for by dear friends when we were unable to care for them ourselves. From the night of the crash to many days later, friends and church family looked after and loved our pets when we had no energy to do so.

You've Got to Get Out of town: While our days were consumed with everything we could do to help our children heal, a group of friends realized that we had no time to be a couple. To solve that problem, they pooled their resources to give us a weekend away.

The Melodic Notes of Encouragement: For years, a small note here and a card there were incredible day brighteners for our family. Those messages often included some encouragement to our family that we were loved, that Reed was missed, or both. Electronic communications are good too, but when someone takes the time to pen a note or word of encouragement, the result can be a game changer.

The Red Bed: One of the most overwhelming things we faced in the aftermath of our darkest day was the barrage of decisions. Grieving is not a rational process, and making decisions following the loss of a loved one can be extremely difficult. There were several instances where friends and family were willing to do the research necessary to help us make an informed decision. Their assistance helped us to be able to sort through mountains of paperwork, in one case, and locate an elusive product in another. No matter what decisions a family is facing having others be willing to serve as guides is an immeasurable gift.

What Have You Done to Your Kids?: Grief retreats for families provide much-needed respite. Grief camps for children provide them a place to grieve and remember their loved one. Sharing information about grief retreats or camps can bring expert resources into the hands of the grieving.

I Pledge My Hands: Acts of service can be extremely beneficial for grieving families. We had help with everything from putting in a ramp to accommodate a wheelchair to assistance working in our memory garden. Completing yard work, such as mowing grass, raking leaves, and removing snow, and larger household jobs, like spring cleaning of windows, walls, and floors is an incredible help.

Well, That Is Deceiving!: Sometimes grieving families are flooded with an outpouring of offers to help in the days immediately following their loss. Over time, the well-wishers resume normal living. An incredible gift is to do something special for the family a few months or years down the road. Offering support when the rest of the world has moved on acknowledges that grief can be a long journey.

Almost Heaven: We were completely blown away when a dear friend paid for a week's vacation for our family. Another friend's family pooled their resources and gave us a very large sum of money to be used for our family's first vacation. While not economically feasible for some, the love given in these gifts was amazing. A valuable lesson to our family was that God designed rest for a beneficial reason.

Gonna Need Some No. 2s: There may be a few days of the year that are particularly painful for a grieving person. One of my dear friends realized this and prevented me the heartache of having to purchase back-to-school items. If a would-be comforter knows of such days (and potentially difficult milestones), offering to do something in acknowledgment of that day or with a grieving family/friend is a great way to be supportive. An example that comes to mind might be the opening day of hunting or baseball (or any other) season. Inviting the family over or offering to do something special with grieving kids is incredibly gracious.

Grace of Strangers: I still remember the pain of receiving the first piece of mail addressed to Reed as if he were still alive. It was agonizingly heartbreaking. Although not completely foolproof, there are a few websites that help remove a deceased loved one's name from direct mailing lists. Offering to take care of that process for someone who is grieving can thwart potential heartache. A few resources are provided in the "Really Good Stuff" section of this book.

Welcome, Teenager!: Reed's final resting place is hundreds of miles away from our home. Several families and individuals have made treks to the prairie to visit the cemetery. We do the same for some friends whose children are buried closer to us. The comforting love song is one that says, "Your child is not forgotten." This song is sung loudly when someone travels that far to "see" Reed. Visiting cemeteries is not many people's favorite thing to do, but for some it is a rite of passage. It is in the remembrance that we honor those gone before us. As a part of one of our children's organizations, we place flags on the graves of veterans every Fourth of July. On one such outing, I watched as our Sally and another little girl took extra special care to clean the graves of young people they knew.

Watch Out, Mary Poppins: With very little energy to expend, friends and neighbors brought us all the items a household needs to run smoothly for many days. Some families may or may not welcome meals for a variety of reasons, but paper products, gift cards, and household sundries are items all families need. Providing these supplies can often be an insulating measure as well, saving families the heartache of immediately having to return to the "real world" while still trying to establish their new normal.

With the Comforter You've Been Given: Expenses add up for grieving families. There were countless people who gave monetarily to help our family. If we worked every day the rest of our lives, we wouldn't be able to repay the generosity. Sometimes God lays the message to give and GIVE BIG on the hearts of the listening. A few individuals did that for our family because at some point they had experienced huge troubles and knew where their needs had been the greatest. God uses every person (and their resources) in divinely appointed ways.

On Easter Rabbits and Turtles: This one can at times seem so obvious, but at other times can be one of the most uncomfortable of all the blessings. I am a firm believer that God places people in our paths for the explicit purpose of loving them for him that day. Oftentimes, this display of love is something small (a compliment or an offer to buy someone a cup of coffee), and other times God has equipped us with talents and skills that can only be used by loving the person he has put in our path. As Aesop once said, "No act of kindness, no matter how small, is ever wasted."

Pizza from California: Although the suggestion in this chapter is somewhat unique to our story, there are other ways that friends and family from far away can provide comfort. In our case, friends ordered pizza for us from the West Coast. Family who couldn't join us for Reed's Run ran their own version of the 5K way out in Washington State. With many businesses having websites or at least phone numbers online, comforters can easily access "gifts of love" from far away.

Chewbacca Seriously Needs a Pedicure: I have read several places about how it isn't the two dates placed in an obituary or engraved on a headstone that matter the most; it is the dash between the numbers which sums up how a person lived. While I agree with that logic, I also know how incredibly painful birthdays and heaven anniversary dates are. Much like the thoughtfulness in other chapters, this comfort suggestion is steeped in understanding the dash. There are so many firsts which grieving families experience, most of them painful. Having someone acknowledge that pain and provide a suggestion for how to remember and honor a lost loved one was a huge blessing for our family.

Really Good Stuff

GRIEF RESOURCES:

Faith's Lodge—a place where hope grows
www.faithslodge.org

Mission: Faith's Lodge: A Place Where Hope Grows supports parents and families facing the life-limiting condition or loss of a child in a peaceful environment to reflect on the past, renew strength for the present and build hope for the future. In its North Woods setting, Faith's Lodge provides a peaceful escape for families to refresh their minds and spirits while spending time with others who understand what they are experiencing.

Located in northwestern Wisconsin, Faith's Lodge was founded by the parents of Faith Ann Lacek, who passed from an in utero umbilical cord accident, to provide a place of refuge and healing for families in their darkest days. From their own personal grief, they have created a place where our family found peace, and we are forever grateful for the time we spent there.

Children's Grief Connection
http://childrensgriefconnection.com/

Mission: Bringing Hope and Healing to Grieving Children and Families Located in northern Minnesota, this organization has undergone some changes over the years but remains centrally focused on their mission to provide support to the grieving. Formerly Camp Amanda, this is the camp our children attended (where the veggie-eaters story originated). Children's Grief Connection now offers a weekend family camp to help support the entire family during the grieving process. They are also associated with the National Alliance for Grieving Children. Many states have similar grief camps.

Camp Love's Embrace
http://camplovesembrace.com/index.php
Mission: A place where grieving children can both grieve and embrace the love they have lost

We were referred to this camp for Cloie, who was not old enough at the time of the bus crash to attend an overnight camp. Camp Love's Embrace is a free overnight camp for grieving children ages seven to fourteen. The camp originated because of the work of a teenage girl who watched the impact 9/11 had on grieving children. Realizing that similar programs abounded on the coasts, she worked diligently to create the same camp experience here in the Midwest.

Both Children's Grief Connection and Camp Love's Embrace were active partners, along with local funeral directors, in the one-day Camp Faith that was offered at our school for children impacted by the bus crash. While we recognize all three organizations above are ones relatively close to our home, we share these to help raise awareness of similar programs and organizations around the nation and the world that provide support for grieving families. Our family is forever grateful we had the opportunity to be a part of all three.

October 15 Remembering Our Babies—National Pregnancy and Infant Loss Remembrance Day
http://www.october15th.com/
Mission: Remembering Our Babies was created to provide support, education, and awareness for those who are suffering or may know someone who has suffered a miscarriage, ectopic pregnancy, stillbirth, or loss of an infant.

In 1988, President Ronald Reagan designated the month of October to National Pregnancy and Infant Loss Remembrance. Due to the diligent work of moms who had previously grieved in silence, October 15 became the nationally recognized day to remember the babies who passed during pregnancy or in their infancy and to provide support for families who are grieving these losses. On October 15, families and friends are asked to light a candle at 7 p.m., regardless of time zone, for a nationwide (and sometimes worldwide) candle lighting ceremony. This website also serves as a forum for events taking place around the world on that day.

Our family has participated in candle lighting ceremonies for the last several years on October 15. It has been our fervent hope that others in our area have a place where they are able to find support for pregnancy or infant loss. We once asked our children if October 15 was too upsetting to them. Their response was poignant. They reminded us that they get to spend every holiday and their birthdays with us, and this is the one day each year dedicated to remembering the three siblings they never had the chance to meet.

"Please, No More Marketing" resources

College Bound Selection Service http://cbssearch.net/
This is the service our family learned of when we contacted the university who had inadvertently mailed a postcard for Reed. Sweet Miss R helped get Reed's name removed from the databases so that we would not face that pain over and over again. A comforter could definitely contact (with the family's permission) this organization to have a student's name removed from the list.

Deceased Do Not Contact Registration
https://www.ims-dm.com/cgi/ddnc.php
I have had pen pals for years. I love to send and receive cards, but there is one thing that I never enjoy: the despised and dreaded junk mail. Nannie had a special place where she placed those unsolicited pieces. She "filed them under 'S'," and as she was a pretty colorful character, you can imagine what she meant. This is the site which was sent to me in the card by Miss R to further remove Reed's name from marketing organizations' lists. This registry was started by the Direct Marketers Association in an effort to help families dealing with the overwhelming task of sorting through all the secondary things associated with the loss of a loved one. This website provides a more thorough listing to have a deceased loved one's name removed from future mailings.

Such a Different Ending

I would have despaired unless I had
Believed that I would see the
Goodness of the Lord
In the land of the living.
Wait for the Lord;
Be strong and let your heart take courage;
Yes, *wait for the Lord.*
—Psalm 27:13–14 (NASB)

ONE OF SISTER'S FRIENDS ONCE HAD A LAUGHING FIT IN ONE OF her elementary classrooms, to which the teacher responded, "Natasha, please laugh in your head." Doing my very best to laugh inside my head is sometimes excruciatingly challenging for me because *I love to laugh.* Much like my young friend, laughing in my head is really not going to happen. Ever. Having a robust sense of humor is a good quality, and many times a saving grace delivered straight from heaven.

Laughter will always be one of my best comfort measures.

My sweetie and I still laugh over things that happened years ago, but my best laughs are saved for my mom. I don't know how it happens. When our funny bones get tickled, look out world! The next thing I know we are gasping for air, reaching for the tissues, and trying to find the nearest bathroom. One time our fits of giggles struck us on the highway, and we had to pull off the road because I was certain we were going to get pulled over and would begin laughing even more uncontrollably before we could explain ourselves. I come from a long line of law enforcement officers, but I don't think even they would find seat belt adjusters as humorous as we did that day.

Laughter like this is restorative for the soul, reminding me never to take myself too seriously.

Then, there is this one man. Even though I laugh in my head when I see him, every time we bump into each other (which is not often), I am transported back to a wintry day before the bus crash. Sawyer and I had left school for a few hours because we needed a quick check-in with his asthma doctor. Our appointment occurred right before lunch, and by the time we would have made it back to school, the cafeteria would be closed. After a quick call to Daniel, my Boy Wonder and I had ourselves a lunch date planned. When you have as many children as we do, we have to capitalize on one-on-one time with them any way we can. Sawyer settled for a lunch date with mom and dad at Hardee's, although given the chance, he probably would have chosen something much more interesting,

The bright sunshine belied the blisteringly cold temperatures outside the large picture windows of our local fast food restaurant. Still shivering, we sat down to enjoy a warm meal. Sawyer told his dad all about our appointments and what was coming up at school that afternoon. Even though we could have hustled through our meal and right back to school and work, we decided to linger for a bit longer to allow our boy to enjoy the playland for a little while. Eventually, we could no longer ignore the realities of the bitter cold or our lives outside the walls of our momentary sanctuary. We all suited up in our winter coats, hats, and gloves, and I ran to refill my Coke for the trip back to school while Daniel ran to the restroom.

I will never (and I mean NEVER) forget what happened next. With my back turned to the area where we had been seated, I heard a ruckus. Not recognizing the voice, I didn't turn around. All I heard was a man's voice saying, "NO! We don't do that!" I rounded the corner just in time to see my sweet little curly-headed, chubby-cheeked boy standing frozen in shock. His little hands were still held out in front of him, cupped where his beverage used to be. I saw the man, whom I had correctly assumed was the source of that voice, now standing in front of the trash receptacles, toss a full cup of soda dramatically into the garbage. As if I were at a tennis match, my gaze flew between my shocked and frozen child to the garbage slinger, swinging toward the gentleman just in time to see his face shift from indignant disgust to shocked horror when he realized what he had done. Almost like Oliver Twist asking for "more," Sawyer still stood with his hands cupped around what I now deduced was his thrown-away cup. Tiny tears were forming in the corners of his eyes.

I. AM. MOMMA BEAR! HEAR ME ROAR!

In one swift motion, the man, almost in tears himself, stepped between my sweet boy, still frozen in shock, and me. "Oh, my word! I thought your son was my son! Look!" (He was gesticulating wildly now.) "Just look, they have the same coats! Oh, what have I done? I am so sorry! Oh my goodness! I thought my son was drinking someone's leftover drink! I will buy you another one! Oh, I am so sorry!"

A quick maneuver got me past the man and to my son about the time Daniel emerged from the bathroom. I am guessing due to the intense exchange, he had heard every word before stepping out to redeem the situation. By this time, all eyes (this is a small town, after all, and I think even the cooks and clerks stepped out of the kitchen and from behind the counter to see what all the fuss was about) were glued to the showdown outside the playland seating. Like the temperature outside, time was frozen for a few seconds.

And then, I couldn't help it.

Although I wanted to roar, I couldn't. A mixture of pity and lunacy just erupted from somewhere deep inside my belly. I could not have stopped the laughter that came bubbling out even if I had wanted to. The tears and laughter continued for the rest of the day. I had to pull it together to teach chemistry and physics later, but the minute the last bell rang, the chuckles came back like a contagion.

This story could have had a very different ending. Both child and momma forgave the man (even though I seriously have to control myself whenever I see him now), but we could have reacted in anger instead of grace. No ill will was intended, and even though I had never before seen my active little boy stopped in his tracks, no permanent damage was done.

Grace covers everything. Like the ultimate trump card, grace alleviated an incredibly awkward moment and provided me with some personal levity for years to come. Even today while writing this, I am chuckling.

The story of my family and our continued healing could have had a very different ending. Our lives have been forever changed. Clearly there are holes in our hearts that will never be filled, but there are also good things that have emerged because of our journey. We have learned the little stuff is worthy of being savored, because these ordinary moments might just become new traditions. We've learned that we have amazing friends and family, who are selfless and loving and are ever present when we need them. I would have never believed it before our darkest day, but I now know it to be true. God is using our story to change the lives of others. This knowledge is humbling and awe-inspiring. Yet the biggest lesson we have learned is of how wide and long and high and deep the love of Christ is (Ephesians 3:18, 19).

Love with no end is truly impossible to imagine. This love so immense led a Father to allow his Son to die on a cross just so he could have a relationship with me (and everyone else). That love—like a bright shining beacon—illuminated our path even in the darkest moments.

Out of all our updates on CaringBridge, there is one comment that still stands out in my mind. The encourager shared a story of how her aunt and uncle faced a series of calamities. There were deaths in the family, bouts with cancer, and other tragedies the family endured. In the face of all this pain, this friend's aunt remained grounded in her faith. One day someone asked the sweet woman how she could continue to praise God in light of everything they were going through. Her answer has stuck with me so much that I have considered painting it on my rooftop.

"Well, the way I see it, the devil and the Lord are duking it out over this household, and as far as I can tell, the good Lord is still winning!"

I love her faith. She didn't wax poetic about all the troubles she had seen. Hers was a love story of a hope invested in what she believed to be true. God's love will conquer every struggle. Someday he will wipe away every tear.

Our story could have had a very different ending—one filled with bitterness, despair, anguish, anger, betrayal, and mistrust. Don't get me wrong. Each of those has been a houseguest on our journey, but at the end of the day, we knew that there was something more. Something so much better. When we had nowhere else to turn, we landed on our knees, waiting for Someone to wipe our tears.

Even after growing up knowing God's story of amazing grace, it wasn't until Reed died that I began to understand how much pain he must have experienced losing his son. The depth of his pain is unfathomable. My "something better" lies in clinging to the one who truly understands our pain and struggles.

As we have watched countless other tragedies unfold since our darkest day, our prayers have been multiplied, understanding in a small way what it is like to walk in the shoes of the grieving and the traumatized. Deep in our hearts, we pray that those affected know God and his son, Jesus. We honestly don't know how we would have made it this far without our faith. Not some glossy suit-and-tie version, but the real anguished cries of despair, the "lay in bed for days but somehow find the strength to get up and go on" faith which brought us closer to God. The hearts that were broken, disappointed, and betrayed are the same hearts that laughed at the memories and cried tears of joy at the blessings.

Someday we will see Reed and our babies again, and while that knowledge was the only thing that kept us going early on, our mission to share God's faithfulness has changed our days. With the sustained love of friends, family, and sometimes strangers, we learned to live again.

Through it all, without faith, I would not have seen God's hand in the littlest things—the revolutionary acts that reminded us just how much we are loved ...

especially when the red bird sings.

Acknowledgments

When I was a little girl, one of my favorite television shows was *Romper Room*. I would watch with anticipation for the end of the show when Miss Suzanne would look through her magic mirror and say that she saw me, naming off first names of children. Only when your hippie parents name you Kandy, much like the personalized pencils I could never find in elementary school, Miss Suzanne never said my name. *It's okay. I think I am over it. I think.*

The stories that filled this book could not have been possible without a tremendous amount of support. Although I haven't named every kindness and every person who has loved our family, my heart knows and will always remember. For every single person who prayed, you are the best part of our healing journey. Many times it was your prayers that allowed us to get up and attempt a day. For those who loved our family in tangible ways through acts of service or through gifts, your energy often preserved ours (which was a precious commodity at times). Please know this book would have never been possible without all of you.

To all my grieving friends, there have been times when I felt as if I was wrestling with God because I haven't wanted to share pieces of our story. I often feel there are parts too ugly or parts that make me look so weak and vulnerable, especially hard when one loves superheroes. Typically I give in to God's gentle nudges for all of you. Thank you for your words of encouragement that remind me you needed to read my words that very day. It is in those moments, I realize this is why God placed the tough stuff on my heart.

To my editorial friend, Jen Spiegel, the moment I saw you add the word *that* so many times to my manuscript, I knew you were the girl for me. Together we shall *that* the world. You are the first person in almost thirty years who was able to attempt to undo what the Florida Department of Education produced. One contraction equaled an automatic F in English class, and you forced me put them back into my writing. The State of Florida worked valiantly to take the "country" out of all of us, and you worked tirelessly to put it back in. Thank you for polishing this book and me until we shined.

To the cheerleaders—Jacki and Nikki—for always being there! To my bleacher besties—Shelly and Deanna—thanks for loving me even when I wasn't around while trying to finish this book and go to school. To Pam, who gave me a whole farm and more love and food than I could imagine to write many of the chapters in this book, you have been a lifelong bundle of positivity. For a girl who thought she would always have only guy friends after growing up with boys, you have all shown me a sisterhood of love!

To my "created" family, Sheldon, Karla, Jeff, Blythe, Mansi, Bruce, Sophie, Elle, Conner, James, Brenda, Milo, Josh, Nicole, Lydia, Bri, Tony, Bug, Jacob, Damien, Darrien, Davontay, and Lucas, you are gifts greater than I ever imagined possible. What God puts together in a family will always amaze me! He didn't join us by blood, but through the blood of his Son, your presence brightened our days when we didn't know how to find the light.

To my family, you are and forever will be the best part of my life. Nannie, Granddaddy, and Papa, you are missed and I hope that y'all and Reed all have the sweet tea and hugs ready when I get there. Thank you for a magical childhood. Mama, all our hours staying up late and laughing are a big part of who I am. I know you always say, "What the good Lord didn't give me in looks, he gave me in talent." You are absolutely beautiful to me, even if you didn't put mustard in the sweet potato pie. Mom, I know you read every blog and are often sharing my work with bigger audiences. Thank you for always pushing me to believe that God has a plan for our story. Daddy, when this book is finally published, you *will* definitely get the first copy. Thank you for always and forever being my biggest fan.

To my siblings—Davy, Kelli, Mary, Rita and Lori—you are loved for all the ways you bring joy to our lives and even more so the stories you add to mine. To my Stevens and Nowatzkis, thank you for making me one of your own. To all my nieces and nephews you bring me amazing joy.

Daniel, thank you for providing time over these years for me to write our story—even if that meant one summer living in a van down by the river. (Okay, it was an RV parked in our driveway while we remodeled, but nonetheless it worked.) If someone would have told me that a blind date would be the best decision of my life, I would have scoffed. But much like many things in life, I would have been wrong. You are the best thing that has happened to me in the last twenty years—even if I didn't dream of you as a little girl.

To my babies in heaven—Noah, Tim, and Savannah Kate—someday I am going to hold you and never let go. Even though I didn't hold you on earth, there has never been a moment I have forgotten about you. To my redheaded wonder Reed, life has never been the same without you. I want you to know that while you are surrounded by the joys of heaven, God has surrounded us with the best he has to offer here on earth. *You will forever be my sunshine.* To my children here at home, thank you for allowing me to share our story, which is often your story. You never ask me to not share or not post, and believe me: I *know* what a gift that is. Sawyer, while you are now an adult, you will forever be my Boy Wonder overcoming every obstacle that comes your way with humility and strength. Thank you for always rising above and showing the world that Stevens are truly *not common.* Erin, you will always be my Sister, and even though you are almost grown, you will forever be the little girl first learning to shoot hoops in the driveway. Your heart for loving the widowed, the orphaned, the forgotten, and the underdog amazes me, especially after all you have endured. Someday, you will be a teacher extraordinaire. Cloie, my mini me and Sally Gal, there is nothing that slows you down. Every single day I see how much you are like Reed and I know that would make him so proud. The best part of this journey is when you just want to snuggle and hold me close. Thank you for always being a beacon of kindness and love wherever you go.

To God, thank you for loving me enough to believe a math-loving, science geek and superhero fan had it in her to write a story. Your love through it all has been the constant that has held our family together.

Thank you for everything, because without you, none of this would be possible.

To the redbird, thank you for being God's best way of loving our family.

If you enjoyed this book and would like to learn more about our wonderful, crazy, beautiful, loved, at times, hilarious, and definitely always faith-filled journey, more stories and how to contact me for speaking engagements can be found at www.realsweetgrace.com.

CPSIA information can be obtained
at www.ICGtesting.com
Printed in the USA
FFHW020814281118
49682016-54059FF